ARKANA

The Secret Zodiac

Fred Gettings is the author of over fifty books, including *The Hidden Art, The Dictionary of Hermetic, Occult and Alchemical Sigils* (Arkana 1988) and *The Dictionary of Astrology* (Arkana 1988). An art historian, he is also an expert on astrology, with a special interest in the history of symbolism and arcane lore.

By the same author

Dictionary of Hermetic, Alchemical and Occult Sigils
Dictionary of Astrology

THE
SECRET ZODIAC

*The Hidden Art in
Mediaeval Astrology*

Fred Gettings

ARKANA

ARKANA

Published by the Penguin Group
27 Wrights Lane, London W8 5TZ, England
Viking Penguin Inc., 40 West 23rd Street, New York, New York 10010, USA
Penguin Books Australia Ltd, Ringwood, Victoria, Australia
Penguin Books Canada Ltd, 2801 John Street, Markham, Ontario, Canada L3R 1B4
Penguin Books (NZ) Ltd, 182–190 Wairau Road, Auckland 10, New Zealand

Penguin Books Ltd, Registered Offices: Harmondsworth, Middlesex, England

First published by Routledge & Kegan Paul Ltd 1987
Published by Arkana 1989
1 3 5 7 9 10 8 6 4 2

Printed and bound in Great Britain by
Richard Clay Ltd, Bungay, Suffolk

Contents

Illustrations

Preface

For occultists, symbols have a real meaning. A symbol that is merely a symbol, merely a copy or image, has no meaning; there is only significance in what can become a reality, in what can become a living force. If a symbol acts upon the spirit of humanity in such a way that intuitive forces are set free, then we are dealing with a true symbol.

(R. STEINER, from a lecture given in Berlin, 2 December, 1904, published in English in *The Temple Legend. Freemasonry and Related Occult Movements*, 1985, translated from *Die Tempellegende und die Goldene Legende*, no. 93 in the Bibliographic Survey.)

This book deals with the esoteric significance of a thirteenth-century zodiac in one of the most beautiful churches in Italy, within the framework of a 'true symbolism' hinted at in the quotation above. Since this study properly concerns itself with topics as diverse as esotericism, mediaeval history and lore, astrology, secret writing, ecclesiastical doctrines and art history, the subject matter is complex, even though I have attempted to write for a general readership. Even so, I doubt that I shall be able to persuade specialists in so many different and diverse fields to accept without reserve the claims I make on behalf of the hidden art of San Miniato al Monte. In view of these doubts, I would like to add a few words by way of preface.

   The esotericist may find some of the points I raise about mediaeval mysticism and occultism questionable – perhaps not so much because there are many disputatious points in the text, but because it is still maintained in certain esoteric schools that some higher truths should not be broadcast in literature intended for non-initiates. In spite of the great wealth of knowledge derived from the mystery wisdom which has been made available to mankind in the past century, not all modern occultists and esotericists subscribe to the post-Theosophical doctrines that the ancients vows of secrecy in such matters belong to the past: the veil has not been rent for everyone. The roots of this belief are essentially healthy, of course, for in attempting to reveal esoteric lore to the uninitiated, it is so very easy to lead towards misunderstandings, and the true esotericist is always reluctant to foster confusion or misunderstanding. The esoteric lore, and the history of the world as seen from an esoteric standpoint, are so very different from non-esoteric lore, and from the conventional notion of world history, that there is very little commerce between the representatives and specialists of the two camps. Fortunately, a large group of esotericists will agree with me that the time is already with us when the ancient mysteries must be brought into open consciousness. It is in this spirit, therefore, that I beg the esotericist, whatever his or her affiliation and opinion, to regard my account of the extraordinary esotericism which may be encountered in San Miniato al Monte.

Again, the specialist mediaeval historian may find some of the things I say about San Miniato to be somewhat imaginative. There is perhaps no easy way of countering such a criticism, save perhaps by pointing out that the thirteenth century represents the flowering of an esoteric lore which the majority of modern historians have failed to evaluate correctly because of the burden of the three centuries of the 'cult of the fact' which they carry on their own shoulders, like a tenacious Old Man of the Sea. I have to confess that one of my criticisms of the modern approach to history is that it is more concerned with archaeology than with artistic interpretation, more concerned with amassing what are often taken to be 'facts', than in developing an awareness that the study of history should be purposive and artistic. The historians of the mediaeval period (such as Neckam, whose influence on San Miniato we cannot fail to observe) tended to see history as something which could be used to point morals, as a study which might indeed be an adornment of man. The factuality of which modern historicism smacks was not really the concern of the mediaeval world, and this (however reprehensible it may appear to the modern mind) permitted the thirteenth-century historian to be more of an artist, more of a moralizer than is possible today. Even so, when we moderns look back some eight hundred years, and attempt to visualize how the minds of mediaeval esotericists, builders and astrologers might have worked, we have to give them the credit of being moralizers, free of the modern tyranny of the fact. Therefore, when I attempt to reveal how the thirteenth-century masons made use of church orientations, sunlight, lapidary inscriptions, art forms and secret methods of writing for moralizing and historionomic purposes, we have a glimpse into their view of history which might confuse or worry the modern historians, whose intentions are quite different. All I can say is that from a historical point of view my hypothesis essentially points to a great union of hermetic lore and theological wisdom during the early thirteenth century. It is a hypothesis which lends credence to a whole mass of otherwise unconnected elements of symbolism, art, belief and literature. The modern notion is that a good hypothesis should be taken as a working model, to be dismantled only when another hypothesis lends greater credence to the observable facts. My thesis gives a convincing account of that extraordinary – perhaps indeed unique – unity between art, symbolism, philosophy, theology and architecture which is one of the outstanding charac-teristics of the thirteenth century. Since my theme is unity, I suspect that the hypothesis I offer may be rejected only if another and more coherent account of this unity is offered in a way which throws greater light on each and all of these different facets of human endeavour in mediaeval Florence.

Modern astrologers may be puzzled by some of my findings. The practical astrologer who is unfamiliar with mediaeval astrological lore will be surprised to find in thirteenth-century astrology so little that he might recognize as his own. He will understand the twelve images of the signs, and the seven images of the planets, perhaps even the sigils for the aspects – but he will recognize little else. His surprise will be the greater because he has been led to expect familiarity: this is a direct result of the numerous superficial 'histories' of astrology which are found in bookshops today, for there is a current misconception in astrological circles that astrology has not changed much in three thousand years. One finds even serious historians of the art claiming that the late Roman astrology of Ptolemy is little different from that which is practised today, when the truth is that little of what Ptolemy wrote has found its way into modern astrological lore, and many of the notions which appear to be the same, on superficial acquaintance, are actually very different. The truth is that it is often very difficult even for specialists to be precise about many of the things which Ptolemy writes about. More apposite, however, is the fact that only a specialist could read a Roman, Byzantine, Arabic or mediaeval European horoscope in the way in which it would be interpreted by its contemporaries. If the differences between Ptolemaic astrology and modern astrology are so considerable, then how much more are the differences between the modern art and that practised in mediaeval times, after which the classical astrology had been made more complex and more redolent of esoteric lore at the hands of the Arabs? Even were the sigils of a particular mediaeval horoscope to be changed so as to be understood by the modern astrologer, it is unlikely that he or she would make sense of the underlying tenets, so different was the astrology of the past from that in general use today. A good astrologer would be able to 'read' a mediaeval figure (the sigils having been translated), but he would only be able to do so in the light of the modern astrological system with which he is familiar, and not in terms of the systems with which the mediaeval astrologers were familiar. This difficulty reaches into the very roots and methodologies of history, and is one we encounter at almost every level of our study of this zodiac of San Miniato.

A few of these differences between the mediaeval and modern astrologies will emerge in the following study, but I should perhaps comment immediately on the extraordinary fact that my researches in San Miniato indicate that without a shadow of doubt the thirteenth-century astrologers concerned with this zodiac used what is nowadays called the constellational zodiac. It is quite possible that they used this 'zodiac of the stars' only for symbolic purposes – for example, in their occult orientations – which were in any case a direct throwback to the temple-lore of the ancient mystery wisdom. It is quite certain from surviving horoscope charts of the mediaeval period that they also made use of the tropical zodiac in their divinatory arts, or judgmental astrology – even so, the significance of this use of constellational material has not been sufficiently remarked by either astrologers or historians. In effect, the evidence that at least one group of builders made use of the constellational zodiac in their secret symbolism requires that we look again at the symbolic intent behind many of the great European cathedrals and churches which use zodiacal symbolism – for example, at Chartres, Vezelay, Amiens, Paris in France, Canterbury in England, Parma, Sacra di San Michele in Italy, and so on. The symbolism of the constellations is different from the symbolism of the tropical zodiac, yet this is not adequately recognized by astrologers or art historians. My proposition may therefore be disturbing for the majority of astrologers – at least for those astrologers who are interested in the history of their subject – not least because it demands a new assessment of old data, and a new view of the mediaeval astrology. If the constellational zodiac were so important in the mediaeval period, then the Arabic star-lore, with its specific interpretation of the fixed stars, is part and parcel of mediaeval church symbolism, and not merely a semi-moribund literary tradition, which finds its way into such later works of art as the Schiffanoia Palazzo or the Chericati Ceiling, through the learned esotericisms of scholars.

Fortunately, the language of the San Miniato zodiac is very clear, and I doubt that any practitioner of the art will deny my basic postulate that the mediaeval astrology was essentially a practical device by which the church builders attempted to relate earth patterns to cosmic patterns. In this, they were no different from their forebears, Christian and pagan alike. The fact that our modern builders no longer attempt to establish such a correspondence is entirely to our loss.

The theologians will probably be the ones most happy with the claims I make about San Miniato. The thirteenth-century symbols with which I deal are thoroughly Christian, for all their pagan origins. There is scarcely a Christian symbol – from the cross to the bread, from the Christos monogram to the vesica piscis – which was not interpreted in a different way during pagan times, and so it is important that we recognize the particular way in which the mediaeval Christians adjusted to their own world-vision the most powerful of the pagan images. It is unlikely that I have written anything about the San Miniato zodiac which will trouble the churchman, since my basic postulate is that this zodiac was laid down not merely to honour certain esoteric truths about the Christ, but also in the service of a church militant against one of the numerous heresies which beset the twelfth and early thirteenth-century Papacy. Whether or not my argument that the San Miniato zodiac was designed specifically against the doctrines of the Joachimites is accepted as valid, I think that few theologians will contend with my general notion that the zodiac we find in San Miniato is no pagan thing, but rather part of a Christian programme of reform and elucidation – perhaps indeed the most remarkable example of such a programme to have survived from the mediaeval world. The interesting personal observation I have made during the past sixteen years of research is that it is very often the professional theologian and priest who has helped me most in regard to the work I have undertaken – it is as though the modern training of theology and priestcraft encourages that special feeling for symbolism and for eternal verities which is essential to a wholesome approach to the deeper mysteries which may be perceived in San Miniato.

It is probably the professional historian of art who will take most exception to my general thesis that the basilica of San Miniato is a product of esoteric or occult art. There are several vested interests why art historians should deny my premises and conclusions, since were they to be accepted, a new approach to mediaeval art and art history would have to be formulated. Having said this, I should say that I doubt that any art historian should criticize my general notion that one cannot approach mediaeval art without some knowledge of the hermetic tradition of magic, astrology and quasi-heretical lore which lay behind it. I doubt that any serious iconographer would claim that all 'religious' art of the mediaeval period was rooted only in religious Christian symbolism – the flotsam and jetsam of hermetic lore, of heretical texts and of popular Christian mythology (such as the Golden Legend and the misnamed apocryphal texts) permeate mediaeval art and symbolism in the most unexpected forms. Many art historians would agree that it is quite impossible to understand correctly a single one of the 666 mediaeval fresco subjects in the Salone della Ragione in Padua without a profound knowledge of occult lore. However, few would go as far as I do, and claim that it is just as impossible to appreciate fully the symbolism of the nearby Arena Chapel (linked with Giotto, in spite of the serious nineteenth-century restorations) without a knowledge of occult lore. In making this claim, I am only too well aware that hundreds of art historians and commentators clearly feel otherwise. In essence, all I am suggesting about the art of San Miniato is that astrological lore is just another of the many rich streams of the ancient knowledge and occult lore which is found in almost all forms of mediaeval art. However, I would like to add a few further observations.

For many years I have held the view that it is quite impossible to understand pre-Renaissance art or literature without a profound knowledge of that mediaeval astrology and occultism with which the cultural and social life of the period was thoroughly permeated. This is perhaps more widely recognized in modern times than it was twenty-five years ago, when I began to lay down the foundations of my later work on San Miniato al Monte by studying systematically the history of astrology, hermetic lore and the history of art, yet even today there is still a long way to go towards establishing an educational programme which will bring to life the symbolism of the proto-Renaissance in the minds of modern students.

The fact is that the mediaeval artist dealt first and foremost with symbols, and he seems to have taken it for granted that such symbols should be beautiful or 'aesthetic'. I must add that a great number of mediaeval symbols were designed to work on several levels, and that in many instances such levels were involved with what we might now call esotericism or 'mystery wisdom'. Those who have versed themselves in the hermetic lore – occultists such as Blavatsky or Steiner – inform us that the ancient symbols should be read on seven different levels. The art historians, all too often unversed in the esoteric symbolism which they profess to write about, rarely deal with such symbols on more than one level.

The uninformed prejudice about the nature of mediaeval art is one of the most serious problems I have encountered time and time again in the past few years, for there are whole groups of influential historians and teachers who, while they might admit that the San Miniato zodiac is beautiful, and that it is undoubtedly one of the symbols used by mediaeval artists to signify the spiritual realm, would deny that it has any other significance. I have actually heard such opinions voiced by specialist historians in the temenos of San Miniato, their words unmindful of the esoteric symbols hovering on the façade above them, and on the pavement at their feet. In making such claims they are simply admitting that they cannot 'read' or appreciate mediaeval symbolism at all. More tragic, however, in making such a claim they are demoting the significance of a vast esoteric mediaeval art and literature of which they are ignorant.

I have written about San Miniato before, and I have already attempted to point out that it is one of the last surviving examples of the true masonic art, built in a time before masons were 'freemasons', and hence capable of working for other masters than the church, or similar hermetically orientated groups. My books and articles on San Miniato, and on the related mysteries of the mediaeval age, appear to have found a wide audience. The response to my work from the general public has been gratifying, and San Miniato has become a centre of pilgrimage for many of those who are interested in the mediaeval mysteries of the zodiac. However, the response from the academic world has been questionable, and at times downright rude. I say this merely as a matter of record, for in fact I had expected little else. In the history of art taught in most of our colleges and universities, there is too great dependence upon literature: art history has become a methodology of archaeology rather than a pursuit of soul-development, which is surely what it should be. It is as though the language of art itself has been lost to the modern academic realm, so that those responsible for teaching the history of art are inclined to attend to the more immediate language of literature in its stead. There is a tragic failure to recognize that the arts of painting and sculpture have different tutelary spirits from the arts of literature. Rather than being prepared to make any attempt to rediscover the lost language of art, the modern academic world appears to take satisfaction in surrogates. Being aware of these limitations, I was not surprised that my views on San Miniato – which in effect postulate a new way of looking at art, a new practice and theory of aesthetics – should not be understood, or should find savage critics, among academics.

The sad fact is that nowadays the majority of people look at art in the wrong way. No longer are people prepared to give themselves completely to works of art: they are not inclined to meditate in front of such works, with a view to hearing the quiet though distinctive language proper to art. The ancient meditative approach, so essential to the growth of soul (which is the proper concern of art), has given way to notions of a quick-service art-appreciation which is superficial in the extreme. We live in a world which no longer has time for art, even time for itself – it is a world of instant art, in which a journalistic art of pre-digested imagery is dominant, a world which, thanks to television and the ad-man subterfuge, strews unwanted rubbish in our subliminal worlds. There is only one end to which this superficiality can lead – the certain atrophy of the human imagination. Meanwhile, even while attending this horrific end, those responsible for education and art more often than not prefer to read books about works of art, choosing to listen to the cacophonous voices of interpreters, rather than to experience art directly. They do this in the conviction that art is a literary experience, rather than a soul-experience. A corollary to this dependence upon literature is that there is now a history of art which is virtually divorced from the true appreciation of art, which, by its spiritual nature, should really be rooted in the meditative life.

Not for one moment do I wish to suggest that we should meditate (in any eastern sense of the word) in front of a work of art – that is with mantras, with chanting or with mental picture-building. Rather, I mean that we should be prepared to approach the realm of art as though it speaks a language of its own, a language which requires an especially attuned sensitivity, and which demands of those who approach it the ability to 'listen' or to 'see' in the inner senses of these words. I feel that one should approach a work of art in such a state of mind as permits that work to induce, in a thoroughly wholesome way, mental pictures within the soul. I say this out of a deep conviction that such was the original purpose of art, and that this was the healing process involved in almost all pre-Renaissance art forms. There was a time when all art was concerned with linking man harmoniously with the spiritual realm. The main purpose of establishing this link with the spiritual – be it through music, words, dance or painting – was to bring healing and solace to the soul. It is worth noting that this concept of art, as a therapy for the soul, changed mainly as a result of the demoting of true symbolism during the Tridentine reforms – themselves subsequent to certain confusions engendered during the Renaissance. It is therefore a concept of art which was undreamed of when the San Miniato zodiac was laid down. In view of this, to approach the zodiacal symbolism in the right spirit, we have to cast off this heavy post-Tridentine hypothesis which denies that symbolism is multi-layered, and deals only with consciousness. Since the Tridentine reforms, there developed a notion of art as little more than an instrument of decoration. However, occultists are aware that decoration does not link directly with the spiritual realms, whereas truely symbolic forms do. There can be no healing in mere decoration, yet most of the visual arts of modern times are more concerned with decoration and its modern collaboration, which is illustration, than with healing. This modern concept of art (which has heaped around itself a modern art that mirrors its own view of art) is almost antithetical to the art of San Miniato which I examine here.

All the evidence insists that the mediaeval artist was involved far more with 'meaning' and with 'symbolism' than with aesthetics. Any art which is not concerned with meaning and symbolism must be fundamentally harmful for the human being, yet the sad fact is that much of the art with which we surround ourselves in modern times is neither redolent with meaning nor charged with healing forces. We have around us an art of 'sensation' if not 'sensationalism'. And yet, as Coomaraswamy says in his important treatment of the mediaeval view of art, 'To speak of art exclusively in terms of sensation is doing violence to the inner man.'[1] I do not propose to discuss here the aetiology of this modern intellectual violence, yet I must note in passing that it is not unconnected with the dependency upon literary surrogates in the study of art, allied to an unrecognized fear (often expressed in conscious disdain) for the esotericism and occultism which flavoured almost all important realms of mediaeval art and literature. Behind this fear there lies ignorance, of course. The study of history is usually partisan, but there is a limit to which we should be prepared to foist the prejudices and ignorances of one age on the interpretation of the art-forms of another.

It is inevitable that an age which has favoured materialism at the expense of the soul-life should have failed to understand the nature of symbols. Symbols are not abstractions, but living forces which speak their own language directly to the soul of man. I came to the conclusion long ago that a work of art of any quality speaks its own language, and that the understanding of art should really seek no support or explanation of its being from other realms. A true work of art speaks a language proper only to itself; it is a cosmos, a created unity, a reflection of a spiritual truth, with no dependence upon other cosmoses for its being or significance. Because of this, I would maintain that the hallmark of a great work of art, such as the esoteric architecture of San Miniato al Monte, is that it may stand alone, without need of commentary or explanation. The symbolism of San Miniato, of which the mediaeval zodiac is the symbolic hub, is of such an order that it is possible to discover a harmonious unity, within both the interior and exterior symbols, which point to an esoteric meaning that has no need of supporting documentary evidence, contemporaneous or otherwise. I would maintain that it is perfectly possible to follow the anagogic symbolism of the basilica and its zodiac, purely from an examination of the symbols themselves, and with no reference to, or dependence upon, the following text. Indeed, it is only by following the mediaeval arguments in marble, rather than in my words, and in attending the anagogic processes toward which they point, that it is possible to arrive at a sense of the mystery wisdom within the basilica, and to experience in a living way the healing power of its ancient art.

The genuine work of art does not seek to be explained. Nor do its therapeutic or meaningful qualities require to be examined only in the light of the intellect. Experience has led me to the conclusion that there is always something ultimately disturbing or harmful in talking and writing about painting, literature or music. In a sense, the experience of real art pertains to personal soul-experiences, concerning which it is irrelevant what others might think or say. I would apply this argument (crudely put in the preceding sentences) to the art of San Miniato, and suggest that even without my own words, my own written guide, the sensitive human being is by his own soul-nature able to experience the working of the hermetic structures within the church. He will be healed and refreshed through his contact with the symbolic structures in the church, even if he is unable to formulate in conscious terms what the symbols are, and what they mean. True art has never really had need of words, and were our educators and mentors more intelligent about these things, then they would ensure that the modern theory of the subconscious (which is really old wine of the initiates in new bottles, and that a disturbed wine to boot) should be applied to theories of aesthetics in a more convincing way. Art speaks to what is now called the 'subconscious' within man, and it is the function of the intellect to give a more or less garbled version of what the guardian of the subconscious permits it to realize.

It is certainly no accident that our own century, which has seen the development of a conception of the unconscious, is now witnessing the reappearance of many of the symbols originated in the ancient mystery centres. The ancient cosmic lore is presenting itself once again, though for the first time in a form recognizable to the uninitiated, designed to be appreciated by the conscious minds of men. As Ean Begg has shown, the Egyptian goddess Isis, herself symbolic of something of inestimable value to the future development of mankind, is resurfacing in the esoteric symbolism of the Black Virgin.[2] The ancient star-wisdom, laid down in a form which is still recognizable in twelve images constructed some three thousand years ago is resurfacing as the external form of man's inner search to relate harmoniously once more with the cosmos from which he was severed some centuries ago.[3] The esoteric lore of the early Christians, formulated in the days when such words as 'resurrection' and 'reincarnation' had very different meanings from the ones ascribed to these words today, is also reappearing in many new esoteric lores, legends and cults, not all of which are of obvious value at the moment, but some of which are preparing seeds for future growth. The interesting thing is that all these reborn ideas have survived not so much in philosophical concepts or in literature, but in forms of art, or in games such as chess, playing cards and (as Stierlin has shown) even in such a thoroughly materialized sport as polo.[4] They have survived precisely because they were designed into systems of art and play which disguised their true intent – the result is that in their outer form of art they were misunderstood, and more often than not ignored as reservoirs of ancient wisdom. Had the materialists really understood the secret symbols of the cathedrals, they would certainly have devised some wholesome-seeming stratagem to destroy their structure. As it is, they have succeeded only in destroying a great deal of those structures, in particular the content of symbols which, while they could not understand them, were obviously redolent with some hidden and potent significance. It was no accident that after the French Revolution, itself guided initially by esoteric schools, Notre Dame in Paris should have been turned into a vast stable for horses, as part and parcel of the demystification technique of the enlightenment.[5] The horse has ever been an esoteric symbol of the higher potential for thought, as Jonathan Swift, one of the great masters of the Green Language (or the 'language of the birds' as one hermetic form of speech is sometimes called) was well aware when he gave us the talking horses, the houyhnhnms which Gulliver encountered in his travels. How fitting, therefore, that horses should be stabled in the most beautiful and ornate symbol of alchemical lore ever built in Europe. Even the symbolic forms of history, of those events which the uninitiated might imagine had been born of random meetings, or by chance, are rarely without their recondite symbolism. The horses of this story represent the intelligence of the human being taking refuge in the fabric of esoteric symbolism. It is only in this century, after Blavatsky and others of her eminence waved the olive branch over the flood of materialism, that it has been wise for the horses to canter back into the world.

In the light of this, we may see that it is no accident that the wisdom enshrined in the mediaeval esoteric complex of San Miniato should be permitted to enter into consciousness in our times. The symbolism appears to have been laid down precisely to inform man that the material world partakes of the eternal. If my theory is correct, and the San Miniato zodiac really did have among its several purposes the confuting of the Joachimite prediction that the Antichrist was to appear, and that the familiar world was coming to an end, then no great power of imagination is required to see the relevance of this message to our own confused world, which bears more parallels with the late twelfth century than we might imagine.

What we have within the basilica of San Miniato, and to some extent on its beautiful marble façade, is a work of art which speaks directly to the soul, or to what the moderns might call the unconscious. Until now, it does not appear to have figured to any great extent in the conscious realm of man. There is distinct evidence that at least two different artists of the fifteenth century were aware of part of the esoteric message which I have unravelled. There is even some indication that one of the Benedictine monks who lived in the adjacent monastery in the nineteenth century was aware of the mysteries of orientation, but on the whole the wisdom within the church has been recognized only by esotericists, who have preferred to keep this wisdom to themselves. The historicism of our time requires that the ancient mysteries be brought back into the light of consciousness – not merely into the consciousness of initiates (who would themselves have no need of such a book as this), but into the consciousness of those people who have not yet sought that special development required to attain initiation.

The seeing soul of the initiate will see, and will certainly have no need of my words. However, even a casual observer of humanity cannot fail to observe that many people are prepared to wander through their heritage of mediaeval churches and cathedrals without making any effort to open their souls, without attuning themselves to any special kind of listening. For all its boastful talk of 'communications' and 'media', the world in which we presently live does not encourage people to commune with art, or even to look with curiosity, or in an open spirit of inquiry, so it is sometimes necessary for individuals to take upon themselves the mantle of guide. Mercury, the ancient symbol of hermeticism, once the messenger-god who ruled communication between the material realm and the higher world, is now demoted to a symbol of commerce on the bronze doors of our banks and financial institutions. I suppose, therefore, when all is said and done, it is in this guise, and for such people who are not accustomed to seeing the hermetic symbols directly, that I write this book. There is no secret in the placing of the small wings on the feet of hermetic Mercury, for he hovered above the earth over which he stood, as symbol of this holiness. There is a sense in which every place upon which we stand is holy, but when we stand within an ancient mystery-centre, as we do if we place our feet on the nave pavement of San Miniato, then we are in a holy of holies, and it behoves us to open our eyes and our souls in a different way. The ancient art of the mystery centres is ever-healing, for it pertains to the true art which mirrors the spiritual realm. The art of San Miniato al Monte is perhaps the last complete representative of thirteenth-century mystery wisdom, and it therefore requires that we approach it in a new way, with a view to receiving from it a much-needed power of healing. If the following text helps one person to a greater understanding of the ancient mystery wisdom as manifest in this basilica, then all my years of labour and research will not have been in vain.

This may seem a very far-fetched method of divination to be employed and recommended by a scientist, but serves to remind us that astrology was the supreme science in the thirteenth century, and that the fundamental natural law almost to the time of Newton was the subjection of the inferior elementary bodies to the rule of the stars.

(L. THORNDIKE, *Michael Scot*, London, 1965)

It is known that there existed Schools of Builders. Of course they had to exist, for every master worked and ordinarily lived with his pupils. In this way painters worked, in this way sculptors worked. In this way, naturally, architects worked. But behind these individual schools stood other institutions of very complex origin. And these were not merely architectural schools or schools of masons. The building of cathedrals was part of a colossal and cleverly devised plan which permitted the existence of entirely free philosophical and psychological schools in the rude, absurd, cruel, superstitious, bigoted and scholastic Middle Ages. These schools have left us an immense heritage, almost all of which we have already wasted without understanding its meaning and value.

(P. D. OUSPENSKY, *In Search of the Miraculous*, London, 1931)

Introduction

If a historian is permitted to express himself in allegorical-mythical terms, we might say that Thoth, the Egyptian god of books, who is actually Hermes Trismegistus, was then entering upon his hidden realm which endures down to our days: the hermetica, the mysteria, the secrets, are set down in books and nevertheless they remain inaccessible to those 'of closed mind'; astrologers, alchemists, natural philosophers, and poets – and in our times also psychologists – are their guardians, the Christian hierarchs and theologians are their – sometimes stern, sometimes mild – adversaries.

(P. SCHMITT, 'Ancient Mysteries in the Society of Their Time, Their Transformation and Most Recent Echoes', from *The Mysteries. Papers from the Eranos Yearbooks*, Princeton, 1971.)

I first encountered the zodiac of San Miniato al Monte some sixteen years ago. With one of those perspicacious insights, all too rare in ordinary life, I sensed from this first view of the zodiac that much of my future life would somehow be involved with solving the problems of symbolism set by its iconography and orientation. I look back over these years now, and ask myself how indeed I knew from the very first experience of the zodiac that it contained problems which had to be solved.

Sixteen years ago, I knew precious little about this remarkable church and its zodiac. As a professional art historian, I knew only that there was a problem of orientation: the basilican church of San Miniato al Monte broke all the mediaeval ecclesiastical rules of orientation. As a specialist in symbolism, I knew that one of the symbols used in the zodiac was a 'deviant', so far as the astrological tradition was concerned: the image for Pisces was not standard. However, beyond such academic details, I knew nothing with my conscious mind of the deep problems of esoteric symbolism which would present themselves in later times. I did not then suspect that the zodiac was merely the centre of a vast cycle of arcane symbolism within the church, a cycle which reflects the deepest levels of hermetic esotericism known to the mediaeval mind.

Even so, this limited knowledge I had of the San Miniato zodiac was somehow sufficient to warrant a tremulous excitement of soul when I first saw it, in the dim

1

light of the basilican nave. If there is such a thing as Platonic 'remembering', then this was surely it, for I felt that I somehow already knew the zodiac, even though I had not been to the basilican church before. It was as if I had a foretaste of what was to come, as though already, in some hidden part of my being, I knew about the mysteries of San Miniato, and had to unravel them from within myself, rather than to seek them in the outer fabric of the church. Probably I was catching a taste of what the orientalizing occult books sometimes call a 'sense of karma'.

Whatever the roots of the experience, however, the personal situation of my life during the next sixteen years permitted me to work in considerable depth on the symbolism of the zodiac, and upon the ramifications of this symbolism throughout the church. My academic background and personal inclinations had encouraged in me a deep interest in the history of astrology, and in particular in mediaeval astrology. These two life-directions combined to make the zodiac of San Miniato al Monte an ideal subject for my research. I soon became obsessed by the zodiac and its hidden significance, and, gradually, as the years passed, my research led to the most extraordinary discoveries which had the effect of changing my view of thirteenth-century art and astrology. Some of these discoveries I have published. Others I have not yet had the courage to publish, for they appear to touch on sensitive areas of contemporary prejudices and ignorances. I found it difficult to write intelligently about the survival of the ancient Sun-Mysteries, and about attempts to counter the heresies of Joachim di Fiore, for a public who knew nothing of these particular mysteries and heresies, and who indeed had only a garbled notion of what mysteries and heresies were at all.

How may I encapsulate in a few words the story of the many things I discovered in this mysterious church? By a series of happy accidents (which, again, the modern occultists might well link with karma), I was fortunate enough to discover that the orientation of the church of San Miniato was so arranged as to permit a ray of sunlight to fall once a year upon important hermetic symbols within the church. I was rapt by the experience, and excited to discover the survival in a Western church of the practices I remembered being mentioned in the early literature of the mysteries. The temple of the cult of Serapis had been orientated astrologically, so that once a year a beam of sunlight fell upon the lips of the statue of the god.[1] The symbolic and anagogic significance of the sunbeam in San Miniato was of the same mystical order, a living proof of the reality of artistic devices which had survived in literature, but not in art. The fact that this San Miniato symbol was linked with the concept of the fish-symbol meant that it was possible for me to tie the 'pagan' zodiac with traditional Christian art, which had made of the fish its most important hermetic symbol. By the time I had completed my survey of this symbolism involved in the annual ray of light, I was convinced that it represented what is perhaps the most profound mediaeval esoteric symbolism known to modern man. It is certainly the most remarkable use of solar symbolism in mediaeval art.

My good fortune did not end with the light symbolism. By virtue of a certain amount of inspired guesswork, and by dint of casting a number of horoscopes for the year 1207 (which year is mentioned in an inscription alongside the zodiac), I was able to show that in this year there was a unique stellar event which was recorded within the symbolism of the zodiac, and within the church as a whole. This was a 'satellitium in Taurus', a gathering of planets in the constellation Taurus, which was in turn reflected in the Taurean symbolism of the zodiac and the basilican church, and linked by theological arguments with the nature of Christ. The connection between the sunlight which fell on the lips of Serapis, and the Bull of Taurus, became more clear to me, for in Christian esoteric symbolism the zodiacal Taurus is directly linked with Serapis, who in the ancient Egyptian mysteries had been figured as a sacrificial bull.

As if all this were not enough, I was able to show that the orientation of the zodiac was also linked in a most important way with this year of 1207. The axis of Taurus had been directed precisely towards a specific point of sunrise over Florence, a point which, because of certain astrological considerations relating to 1207, may be said to be the anagogic direction of Taurus.

The outline of my exciting findings, and a somewhat simplistic argument in explanation of these, were published. The treatment of the zodiacal symbolism appeared first in an article I wrote for a scholarly journal, in 1978. This material was then marshalled into a more accessible form, and incorporated into a treatment of the sun-symbolism, in two chapters of a book I wrote on esoteric trends in art, also published in that year.[2] Signor Aldinucci, the Father-Abbot of the Benedictine monastery now housed in San Miniato, a man of profound insight and breadth of knowledge, read my book and on the strength of this invited me to prepare a short guide to the mysteries of the zodiac and the esoteric symbolism of the church, which might be sold to visitors. This text (in four languages) was published in 1981, and it is this which has attracted the most attention – and, I might add, misunderstanding – in recent years.[3] However, the living feed-back and exchange of ideas which has resulted from this booklet has enabled me to reformulate certain of the propositions which I hade made about the symbolism of San Miniato al Monte, and it has therefore contributed in no small way to the present new text.

The response of a few historians to my published findings concerning the zodiac of San Miniato has been cautious. Some responses have been directly hostile, and others have failed to evince much real understanding of the principles involved in esoteric history or in mediaeval astrology. That is probably inevitable, of course, for the principles of esoteric historicism are different from those of the exoteric historicism, and much of what has been discovered or published by modern esotericists about the nature and purpose of mediaeval art[4] actually challenges the prevalent view of the history of thirteenth-century art. Certainly it requires that scholars amend their view of both the significance and importance of thirteenth-century astrological thought.

However, the response to my propositions have not all been framed negatively. Some scholars do admit the validity of my view of San Miniato al Monte as a hermetic centre, with the zodiac of San Miniato as the meaningful hub of a wheel of anagogic symbols. The more helpful among these scholars have wisely pointed out that if my proposition about San Miniato is to find a wider academic support, then I should seek to provide some sort of documentary evidence in support of my theory. To be fully supportive, such documentation would have to be contemporaneous with the zodiac itself. In effect, it is suggested that if I wish to gain support for my notion that the San Miniato zodiac represents a hermetic foundation chart, linked with annual, diurnal and epochal rhythms, I will have to find something akin to the thirteenth-century horoscope which I claim was used for laying down the zodiac in 1207.

The chances of such a document having survived the vicissitudes of time are of course very remote. Consequently, while I have looked for such a chart in the obvious places, and even in some of the less obvious places, I have never really expected to find one. Indeed, it has always been my contention that such documentary evidence is unnecessary. I feel there is no real need for a contemporaneous documentary evidence to support what I have claimed regarding the symbolism of San Miniato. I insist that all the needed evidence for what I claim about the zodiac is built within the stone and marble of the church itself. I emphasize this point, and attempt to make my own philosophical position clear, because in the past few months the unexpected has actually happened. The extraordinary fact is that I have been fortunate enough to discover contemporaneous documentary evidence which supports entirely the claims I have made about the symbolism of San Miniato al Monte.

What I have discovered is not itself a mediaeval horoscope for 1207, but something even more significant. I would not be a serious historian were I not to regard such evidence with respect, even with awe, and were I not to publish such evidence in support of my arguments. Yet, having discovered it, and having set out to make use of it in a published form, I must reiterate that I do not regard it as a necessary part of my argument, which is aimed at showing the zodiac and its related symbols to be of esoteric content. However, this documentary evidence is certainly an unexpected bonus, a welcome support for an argument which has been attacked more by prejudice than by learning.

By one of those curious quirks of destiny which most of us encounter at some time or another, this documentary evidence has been under my gaze ever since I first walked into San Miniato al Monte, over sixteen years ago. However, as is the way of things, for a long time I did not see it for what it was – I simply did not have the vision to recognize its true significance. Perhaps this is understandable, for the documentation does wear a most cunning disguise. The evidence consists of an inscription in Latin Leonine hexameters, set in a marble slab (over three metres in length), placed close to the zodiac itself (figure 1). The sense of this

1 The thirteenth-century Latin inscription in the nave of San Miniato al Monte.

inscription is not very clear, however, for the mediaeval Latin is not easily translated. After some initial difficulties, I have succeeded in translating this Latin, and in so doing I have discovered to my surprise that it incorporates a remarkable mediaeval code.

When translated and decoded, this inscription reveals the exact time and date on which the zodiac was laid down, and mentions the names of the planets involved in the satellitium in Taurus. The date contained within this coded Latin corresponds precisely to the date I had arrived at independently, and published in 1978, over nine years ago. It is, of course, the date on which the unique gathering of planets took place, on 28 May 1207.

It is this latest discovery – the significance of the inscription as a 'lost' code, and its relevance to the symbolism of San Miniato – which would be sufficient reason for publishing a further book on the zodiac of San Miniato. However, there is one other important and additional hypothesis which my findings have enabled me to formulate. In examining the inscription with regard to its encoded message, I naturally paid some attention to the numerological significance of its structure, in the knowledge that this would have played a most important part in any system of code or esoteric structure of the mediaeval period. The curious form of the inscription (figure 1) arises from the fact that it is a seven-sentence inscription presented in three lines. It is partly this structure, and the relationship of the hermetic numbers 7 and 3, along with the fact that these together contain a carefully controlled number of letters, which has enabled me to establish a relationship between the inscription and the numerological system of Joachim di Fiore, which had been widely disseminated in the decades prior to the completion of San Miniato al Monte. Having established this connexion, I rapidly came to the conclusion that the encoded message, and indeed the entire symbolism of San Miniato, was not merely symbolic in an anagogic and ecclesiastical sense, but was entirely purposive in a historical sense. Something of the significance of this will be revealed within the following text, but for the moment we should note that it is my view that the zodiac and its inscription were constructed with a view to counteracting the pernicious doctrine arising from the contemporaneous teachings and literature of the Joachimites.

This code, and the conclusions I draw about its anti-heretical purposes, would be sufficient reason for publication of a new survey of the San Miniato zodiac.

5

However, there are one or two other reasons why an examination of the zodiac in a fresh light will prove of interest to the reader.

First of all, times have changed. When I first began work on the San Miniato zodiac there was not the same open interest either in the history of astrology, or in the fact of esotericism as there is now. The ground-swell of popular interest in what the genuine occultists call 'romantic occultism', and the proliferation of silly notions about the nature of occultism and esotericism which followed in its wake, appears to be weakening, and this has left behind a serious spirit of inquiry into genuine occultist and esoteric lore. This alone means that my approach to the study of the symbolism of the zodiac might be made in a different way. I might take for granted in my modern readers certain assumptions which I could not take for granted even a decade ago. Additionally, the many personal letters I have received relating to my first book (out of print since 1979), and the appreciation shown for the occasional lecture I give on the zodiac, all point to the need for a more complete treatment of the zodiac. The developing interest in astrology, and in esotericism, indicates that the material made available in the following text will find a receptive, if not uncritical, audience. For this reason, the first and second chapters consist of a recapitulation of much of the material which I have already published, though each of the points I make is more securely linked with what is known of the esoteric and astrological lore of the thirteenth century, especially in connection with astrological practices and beliefs.

Second, the esoteric background to mediaeval astrology, and its connexion with theological symbolism is not well understood at the present time. To help remedy this, I have attempted to clarify certain issues relating to the history of astrology, particularly in connection with the misconceptions about the astrology which was introduced into Europe by way of Arabic lore, and which has (with many deviations and additions) grown into the familiar if fissiparous forms which are practised in modern times. No serious astrologer, or historian of astrology, can afford to ignore the esotericism and theologizing which accompanied the introduction of astrology into the western world. I hope therefore that the following text will contribute in some small way towards clarifying some of the issues involved in this seminal period of our history. For this reason, the third chapter deals in a simple way with what is relevant in the known history of astrology in the twelfth and thirteenth centuries, specifically in connection with its widespread influence on the zodiacal symbolism adopted by the cathedral builders of the Middle Ages.

Third, the implications of what I have written concerning the so-called 'foundation chart' of San Miniato, and its link with the constellation Taurus, have not been fully realized, even by specialists. To some extent, therefore, my original argument requires expansion and clarification. What I claim is that the orientation of the marble zodiac is not towards the tropical zodiac favoured by modern astrologers, but towards the constellational zodiac, which is the 'visible' zodiac of asterisms. This conclusion requires that many of the modern notions relating to thirteenth-century astrology be examined in a new light. The idea of a constellational astrology raises several important points, for it is generally taken for granted that the mediaeval artists, sculptors and astrologers used the tropical zodiac in their symbolism, yet the evidence of San Miniato (which is by no means an isolated case, as the following examination makes clear) contradicts this. In admitting that the symbolism of San Miniato is rooted in constellational astrology, we are actually opening ourselves up to reinterpreting much of the arcane symbolism which is found in many of the mediaeval cathedrals, such as the cathedrals of Amiens, Paris and Chartres, the Madeleine of Vezelay, the baptistries in Florence, Bergamo and Parma, and in such astrological fresco cycles as survive in the Salone of Padua or the Schiffanoia Palace in Ferrara. For this reason, the fourth chapter, while restricting itself mainly to considerations of the 1207 chart, deals with certain matters relating to astrological practices of the period under examination. In particular it touches upon the mediaeval use of constellational imagery and all that this implies in contrast to the more familiar symbolism of the tropical zodiac.

The fifth chapter deals in considerable detail with the secrets of the San Miniato inscription, which I succeeded in fully translating only in 1985. Since I intend the decoding of the inscription to be clear to the general reader, rather than merely to specialists, I have felt it only fair to preface a detailed analysis with a brief examination of a few other Latin codes which were used by contemporaneous writers who were themselves involved in esotericism or astrological work. My claim is certainly not that a coded inscription is unique in mediaeval art, but simply that this particular code supports in every detail the points I made long before I was familiar with the meaning of the inscription. It may be argued that my interpretation of the lingua ignota of the inscription is fanciful: it has indeed been argued that my interpretation of the symbolism of the San Miniato zodiac is fanciful. There is little I can say in response to such a charge, save perhaps to suggest that there is no real harm in wholesome imagination (a thing so foreign to the modern soul that Coleridge was constrained to invent a new word to denote it), and to remind those who object that our present notion of knowledge requires that before one hypothesis may be regarded as inadequate, a more satisfactory hypothesis must be presented in its place.

The far-reaching conclusions drawn in the final chapter are entirely personal, and perhaps even self-indulgent. They may be read as placing too much importance on the feeling which San Miniato has evoked on my soul and mind. Even so, a panoramic survey of the esotericism of the Palladium (which in some ways merges into the derived Grail symbolism) in relation to the Sun-Mysteries may prove of interest to the modern reader. As will become clear to anyone who appreciates the following text, the history of our civilization as represented in esoteric literature is very different from that represented in ordinary literature. This in itself gives rise to two different streams of historicism, which (in this last chapter, at least) I am in danger of merging, to the detriment of both. The method by which I attempt to suggest a connection between San Miniato and the larger esoteric tradition of the Sun-Mystery of the Palladium, really belongs to the esoteric approach to history. It is perhaps out of place in a book of this kind. However, having led the reader to a point where the esoteric symbolism of San Miniato begins to take on a formal order and urgency of its own, I felt it necessary to step in a direction where even initiates might fear to tread. I think that the time is coming when specialists in occult lore will more and more find it necessary to take risks of this kind.

Both of the chapters dealing with technical aspects of astrology may in parts appear obscure or even obtuse to the general reader, so that I have taken the liberty of attaching a short glossary (Appendix 1) of those specialist terms which are used in the text, in order that my arguments may be followed even by those unversed in astrological lore. This glossary is derived from the more extensive glossary of terms in my *Dictionary of Astrology*.[5] Further supportive material is set out in other appendices – for example, there is a useful chronology of events (Appendix 2), touching directly upon the building of San Miniato al Monte, and its contiguous monastic building (formerly the Bishop's Palace), and a further Appendix 3 giving all the relevant data and measurements connected with the zodiac, its horoscope and related astrological symbolism within San Miniato. There is also appended useful material relating to other zodiacs, such as those in the Sacra di San Michele, high in the hills alongside the Val di Susa, and in the circular thirteenth-century zodiac in the baptistry of Florence, with its curious solar-centred 'alchemical' inscription (Appendix 4). Appendix 5 is given over to providing useful documentation relating to the important symbols of San Miniato. Sometimes this material is presented in the original Latin, but where good translations are available, I have used these, with grateful acknowledgments. Such material is not essential to my argument, of course, but without doubt it will be found useful in the context of this elusive area of research.

Finally, a word about the notes. It may be felt that I have been too liberal with my references to authorities, both ancient and modern. However, the fact is that I do not seek to argue fallaciously by what the mediaeval logicians called 'argument by authority' at all. Rather, I feel that the history of symbolism in general, and the history of astrology in particular – the very area in which I work, and in which I take the greatest pleasure – have in recent years been given a bad reputation by inept and irresponsible scholarship (which, of course, is scarcely scholarship at all). I would like where possible to remedy this deficiency, by spelling out, in terms of supportive literature and notations, the rationale by which I arrived at my conclusions. Additionally, I am all too well aware that many of the points I make in the following text may appear fanciful to those who are not familiar with the occult and esoteric literature of the Middle Ages, and I would therefore like to make available to those who have doubts a list of reliable or relevant texts by which they may check my own facts, or even elaborate supportively upon them, with a view to amending my opinions, if they feel so inclined.

In conclusion, I would like to thank the Benedictine monks of San Miniato al Monte, who have given me moral and intellectual support during my years of research and meditation. In particular I would thank the Father Abbot Aldinucci and Father Christopher for their personal help and friendship. I would like to thank Professor Ranchetti for his hospitality, and for his willingness to share his profound insight into mediaeval history. I would also like to thank Dr Angus Ross for his willingness to read and criticize my text with such humour and delicacy: any factual errors within the following material are certainly not of his making. I would also like to thank Professor Kendall, whose extraordinary knowledge of mediaeval Latin hexameters I found so refreshing: it was a passing reference he made to a thirteenth-century inscription in Saint Trophime at Arles which nudged me into realizing (not before time, I might add) the true nature of the San Miniato inscription. In mentioning by name these scholars and friends who have helped me on my way, I need hardly say that I do not wish to associate them with any of my views, and in particular with any errors which have found their way into the following text.

Florence, 1986

1 San Miniato al Monte, Florence

Astrology must be something social. . . . In a true Astrology only what is universally human is considered and not the satisfaction of the egoism of the human being.

(E. VREEDE, *The World of Stars and Human Destiny*, 1926)

When we glance down at the circular zodiac in the dim nave of San Miniato al Monte (figure 2), we are looking across a great distance of time, and through a vast confusion of intellect, towards what C. S. Lewis has called a 'discarded image'.[1] It is as though we have arrived some 800 years too late to fully appreciate the meaning of this zodiac, which radiates its intense power of symbolism through the basilica, for we have lost the old power of mystical vision which was the birthright of the mediaeval man. Yet, even at this great distance of time, there still remains in the silence of the zodiac a wonderful sense of the miraculous. The zodiac addresses the sensitive realm of our emotional life, rather than our intellects or minds. The ancient esoteric symbolism was not designed to speak directly to the intellects of men: rather, it was the pride of the human intellect which later relegated such things as this zodiac, and made of them discarded images.

The curious Latin inscription set in the marble floor not far from the zodiac informs us that the celestial image was put in this place in the year 1207. Even for those who cannot read the Latin script, the date at least is clear in the Roman formula MCCVII (figure 1). The sack of Christian Constantinople by the crusaders, some three years earlier, was still a pain to the souls of its designers: they might even have been themselves refugees from the pillage of that tower-capped city, for some scholars trace Byzantine elements and symbolism in the decorative florations of the marble zodiac and the related intarsia work of the nave.[2] This tragic event had thrown the mediaeval world into confusion, for the expressed aims of the fourth crusade had been the recovery of Jerusalem from the hands of the Arabs, yet its achievement, thanks to the immoral wiles of the Venetians, was merely to make Christ's burthen the heavier. The Pope of that time, Innocent III, thought and acted on a grand scale. He had recently put the whole of England under a sort of excommunication, and, needing an excuse or

10

2 The zodiac in the nave pavement of San Miniato al Monte.

theological justification for a new feudal arrangement in France, he was already negotiating another 'crusade' which would change the religious face of southern France. This crusade, which was not a crusade, would eventually result in the cruel destruction of the Knights Templars, founded at the beginning of the previous century, ostensibly to protect the pilgrimage routes to the Holy Land, but now almost openly involved in financing and lending moral support to the building of cathedrals throughout Europe.[3] In only two years' time Europe would lament yet again to the use of Christian arms against Christian, at the news of the destruction and rapine of the Albigensians.

Wars to the east, and wars to the west, and great difficulties to south and north – especially to the north. Even in 1207, these builders in San Miniato could see and hear around them the terrible results of the struggle between the powers ecclesiastical and temporal arising from the ambitions of the Papacy, which we remember through the Italianized German made famous by Dante – the Ghibellines and the Guelphs. In later times, historians would see Innocent III as the chief architect of the thirteenth-century papal power and magnificence, whilst others would trace to his policies many of the wars and whitch-hunts which would rip Europe apart in the following three centuries.

Yet, for all the violence one sees on all sides of the Christian world, the first years of the thirteenth century were a watershed in Italian history, and the

11

following decades measured the construction of an important crossroad in the history of Europe. The seeds had already been laid down for the rebirth of that imaginative life which was to mark the greatest period of intellectual inquiry and freedom of thought which Europe would experience in many centuries.

In only a few years' time, the determined will of Francis of Assisi led men to change the spiritual direction of the Church, with that silent example which proves even more dangerous than words. For all that Joachim di Fiore had already predicted that the End of the World would come in the middle of the century, there was a seminal creative power in the air, a creativity which soon flowered in the rhythms and sound-words of Dante, and sprouted wings on the fine pencils of Giotto. A thousand new churches and cathedrals were being built throughout Europe, so that already it seemed to those who recorded the times as though the whole world were taking on a new white mantle of marble.[4]

Of these many churches which were built in that first decade of the thirteenth century, one of the most lovely is the basilica of San Miniato, which still houses among many other unspoiled mediaeval symbols this most remarkable of all mediaeval zodiacs. The church, with its glistening façade of coloured marbles, overlooks Florence from that hill on the oltr'Arno, which in the mediaeval era was called the 'Mons Florentina'. It was the hill which the Armenian prince Miniatus is said to have climbed after his decapitation in the Roman arena in Florence below, and it is in the earth of this hill that he was first buried, along with many of the early Christians of those first difficult centuries of our era. It was into this same mountain that the crypt of San Miniato al Monte was dug later to receive his bones, which, it is said, still rest in the casket below the crypt-choir of the church. There is something symbolic of the Christian faith in the fact that the bones of the Armenian prince, who was later recognized as one of the Saints, may still be seen in the crypt, whilst the Roman arena itself, the symbol of Roman paganism, has disappeared, leaving only traces of its elliptical form in the street curve of via Torta and its extensions, to the west of Santa Croce.

Built almost in its present form at the beginning of the thirteenth century, the architecture and symbolism of the basilican church record a remarkably successful, and perhaps even unique, attempt to establish a harmony between esotericism, astrology and theology. It is one of the few European esoteric centres to have remained relatively undamaged by the passage of time. One might almost attribute this to the magical efficacy promised in the curious Latin of the 1207 inscription, which insists that the building would be preserved from the ravages of time itself.[5]

San Miniato is a quite extraordinary building, and the visitor requires no especially attuned sensitivity to feel something of the profound mystery which emanates from within its lovely interior. Yet, there is a sense in which all modern visitors are foreigners to this extraordinary place, for there has been nothing in our educational programme to prepare them for the impact which this remarkable building has on the soul. Modern man has been encouraged, by the failure endemic to our educational systems, to experience art mainly in terms of aesthetic effects. He has been encouraged to balance in his heart and mind the emotion of beauty, and ascribe it to external qualities – all too often at the expense of the meaning intended by the artists who created the works in the first place. The mediaeval mind did not think or feel in such ways, however: mediaeval man was encouraged to view art almost exclusively in terms of symbols, which in the view of Saint Augustine were intended to point in multifoliate forms to the spiritual realm above.[6]

The mediaeval mind took it for granted that his symbols should be beautiful, yet by no means did he see such beauty as the end of art. The purpose of mediaeval art was meaning: it is in this radical difference between the worlds mediaeval and modern that our difficulties arise. The mediaeval man, for whom the basilica was designed, would undoubtedly have found himself more deeply moved, more involved in its symbolic language, than even the most sensitive of modern visitors. It was designed for men and women who thought, felt and breathed symbols, in exercise of their triune being of mind, soul and body. In comparison to mediaeval man we are really lopsided shadows, for we are governed by our thinking brain which grips feet and fingers around our head and shoulders like Sinbad's Old Man of the Sea. Because of this demonic grip of intellect, it is difficult for us to see the mediaeval symbols and art forms in the right way – that is, as they were meant to be seen, by those who created them. Men are different now, and if we forget this simple fact, we may fail to grasp the meaning of this symbolizing zodiac, which is nothing more than a symbol of a mediaeval esoteric cosmology, laid down in extraordinary patterns of marble slabs.

For all the changes which reverberated around the San Miniato builders, there was security in their souls: almost every man and woman of that time felt bathed in the sustaining light of the spiritual. It was taken for granted by all levels of society, and by all levels of morality, that the world was linked in a great chain of being held safe in the hands of angels. Few even doubted that the earth itself was the central stage of the great act of Redemption, with human beings as the millions of extras saved for all eternity from the work of the Devil, waiting in the wings, or beneath the trapdoor of the stage. We moderns are perhaps less confident and secure, and few among us take for granted the abiding presence of the angels in our daily lives. We do not live within a world where the seen miracle is a daily expectation, viewed as the necessary interpretation of the penetration of one of the nine orders of the angelic realm into the everyday world of man. If there are still miracles around us, we no longer see them – though perhaps only for want of proper eyes. We are not as confident about the spiritual basis of the cosmos as mediaeval man, and we do not build with the same revolutionary fervour and grace. We do not construct buildings to last for eternity, in the sure knowledge that eternity is not to do with time, but with beauty, and the moral life. Nor do we lay our first stones down to mark the movement of the stars, nor dedicate our

13

buildings to the gods. The horoscopes which in ancient times linked new buildings with the sweep of planets and stars, as though architectonic forms were living beings, and the related magical dedications to saints and God, are no longer understood or used. They have degenerated to plaques bearing the names of soon-forgotten mayors and aldermen.

It would seem that we are as far away from the spirit of the 1207 zodiac as it is possible to be. We cannot drink in its meaning in the same way that a mediaeval pilgrim would do, feeling ourselves prepared to allow its healing influence to work directly upon our three bodies of spirit, soul and physical. Now that we have discarded that simple-seeming (though infinitely complicated) mediaeval image of the world, the San Miniato zodiac has become something of an intellectual puzzle to our minds. This celestial figure is more of a question mark in marble, than a regenerative fount of life which refreshes our emotions. In truth, it is for us no longer the 'celestial power' which the inscription proclaimed it to be.

Because of this historic fall from grace, and its consequent loss of cosmic vision, we have to remember the distance in space, time and spirit which removes us from the zodiac. If we forget this separation, and our own alienation from the mediaeval art-forms, then we shall fail to understand the miraculous power of its symbolic language. This would be to our great loss, for the symbolizing of the church points to a depth of art which has almost disappeared from our world. It points indeed to an esoteric art, an 'objective art', which is mentioned scarcely at all in our official histories of art, and is remembered only in a handful of occult texts largely unknown to historians.[7]

Fortunately, a few of the San Miniato symbols still speak in a way which we spiritual alienates may understand, even now. One or two of the occult symbols incorporated into the fabric of the basilica are immediately apparent even to the casual eye of moderns. Such, for example, are the astrological symbols in the nave zodiac, and a few of the esoteric symbols in the marble floor of the nave: some art historians even claim to be able to trace a connection between the pavement of dove-symbols with Indian legends,[8] unwittingly disturbing with their footnotes a whole realm of esoteric lore. Some historians interpret the powerful redemptive image of the eagle crushing a serpent in its talons, central to the nave pavement, as a Christianized throwback to wisdom which once belonged to initiates.[9]

Other hermetic and occult symbols are less evident, however, even to the trained eye of the historian and occultist, and it is this which makes the esoteric content of the church at once the most elusive and exciting in Europe. The series of complex occult and theological symbols in the church defies an ordinary approach to its iconographic problems and secrets. Such an approach is simply not adequate, for the architects who designed San Miniato al Monte, and laid within it a hermetic system of symbols, spoke an artistic and spiritual language which is no longer understood by the majority of people.

San Miniato must be approached with an attitude of mind which in modern times might be called 'holistic', but which in mediaeval times was called 'contemplative'. The contemplative mind was the thinking mind made fecund and creative by insights afforded by spiritual disciplines, or by the grace of God. It was wisely recognized that a mind not so activated was barren and moribund. The architecture of San Miniato was designed to speak to the whole man, rather than merely to his intellect. The many layers of astrological and theological symbols within the church must ultimately be apprehended in that single sweep of vision which most easily arises from quiet meditation, yet the modern outlook, fostered by the innate intellectualism of our educational systems, largely prohibits such a vision. The majority of visitors are inclined to follow the modern norm, and attempt an approach to esoteric symbols as though they were so many pieces of a jigsaw puzzle that might be assembled by means of a systematic intellectual effort, in the hope that from such discrete examination, a whole picture will eventually be formed in the mind. However, the ancients rarely constructed their esoteric works with such an approach in view – they did not design them to be considered by the human intellect alone, but rather by the whole man, exercising his triune nature of thinking, feeling and will-life. A frontal and intellectually biased approach to these symbols is inappropriate: the modern intellect is inclined towards a critical analysis which is generally fissiparous in direction. A frontal approach of the intellectual kind merely puts the mysteries themselves into dignified retreat. The only possible way to reach into these ancient secrets is to allow them to speak in their own tongues: in effect, this is the only valid approach to all art, though this is no longer recognized in modern times.

Without doubt, it is the marble zodiac which is the hub of San Miniato's rich symbolism. This is certainly the most remarkable zodiac in Europe, and perhaps in the entire world. The Latin inscription calls it a 'numine celesti' – a divine power of the Heavens – and, as we shall see, it is so called with very good reason. A careful study of the zodiac in relation to the symbolism of the interior, and to the façade of the church, reveals that this is much more than a huge zodiac. It is really what P. D. Ouspensky would have called 'a philosophical machine',[10] for its meaning links in a most extraordinary way with many of the hermetic and astrological symbols within the basilica, and on the façade, providing an opportunity for the most profound contemplation of Christian and occult mysteries. There is scarcely a stone of the original basilica which does not play its part in the profound symbolism of the zodiac. As we shall see eventually, this symbolism so unites the interior and exterior of the church that they together participate in three rhythms: first, in the daily apparent movement of the sun; second, in an astonishing annual phenomenon of the sun, when the solar body stands in a particular relationship to Florence, and third in a distinctly powerful configuration of planets which might be regarded as signifying a new age, such as that which was inaugurated in Florence after the building of San Miniato. This zodiac affords a most subtle display of an occult symbolism which would probably

15

have been understood with relative ease by the majority of ordinary mediaeval worshippers, but which nowadays proves elusive for the modern mind, unless prepared by special instruction.[11]

Those who are not familiar with the hermetic and occult basis of much early Christian symbolism may be surprised to find a zodiac within a church. The majority of moderns tend to think of the zodiac and related astrological ideas as being somehow pagan. However, the truth is that the zodiac, and its attendant astrological symbolism, was to some extent 'Christianized' in the twelfth and thirteenth centuries. Even in the popular textbooks, mediaeval astrology was Christianized to a point where each of the twelve signs, the seven planets and the Ptolemaic spheres, were permeated with specifically Christian ideas and ideals. The story of this conversion of the pagan zodiac is a complex one, and will be sketched briefly in a separate chapter: it is sufficient here for us to note the presence of this zodiac, as a Christian and entirely non-heretical device in the nave of the church.

San Miniato is by no means unique in having a marble zodiac set into its fabric. Another marble zodiac, of similar date, is found embedded in the octagonal floor beneath the radiant splendour of the tesserae of the Florentine baptistry – though this zodiac, unlike that in San Miniato, is no longer in its original position.[12] It was indeed almost a commonplace for the mediaeval builders to incorporate zodiacal and stellar forms into the fabric of their churches and cathedrals – especially when they were intent on pointing to some esoteric strain in their Christian symbolism. So well established was this strain of occult-astrological lore in mediaeval Christian art that it still survives in a wide variety of mediaeval symbols in ecclesiastic and public buildings throughout Europe. For example, much of the more interesting symbolism in Chartres cathedral, in Vezelay, in Notre Dame, Paris, in Canterbury cathedral, and so on, is occult or astrological, whilst the entire interior of the Salone in Padua, the baptistry in Parma, and that in Florence, along with the nearby campanile of Giotto, depend upon an astrological lore which is foreign to modern visitors, yet which would have been quite clear to the mediaeval people for whom they were designed.[13]

The fact is, as we shall see in Chapter 3, that the zodiacal symbolism, like the star-lore of the Arabian astrology, was thoroughly Christianized by the late twelfth century, and was used to quite remarkable ends in many different mediaeval and proto-Renaissance works of art. However, this 'Christianized' version of astrology should not itself disguise the fact that, in terms of ordinary history at least, the zodiac, planets and planisphere were originally pagan, and directly linked with the initiate wisdom of the Mystery Schools. The surviving marble zodiacal imagery on the Egyptian planisphere of Denderah (now in the Louvre, and still, in spite of all, wrongly called a 'zodiac'), the numerous Babylonian astrological stelae, and the large numbers of Hellenistic and Roman references to the use of astrological orientations and horoscopes in papyrus fragments, make this quite clear.[14] The undeniable truth is that whilst remarkably few changes have been made to the basic twelve zodiacal images used by astrologers since pre-Christian times, the meanings attributed to those images have changed considerably with the passage of time. Only an occultist's approach to history could adequately clarify the nature and importance of these changes to the development of western cultural life.

The occultist's view of history is somewhat different from the conventional view. Put briefly, we might say that the occultist is inclined to see the general sweep of history as being guided by Schools of Initiation. Such schools are viewed as being the legitimate descendants of the ancient mystery centres, often interlinked with the Christian Church, but sometimes working separately from the modern initiation of Christianity. It is held that periodically (or as required by the exigencies of history), these schools inject into the stream of history such ideas and innovations as are considered necessary for the maintainance of culture, or for the influencing of needed changes, in dominant civilizations. Many occult historians claim that all significant movements in literature, art and cultural awareness were directed by such esoteric schools, who at the appropriate moment provide data, symbols and ideas to enrich and maintain ordinary civilized life.[15]

All the important symbols used in religion and art are said to have been derived from such occult schools, and among these are the zodiacal and planetary symbols of astrology. The occultist Steiner, who has left us the most satisfactory account of the influence of esoteric schools on our western culture, makes the point that the imagery of the zodiac (an imagery which has influenced human thought and art for at least 2,500 years) originally proceeded from such esoteric schools in Babylon.[16] Having stated what must be the obvious to any historian of the subject, Steiner then goes on to make a most remarkable claim – that the images of the zodiac and the constellations, bequeathed to humanity by esoteric schools, were so designed in the pre-Christian mystery centres as to establish a symbolism that would reflect the esoteric wisdom which would eventually stream from early Christianity. Steiner, presumably by way of example, specifically links the choice of the image of the celestial Virgin with the later cult of the Virgin Maria, and the sign Pisces with Christ himself. Steiner's claim is a momentous one, so far as conventional theory of history is concerned, yet the art-historical evidence suggests that the symbolism of the zodiac – ostensibly 'pagan' – was indeed readily assimilated into early Christian theology and art, almost as though such occult symbolism had been designed for such a purpose. Steiner's example happens to be an apposite one for our own purposes, because a deal of the significance of the San Miniato symbolism rests precisely on the esoteric meaning inherent in the connection drawn between Christ and Pisces.

Several strains of occult and astrological lore were so well ingrained in early Christian art that a few have survived even in our modern symbolism – their origins largely forgotten. This survival is in spite of the later reaction of the established Church which, for good historical reasons, attempted to stamp out from theology and art all reference to hermetic lore and astrology. A good example of such an 'occult' survival is what modern symbolists call the 'Stella Maris', the star which is often found on the shoulder (sometimes on the mapharion) of Maria in icons and mediaeval religious pictures. No satisfactory explanation for this star has been given by conventional historians, though occultists recognize that it is actually derived from astrological sources.[17]

In the early images of the constellation Virgo we find the predominant fixed star Spica, which is now known to be a binary. Spica was the 'Ear of Corn' in the hand of the celestial Virgin. Historians link her with Isis, the goddess who also clasps to her body either wheat-ears or the young Horus child. Occultists recognize this pagan image as a prototype for the later image of the Marian virgin image, in which the 'Ear of Corn' is transformed into the Child – who is, of course, the Bread of the Eucharist. Some mediaeval images of Maria even show her with ears of corn scattered over her dress as symbolic motifs – reminiscent of Astraea, with whom the myth of the origin of the constellation Virgo was linked (figure 3). Aside from its symbolism in painting and sculpture, the actual star Spica was also seen in Christian terms, for the Venerable Bede identified the whole constellation of Virgo with the prototype of Easter, at which festival the stars of the constellation shine so brightly in the eastern evening sky – the brightest of the stars being Spica.[18] In the star-lists of the astrologers, this same Spica was adopted as one of the so-called 'fifteen stars' – the only fixed stars to be accorded special sigils, and related specifically to the sympathetic magical arts involved with the manufacture of talismans and charms.[19] The sigil for Spica ♍ was graphically linked with the sigil for Pisces itself ♓ and with the ancient Egyptian sigil for 'god' ☉ , which in modern symbolism has become the symbol for the sun.[20] This connection between Spica and Pisces arose from the idea that Christ himself was prefigured in the image of Pisces, so that Virgo was visualized as reaching out across the zodiac, to draw the Pisces child towards herself. It was no accident that the theologian Albertus Magnus, writing in the very century in which the San Miniato zodiac was laid down, should place the Ascendant of Christ's horoscope in Virgo: by then the symbolism to which he pointed was at least 2,000 years old. Thus, Spica as the image of an ear of corn, itself derived from a fixed star, and with its several connotations of 'Christ' and 'Bread', survived as a star-symbol on the shoulder or mantle of the Maria Virgin. We shall eventually observe profound symbolic parallels to these ideas on the façade of San Miniato itself.

Many such symbols – some of them misunderstood, and few of them fully appreciated by modern historians – have in a similar way survived from ancient streams of occultism and magic into our culture. We might, for example, add to the Spica symbol such things as the magically inspired use of lapis lazuli (ultramarine) for the traditional colours of the Virgin's palla, the symbolism of the halo (why should the Greek word be derived from the 'threshing floor' circle trodden out by oxen?), the images of the four Evangelists, the Seven Virtues and

3 *Fifteenth-century woodcut of the Madonna with robes covered in heads of corn, with reference to the celestial Virgo.*

the Seven Vices, and so on. Each of these was originally involved with pagan occultism. It is, for example, no accident that such lapis lazuli stones were used for the eyes in the three figures of the lectern in San Miniato (figure 4). Certain strains of occult influences in art are partly recognized by non-occultist historians, of course – some attention has been paid to the survival of astrological images in the façades of the great cathedrals and churches of France and Italy, in such places as Paris, Chartres, and Vezelay.[21] Such occult symbolism is sometimes recognized, but all too often historians fail to understand its deeper significance, seemingly being inclined to regard such occult symbols as 'decorative'. In such attitudes we may note the failure to grasp that the art of the ancients was fundamentally

19

4 The thirteenth-century lectern on the pulpit in San Miniato al Monte.

different from modern art, in which there is all too evidently a place for 'mere decoration', as Kandinsky lamented in the greatest of his books.[22]

The modern occultists, who so profoundly influenced Kandinsky, and therefore contributed greatly to the modern school of painting, recognize that such symbolism is always intended to express a deep meaning. Such survivals into mediaeval art of the ancient zodiac indicate that this twelve-arc circle, whose very etymological significance has been mislaid in modern times,[23] represents the highest symbolism of the ancient mystery cults, and (significantly) required only slight changes to become perfectly integrated into the new mystery wisdom of Christianity. The mediaeval artists were presented with the ancient astrological imagery by way of the Arabs, and were not slow to see the spiritual significance of a circle of symbols which proclaimed a connection between the Heavens and the Earth. The mediaeval artists – and in particular the cathedral builders – soon learned to exploit certain of the spiritual ideas within the zodiac for their own purposes of revealing what we now call the

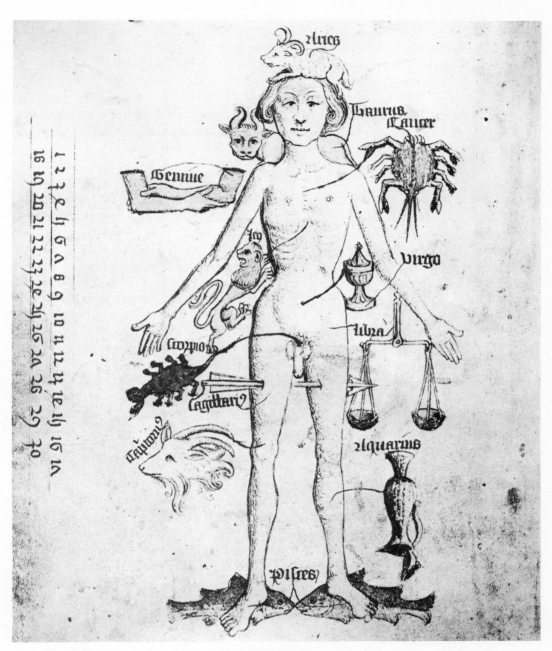

5 *A fifteenth-century 'zodiacal man' from a manuscript in the British Library.*

'doctrines', but which the mediaevals still called the 'mysteries' of the Incarnation and the message of Christ. It was Tertullian, one of the earliest apologists, who translated the Greek word 'mysterion' into the Latin 'sacramentum', a term still used in the liturgy and literature of the West by people oblivious to its direct link with an ancient and almost forgotten wisdom of initiation.

We find in the astrological theory, which the mediaeval artists and designers inherited from antiquity, what is properly called the 'melothesic figure' – popularly, the 'zodiacal man' (figure 5). In this figure, each of the twelve signs of the zodiac was linked with a particular part of the human body, and sometimes even with an inner organ or function. Since the zodiac was itself at the periphery of the known cosmos, it was a symbol of the extreme spirituality of our cosmos, and it was indeed specifically linked with the highest angelical beings of the traditional Christian hierarchies – with the Seraphim and Cherubim. Christ, who was believed to have descended from heights beyond even these exalted beings, was linked with the highest spirituality expressed in each of the twelve signs of the zodiac in turn. In an esoteric sense, therefore, the zodiacal man in mediaeval art is really a debased symbol of Christ, carrying much the same force as the old image which depicts Christ standing 'incarnate' in the midst of the four elements, Himself the 'Quintessence' or 'Fifth Element' at the centre of the four traditional elements of Earth, Air, Fire and Water.

In the course of our examination of San Miniato al Monte, we shall study in some depth the Christian symbolism of only two of the zodiacal signs – Pisces and Taurus – but we should remember that as archetype, Christ was regarded as the perfection of all twelve. Just as he had 'rule' over twelve human disciples on earth, so he had 'rule' over the twelve signs of the zodiac in the heavens: the great Clemens, writing from a living memory of the life of Christ, had no hesitation in equating the twelve disciples with the twelve signs of the zodiac, with Christ as the central sun. The link between Christ and the zodiac formed a convenient connection with that which was seen as existing between man and the zodiac, through the melothesic figure. Just as the sun marked out the true zodiac, so Christ marked out the true man, and He is the guide who gives his light to the faithful. The remarkable twelfth-century scholar Alexander of Neckam said precisely this in his encyclopaedic account of symbolic analogies.[24] By such reasoning, the body of Christ, through the numinous power of the zodiac, merges with the body of man, to become a single united symbol within the church. Both were related in movement and significance, each was harmoniously linked with the movement of the sun, in its daily rising and setting, and with its annual creative passage which marked out the seasons of the year. It is this magical connection between zodiac, man and Christ which the design of San Miniato exploits, with a brilliance that exceeds even genius. It is this which most clearly reveals the basilica of San Miniato as the supreme expression of a systematic effort to Christianize the pagan astrology, and to put the resultant esotericism to the service of mediaeval theology.

2　The secret symbolism of the zodiac

Come, I shall show you the Logos, and the mysteries of the Logos, and I shall explain them to you in images that are known to you.

(CLEMENT OF ALEXANDRIA, *Protrepticus*, XII, 119, i. quoted by H. Rahner, *The Christian Mystery and the Pagan Mysteries*, 1944.)

The marble zodiac of San Miniato al Monte is unique for a number of reasons. Not only is it the largest marble zodiac in Italy, and probably the oldest marmoreal survival of a complete astrological lore, it is also the only floor zodiac to be precisely dated. The date, recorded in Roman numerals as 1207, is found in the inscription on the marble floor between the zodiac and the church's central portal (figure 1). As we investigate the occult meaning of the zodiac, we shall discover that this date is itself of great importance, and relates to much more than merely the year in which the zodiac was laid down in the church. Indeed, we shall find eventually that the Latin inscription which contains this date is of considerably greater importance than has hitherto been realized, for it contains within it a code which, when interpreted, lends documentary support for the theories set out in this present book. So important is this inscription, indeed, as so fascinating its code, that a whole chapter has been devoted to an examination of its meaning – see Chapter 6. A reader who may feel tempted to leap ahead to this chapter is advised, however, that a complete understanding of the significance of the code may only be gained by someone already familiar with the esoteric background to the zodiac and church as a whole. It is the purpose of the following chapters to establish such a familiarity in the mind of the general reader.

The twelve images of the zodiacal signs in the San Miniato zodiac are, with certain important exceptions, standard mediaeval images, and therefore very little different from those still in use today. The images themselves are virtually simple silhouettes in marble, set against an ornate arabesque which points to an oriental influence (figure 2). On the basis of this orientalizing quality of the zodiac and the related symbolism, it has been suggested by some scholars that the zodiac might have been imported from the east – in particular from Constantinople, which had been sacked by the Christians persuaded from their intended Fourth Crusade, in

1204. However, stylistic considerations, as well as the general significance of the zodiac in regard to the symbolism within the basilica itself, appears to rule out this suggestion. There may be little doubt that the entire zodiac was designed locally, to meet the very precise requirements of the hidden symbolism envisaged in the whole of San Miniato. It was, indeed, designed as an integral part of the church ornamentation, and was no isolated fragment, no mere booty of that lamentable destruction of Constantinople.

The twelve signs are distinctly European in style, in forms which suggest that they have been derived from some manuscript tradition. The single exception to this is the sign Pisces, which departs radically from the ancient tradition, in a deviation which, as we shall see, is one of the clues to the occult symbolism of San Miniato (figure 6).

6 *Detail of Pisces from the nave zodiac of San Miniato.*

In mediaeval astrology, the zodiacal signs were associated not only with the twelve human psychological types, but also with specific parts of the human body, in what is called the 'melothesic man' – the 'zodiacal man' of popular thought (figure 5). A tabular list of such associations in the mediaeval astrology is:

Aries (Ram) – head	Taurus (Bull) – neck and throat
Gemini (Twins) – arms	Cancer (Crab) – chest and breasts
Leo (Lion) – heart	Virgo (Virgin) – stomach, womb
Libra (Scales) – pelvis	Scorpio (Scorpion) – sexual parts
Sagittarius (Man-horse) – thighs	Capricorn (Goat-fish) – knees
Aquarius (Waterman) – lower leg	Pisces (Fishes) – feet

There are other related associations – for example Capricorn has rule over the skeletal system – but we need not consider these at this point. In any case, we shall find in this study that our main interest will revolve around the link drawn between the Taurean rule over the throat, and the Piscean rule over the human feet. To stop short at such associations, however, is to miss the whole tendency of mediaeval thought, which is towards allegorizing, towards establishing anagogic connections between things. We find examples of this allegorizing in the writings of Alexander of Neckam, who was alive whilst the zodiac was being laid down. We find a similar predisposition to establish anagogic connections between the parts of the body and theological texts in the thirteenth-century work on magical sigils by Arnaldus de Villanova.[1]

In that part of his text which deals with the zodiacal sigils, Arnaldus is intent on recording the procedure for making a series of 'gamalei' or magical stones, as well as occult 'seals', which were supposed to exercise a prophylactic influence over health. The procedure he records for making the seal for Taurus is designed to counteract illness of the head, including ophthalmia and disorders of the eyes, as well as all maladies connected with the neck and throat. This connection would have been obvious to any mediaeval reader, since Taurus was known to have rule over the neck and throat. Additionally, Taurus was ruled by the planet Venus, which had dominion over such things as the physical body, music and singing. As a result of these associations, the connection between the sound of the voice (with what we might call the 'larynx') was taken for granted in mediaeval astrological lore. Arnaldus instructs the seal-maker to write around the circumference of his gold or silver seal 'benedictum (sic) sit nomen Domini Jesu' (Blessed be the name of Lord Jesus): we see in this the esoteric link with the 'name' or with the 'word' arising from the Taurean ruleship over the throat and speech. The association between the 'physical body' (rulership of Venus), and the fact that Taurus was the first of the Earth signs, would point to the idea of 'incarnation', and in particular to the Incarnation of the Word, the Logos.

Within the Christianized zodiac, Taurus the bull was seen as an image of Christ in his role as the incarnating god, sacrificed in the Redemptive act. The early symbolism of the 'Bull' was, of course, linked with the Mithraic mysteries, which in the early centuries of our era struggled with the Christian initiation wisdom for dominance. It is also possible that a link between Taurus and the ancient mystery wisdom of the Egyptian Serapis was contained within the esoteric lore. The central

7 *Roman relief of Mithras killing the bull, surrounded by images of initiation grades. British Museum.*

image of the Mithraic cult was that of a bull, which was being sacrificed by Mithras, who cuts its throat to allow the blood to run to earth: sometimes a scorpion and snake are shown attacking the genitals of the bull (figure 7). The astrological symbolism is fairly apparent in this image, since Taurus and Scorpio oppose each other in the zodiac. However, in many Mithraic tauroctonic images, the zodiac is also figured completely, as a sort of cosmic background. The idea of the bull having its throat cut links with the image of Christ, who spills His blood to redeem the earth. As we shall see, it is certainly no accident that we find a most remarkable fifteenth-century survival of this tauroctony in San Miniato itself, an important point which will be discussed in Chapter 3.

The bull of the ancient Mithraic mysteries was not the only link with the astrological image of Taurus. We have already noted that the wisdom of the Egyptian Serapis was concerned with the consecration of a sacred bull, chosen by the priests because of certain physical characteristics, which included a marking on the head (which survives even into mediaeval images of the bull used in ecclesiastical art). The god Serapis was derived from the Osirified Apis bull of the

26

Memphite cults of Egypt, and was therefore linked with the ancient solar mysteries. Although not specifically linked with the zodiac, the temple of the cult was orientated according to astrological principles, and (as we shall see) contained the germ of a symbolism which survived into mediaeval art.

Since the cosmic Bull had rule over the human neck and throat, it also had rule over human speech: it is recorded that the temples of Serapis were so built that, during a certain time of the year a beam of sunlight fell on to the lips of the statue of Serapis within the temple. The lips were of course the outer symbol of the word, and the Egyptian hieroglyphic 'ru' ◯ which was used to denote the lips, as well as the birth passage, was adopted into the early Christian symbolism of the ankh cross ☥. In the Christianized zodiac this rule was extended to the Word itself, and became an important element in the symbolism of pulpit lecterns from which the Word of God was read.[2] As we shall see, it is such a symbolism as this, which draws a connection between the 'Word' or 'Logos' and Taurus, that is exploited to the full in the lectern symbolism of San Miniato al Monte. Taurus was used in the secret zodiacal symbolism of Christianity as a symbol of the incarnate word, the Logos, but this level of zodiacal symbolism appears to have been missed by the majority of modern art historians.

Whilst Taurus was concerned with the descent of the Word into matter, Pisces, represented by the two fishes, was concerned with the ascent of the spirit back into the spiritual realm of the heavens. The idea is that the Piscean lives in the 'watery' fluidity of the poetic world of what we would now call the subconscious (the mediaeval terminology was less ambivalent and ambiguous). This was one reason why the zodiacal sign and constellation were universally imaged as fishes. The fish of the mystery wisdom was, however, of a slightly different order, for the fish-man of the Babylonians is widely recognized by esotericists as being an image of the initiate, one who is at home both in the material world (the human body) and in the spiritual realm (the fish). Many of the ancient myths connected with fish-men, or mermen, even the biblical story of Jonah and the whale, are interpreted as references to initiation rites. The fish was not only used as an acrostically based symbol for Christ (see the notes on Augustine in Appendix 5), but also as a symbol of initiation, sometimes in the image of the man-fish, at other times in the image of the man being swallowed by a fish.

In particular, the imagery of the sun-god Christ was linked to Pisces both by the ancient fish symbolism,[3] and by associations with Pisces as a 'resurrectional' or 'excarnating' sign. It was therefore the opposite of Taurus, which was seen as an earthly 'incarnating' sign. Some of the mediaeval images for zodiacal and constellational Taurus attempt to combine the earthly and the fluidic proper to the Christian initiation symbols, by making Taurus into a bull-fish (figure 8). This particular image, while definitely pertaining to the initiate-art, was in fact derived from Arabic astrological lore.

Just as the instructions for seal-making recorded by Arnaldus throw light on the astro-theological connotations for Taurus, so do they throw light on the

8 Roundel of Taurus the Bull (with fishtail) from the narthex portal of Sta Madeleine at Vezelay.

associations which may be drawn for Pisces. The seal for Pisces is involved with curing and preventing maladies of the feet, which were, of course, ruled by this sign in the images of the melothesic man (figure 5). Pisces was ruled by the planet Jupiter, and from very early times the associate house of Pisces was linked with the idea of the spiritual realm, of which Jupiter was himself the ruler. 'Qui credit in me etiam in mortuus fuerit vivet (sic)' (He who believes in me will find life even in death) is one of the quotations which must be written along the circumference of the Piscean seal described by Arnaldus. The connection between 'resurrection' or 'eternal life', or 'life even in death', and the sign Pisces was therefore self-evident to a mediaeval astrologer or magician. St Mark was one of the names evoked on this seal, which reminds us that his Gospel is the one which deals mainly with the three years of Christ's ministry, terminating in the week of the Passion, the Resurrection and Ascension. These further associations with the 'renewal' theme of Pisces, remind us that the central doctrine of Christianity rests on the fact of Resurrection, however this fact is interpreted.

In the Christian zodiac, as in the pagan zodiac, the two fishes of Pisces appear to be associated with the idea of the spirit and soul. Certainly the two fishes are linked together by the cord which they each hold in their mouths, and certainly this relationship of the two tied fishes was interpreted by alchemists and the later Rosicrucians in terms of spirit–soul dualities. What was later called the 'silver cord' was in mediaeval star-lore usually called 'Nodus' or 'Nodus Coelestis', the heavenly thread.[4] The standard mediaeval image of Pisces expresses this idea by showing the two fishes swimming in opposite directions, as may be seen in a zodiacal roundel from a twelfth-century Benedictine establishment, at Sacra di San Michele, Val di Susa (figure 9). The contemporaneous zodiac in the baptistry in Florence also clearly shows the Nodus in the mouths of the two fishes, both swimming in opposite directions (figure 10).

9 Twelfth-century roundel of Pisces from the constellational arch in Sacra di San Michele, Val di Susa.

It has been suggested that this 'Nodus' symbolism is designed to reflect the idea (so perfectly expressed in Neoplatonic literature) that soul is not always in accord with spirit. The soul falls in love with the physical body, and seeks union with this, rather than with the spirit which it is supposed to serve faithfully. For this reason, the soul is tied to the spirit for the duration of a lifetime. Whether this Neoplatonic notion did influence the symbolism of Pisces or not, the spiritual nature of the fishes was adapted by the mediaeval image-makers as relating very distinctly to the spiritual nature of Christ. In any case, from the very earliest times, Christ had been linked with the image of the fish. The drawings of fish in the catacombs were symbols for Christ, and a whole battery of more or less esoteric interpretation was erected to account for this symbolism. A sample of this esotericism, derived from a Sibylline prophecy, is set out in the notes on Augustine's acrostical treatment of the fish in Appendix 5.

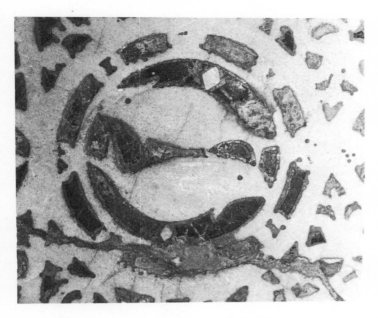

10 *Thirteenth-century roundel of Pisces from the floor zodiac in the Baptistry, Florence.*

The anagogic symbolism of the image for zodiacal Pisces reflects the Neoplatonic and Christian esotericisms, connected with both the symbolism of the 'Nodus', and the Sibylline image of the fish as 'Soter', 'Saviour' and Christ. The sculpted fish of Pisces in such places as Canterbury, Vezelay, Amiens, Sacra di San Michele and even in the contemporaneous baptistry zodiac in Florence, all have this 'Nodus Coelestis' in their mouths. Virtually all known pre-twelfth century manuscripts insist on this 'Nodus' as part of the symbolism of the Pisces imagery, even though it was really derived from the asterism of Pisces, and not from anything intrinsic to the sign. It was a name first given to the binary alpha of the asterism, the 'Al Rescha' (the Arabian word for 'the cord') the 'Desmos' of some mediaeval manuscripts, thanks mainly to Aratos. It is, however, very significant that the San Miniato symbolism chooses to ignore this ancient tradition.

In the marble zodiac, the two fishes are presented as facing in the same direction, and are not linked together by a cord (figure 6). As we shall see, there is nothing accidental in this deviation from tradition, for it affords a clue to the first series of hermetic lines of direction which radiate from the zodiac.

We have already observed that Pisces has rule over the human feet in the melothesic man. When we look down at the Pisces-Christ, figured in the cold marble image of two fishes, we ourselves begin to merge with the extraordinary symbolism of the church. We ourselves are standing upon the image of the Sun (figure 11), at the centre of the zodiac.

On first reflection, it may strike us that a sun-symbol is a most curious thing to find at the centre of a mediaeval zodiac. The mediaeval cosmos was nominally geocentric, and we should therefore reasonably expect to find a symbol of the

11 The solar centre of the zodiac in San Miniato al Monte.

earth at the centre of the zodiac. The two largest frescoes which may still be seen in northern Italy – in the Campo Santo of Pisa, and in the Duomo of San Gimignano – do indeed show the earth at the centre of the spheres. In fact, however, our view that the mediaeval cosmoconception was 'geocentric' is itself based on a misunderstanding of the mediaeval mode of thought. As any reader of Dante will recall, the centre of his cosmos was Hell, which itself lay at the centre of the earth. C. S. Lewis, in his entertaining study of mediaeval lore, points out that the pre-Copernican cosmos was not geocentric, but diabolocentric, the central hell being encased within the material structure of the earth.[5]

In this San Miniato zodiac we find neither a central earth, nor a central hell – we find instead a sun-symbol (figure 11). The concept of a heliocentric cosmos, raised initially by Greek philosophers, had to wait until the sixteenth century to simplify the over-complex geocentric Ptolemaic model, and to eventually readjust the model of our universe. We may therefore assume that the symbolism of the central Sun has nothing to do with a new model of the universe, but points to an inner meaning within the framework of orthodox Christian symbolism, just as does the sun image which is at the centre of the thirteenth-century zodiac in the Baptistry in Florence (figure 12), with its alchemically derived inscription (see Appendix 4).

Whatever it was, the mediaeval cosmos was certainly not heliocentric, and according to all the theory of mediaeval astrology there should be no sun in the middle of the zodiac. We must therefore assume that the designer was wishing to express some extraordinary, or even heretical, idea. We must ask ourselves, then, why did the mediaeval architect put a Sun in the centre of the San Miniato zodiac?

31

12 The solar centre, with hermetic inscription, in the floor zodiac of the Baptistry, Florence.

He put the image of the Sun there precisely because the astrological symbolism which runs through the church (and which marks this building out as one of the most remarkable structures to survive from ancient times) was concerned with the Sun. Its sequences of symbols are ultimately involved with the great solar cycles of day, year and epoch. As we shall see, the movement of the sun through the heavens, the sunlight itself, and the image of Christ as a being from the Sun, or from the solar sphere, is perfectly integrated into the symbolism within the church interior, and even on the façade. The defiant and seemingly inexplicable solar centre of the zodiac is perfectly in accord with the secret symbolism of San Miniato itself.

In fact, it is this solar centre which points to the hermetic antiquity of the San Miniato zodiac, and gives us a first inkling that there may be hidden in its structure a connection with ancient Sun-Mysteries. Several of the late-antique models of the zodiac and of the melothesic man are shown as centred upon a personification of the Sun. A fine example of such a melothesic image, preserved in the Bibliothèque Nationale in Paris (figure 13), shows a personification of the Sun which is sufficiently god-like to persuade the modern art historian Saxl to write of it, 'the drawing is evidently a copy of some very interesting record of that sun worship which Julian the Apostate still professed'.[6] I shall return to this interesting point in

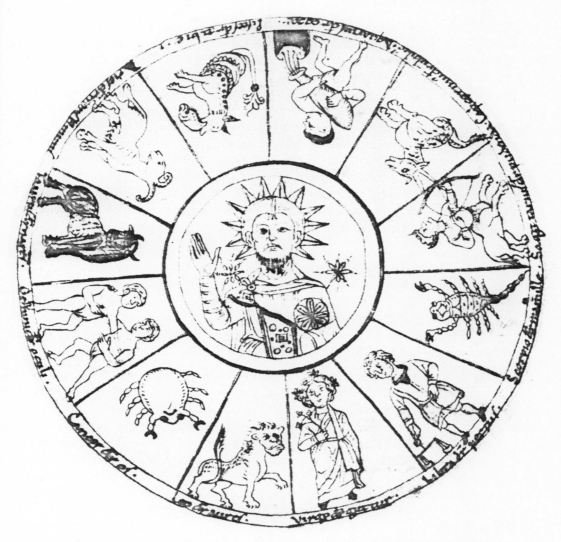

13 Tenth-century (?) copy of a classical zodiac and melothesia, with the sun-god at the centre.
Bibliothèque Nationale, Paris.

my final chapter, but in passing we should note the curious image of Pisces in this melothesic series, which shows a hybrid Capricorn-like creature swallowing a fish. No doubt the mediaeval copyist would be aware of the extent to which an image could mark an heretical (i.e. anti-Christian) strain in the late-classical artist who drew the original. One wonders if these two heretical strains were the reason why the mediaeval copyist or a later commentator should write at the head of the drawing 'Secundum philosophorum deliramenta notantur duodecim signa ita (sic)' (according to the absurdities of the philosophers, the twelve signs are written

33

thus).[7] This marginalia was taken by Saxl to be a mark of the lack of understanding of the ancient conception of the microcosm. Quite the opposite might have been true: it is quite possible that the mediaeval copyist recognized the heretical strains in the original drawing.

Such diagrams should naturally lead us to suspect that in mediaeval literature (as in early Christian literature), the Sun would be linked with Christ himself. The English theologian and symbolist Alexander of Neckam developed this idea in a manuscript which was circulating widely at the same time as the San Miniato zodiac was being laid down. He pictured Christ as the Sun, and the faithful of the church as the Moon, receiving as a gift the light from the sun.[8] In one way or another this idea of the 'solar Christ' is one of the oldest in Christian literature, being mentioned even by the early Clemens.[9] As Steiner put it, in a lecture given on the relationship between astrology and the Christ mysteries,

> The followers and representatives of the Christian impulse were not always so
> hostile as they often are to-day towards the acknowledgement of this
> relationship between the Sun-Mystery and the Christ-Mystery. Dionysius, the
> Areopagite, . . . calls the Sun, 'God's monument', and in Augustine we
> continually find allusions – even in Scholasticism we find such allusions –
> referring to the fact that the outwardly visible stars and their movements are
> images of the divine-spiritual existence of the Christ.[10]

For the moment, then, we must visualize ourselves standing in the centre of the zodiac, with the curious image of the Sun beneath our feet, alongside the Piscean image, which is yet a further symbol of Christ. For the symbolism to take root in our mind, we must recall that in the melothesic man, the feet are themselves ruled by Pisces. We stand alongside Pisces (as image of Christ) with the Piscean part of our being resting on the marble sun (as a further image of Christ). As we look down at the image, we observe that the Pisces symbol on the floor is not quite normal – the two fishes are parallel, rather than swimming in opposed directions. Is this intended as a clue to some other symbolism in the church?

We shall find an answer to this question if we leave this solar point, walk up the nave and mount the stars to the raised 'choir' above the crypt (from Z to F, in figure 14). Between the monastic part of the church and the raised corridor in which we stand is a high wall, pierced at the centre by an open doorway. On each side of the doorway, neatly imaged in the intarsia of the wall, and slightly above our heads, are two friezes of demonic beings and creatures, terminating in two small vertical fishes which flank each side of the doorway (figure 15). These fishes are stylistically the same as those in the nave zodiac: they are parallel and vertical. These fishes are also free of the usual nodus, as in the zodiac below, but in this case they are separated by a space, for they are placed on either side of the fascias of the door jambs.

What is the significance of this space between the two fishes? Surely, we can take

34

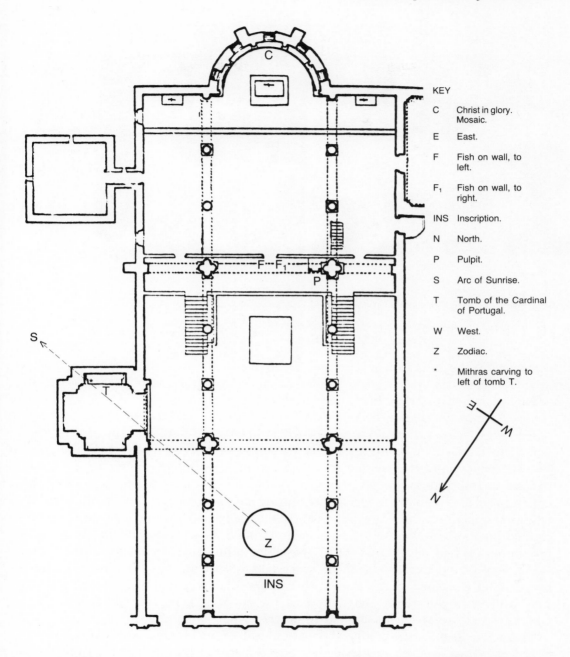

KEY

C   Christ in glory.
    Mosaic.

E   East.

F   Fish on wall, to
    left.

F_1 Fish on wall, to
    right.

INS   Inscription.

N   North.

P   Pulpit.

S   Arc of Sunrise.

T   Tomb of the Cardinal
    of Portugal.

W   West.

Z   Zodiac.

*   Mithras carving to
    left of tomb T.

14 *Ground plan of the basilica of San Miniato al Monte. C marks the position of the mosaic (Christ in Glory); E is the east; F marks the positions of the fishes on the wall; INS is the position of the inscription; N is the north; P is the pulpit; S marks the centre of the arc towards sunrise in May; T is the tomb of the Cardinal of Portugal (the ★ indicates the position on the side of the tomb of the bas-relief of the tauroctony); W is the west; Z is the zodiac. (See Appendix 3.)*

15 *One of the two fishes at the sides of the entrance into the 'choir' of San Miniato.*

it that, since the Piscean fish represent the image of Christ, we are in effect being invited to enter the space between them, to enter, as it were, into that space which is the symbol of the very body of Christ?

The symbolic invitation to 'enter' into the space between the two fishes is itself replete with symbolic power for the mediaeval visitor. This wall, pierced by the door before which we stand, marks the main division of the church – F–F_1 in figure 14. The nave below is reserved for the lay congregation, whilst the apse 'choir' beyond is reserved for the community of monks. To pass through the door is tantamount to becoming a monk, to putting behind one the cares of the world temporal in favour of the cares spiritual. In the mediaeval terminology, a man who entered the monastic life, or a woman who took her vows, was called a 'religious', for he or she had decided to 're-tie' (re-ligio) himself or herself to Christ. The symbolism of the two fish, and the space between them, was therefore far more pregnant of meaning in the thirteenth century than it possibly could be today. Even today, however, we may interpret the space as being the 'inner space' of Christ, which we are being invited to enter.

These two fishes are slightly above the head of an average man: to see them clearly we must look upwards. In the nave zodiac, we found the fish at our feet, and we were therefore required to look downwards. Now the fish are lifted above our heads: we are being invited to look upwards into the beautiful mosaic above. This second pair of fishes obviously relates symbolically to a higher part of our being. Their symbolism as it were invites us to enter into the being of Christ, who

36

is portrayed in the apse across the 'choir', seated in glory between Maria and San Miniato (figure 16). Since we have climbed the stairs to the raised 'choir', we are now literally standing in a higher part of the church, and the power of symbolism is directing us to enter a higher part of ourselves. In following this subtle Piscean symbolism, we are being drawn upwards, and are ourselves participating in the 'excarnating' power of Pisces, in that we are being lifted (in our thinking and spiritual experience) into the realms above.

In terms of the mediaeval view of man, we may observe here an interesting progression. The mediaeval vision saw man as a reflection of the Trinity – in his being, man was triune. Man had a physical body, he was a living spirit, and, as mediator between spirit and body, he had a soul. This physical, spiritual and soul-life corresponded to the 'vegetative', 'intellectual' and 'sentient' parts of his being.

16 *The mosaic of Christ in Glory between the Virgin and St Miniatus, in San Miniato al Monte.*

The two fishes of the nave zodiac, set in the marble floor (figure 6), clearly relate to the lowest principle – to the vegetative body. These are set in the lowest part of the church, and are schematically related to our own feet, the lowest part of our body.

The higher pair of fishes, set in the marble wall (figure 15), relate to the sentient part of our being, to that which mediates between the earth and the Christ. These fish are almost above our heads, and there is a space between them, a space into which we are being invited to walk, as though into the body of Christ, which symbolically is the church itself. The two wall fishes invite us literally to enter that space which will enable us to live the religious life. In view of this progression 'upwards' and 'inwards' (into the soul-life), we must reasonably anticipate a third unit of Piscean symbolism, which will link directly with the highest of the triune nature of man – with the human spirit itself.

Where is this 'higher' Piscean symbol of pure spirit? By virtue of their placing, the two wall fishes invite us upwards and inwards: if we follow the direction they indicate, then we find ourselves looking up at the iridescence of the fourteenth-century mosaic above our heads. This apsidal mosaic shows Christ in glory between Maria and San Miniato (figure 16). As we might anticipate, it is this mosaic that contains the hidden symbolism which, by means of Piscean associations, points to the highest spiritual nature of man.

The basilica of San Miniato has been so orientated that at the end of August,[11], the sun's rays fall in a thin stream of light through the most easterly clerestory window and begin to cut a swathe of light up towards the mosaic. Slowly, as the sun sinks, the light reaches the left foot of Christ, and remains there, shimmering in a glory of gold. One sees the sunlight spread across the north wall of the church in a wide band, then slowly gather in upon itself, as it moves along the eastern wall below the apse zodiac, until it concentrates into a thin shaft of sunlight, to throw a pattern of light which fits exactly over Christ's foot, transmuting it into an area of golden light.

The movement of the light is arrested on this foot: the sunlight glitters there for a minute or two, and then makes no further upward movement. The angle of the window frame has been so designed as to permit no further movement against the inverted dome of the apse. Gradually, the gilded vision fades away, leaving the mosaic tesserae in their original earthly colours. As the sun sinks further to the west of Florence, the sunlight effect is lost, the golden shimmer on the foot fades, and the wonder is over until the following April.

Words are just not adequate to describe the awesome spiritual silence which falls over the church during these few moments of solar alchemy. No poet might describe the intense spiritual experience one has in the face of this majestic and momentary work of art. One recalls the admiration which Otto Demus records for the use of sunlight which he has observed in the mosaics and frescoes of certain Byzantine churches, yet at the same time one realizes that this San Miniato magic is without doubt the most extraordinary use of an almost forgotten art-form to have survived from the mediaeval era.[12]

Inevitably, as we contemplate this art of light, which touches light to Light, we call to mind the Serapis cult of the Egyptians. We have noted that the temple of Serapis, who was derived from the bull cult of the Egyptians, was orientated 'according to astrological principles'. Schmitt records that the temple was orientated for its nocturnal rite towards the star Regulus (in the constellation Leo), which was ruled by the sun-god Helios. The orientation was directed in such a way that at a certain time of the year the sunlight would fall on the lips of the statue of Serapis, housed within the Serapeion. For all the distance in time which separates the Serapeion from San Miniato, the parallels which may be drawn between them are still exact. The symbolism of San Miniato al Monte is certainly not concerned with the cult of Serapis, but there are sufficient connections here, between solar factors and the symbolism of the Logos, for us to draw a link between the esoteric art used in the structure of the Serapeion and that used in San Miniato.

One observes that here, in this miracle of painting with sunlight, we have a complete reversal of what we experienced in the nave zodiac. In the nave below, we ourselves had stood with our foot on the Sun, looking down at Pisces Christ. In the apse mosaic, it is Christ who sets His foot on the Sun, and who looks down at us. This is a quite extraordinary use of Piscean symbolism, engineered to point out the highest principle in man – the human spirit, united with Christ.

With the solar finale of this Piscean experience, the triune nature of man is completed, and we are lifted out of ourselves. In our thinking or 'contemplation', we are carried in our imagination into the movement of the Sun around the Earth, as it sinks over Florence. We are no longer caught in the earth-bound image of the marble zodiac, but are carried upwards into the spiritual realm of the zodiac which is marked out by the Sun. We merge with the ever-moving image of Pisces, which is the Christ, guardian of the human spirit.

A fantastic precision of design and engineering was required to ensure this miracle of light, which proclaims the spiritual aspect of Pisces Christ. Having conceived this symbolic use of the Sun's rays within the church, the designer of the church had to bear many factors in mind. The fact is that the position of Christ's foot within the curve of the mosaic (even the angles of the tesserae which compose the foot), the angle of the clerestory window and the position of the Sun on this day, are so related to the orientation of the church that the solar disc set at infinity touches the lowest point of the solar Christ portrayed in space and time. When the sunlight transforms the tesserae of the foot into an area of shimmering light, the intention of the designer is to express the most highly spiritualized concept of Piscean symbolism – Christ's connection with the zodiac, and His power over death. The experience is at once uniting the sunlight with the sun Logos, the lowest point of this Logos with the highest part of man, the splendid vibrance of the apse mosaic with the quiet darkness of the nave zodiac. Without any doubt, it is the most sophisticated use of Piscean symbolism in the world.

The study of the magical light effects of San Miniato al Monte is not yet complete, for it will require some years of careful calibration to establish the precise rhythms, and their relationships to the ecclesiastical calendar. However, it has already been possible to establish that each of the three main constituents of the internal zodiacal symbols are each in turn illumined by a direct ray of sunlight twice a year. The sun at the zodiac centre, the left wall fish and the left foot of Christ in the apse mosaic, are each briefly lighted by a single ray of sunlight, the first cast through the doorway, the other two cast from upper windows.

For reasons which will become clear later, the most important of these light effects in modern times is that connected with the marble fish (figure 15) upon the wall which separates the monastic part of the church from the lay congregation. It is this fish which we note as relating to the 'emotional' symbolism, requiring the onlooker to enter directly into the fish-body of Christ. Twice a year, a ray of light from one of the two lower windows in the church falls directly upon the left-hand fish. While the ray of light inches forward across the raised floor of the church for an hour or so, when it touches this part of the vertical wall the movement is so rapid that it rests upon the fish for only a few seconds, before slicing off, to fall into the darkness of the choir area.

This light effect is now best witnessed from either of the stairways leading up to the higher part of the church, or by standing directly alongside the wall itself – almost in the path of the sunlight. However, one must recall that before Michelozzo built his cappella, it would have been possible to observe this anagogic use of lighting as it was intended to be seen, while standing on the centre of the zodiac. From this position, low in the nave of the church, the movement of the sunlight would take on a very deep mystical significance, for we should be able to watch the light emerge as though from nowhere (it being hidden in the well of passageway between the frontal wall and the wall bearing the intarsia decoration of the fish). In this symbolism the emergence of a sudden shaft of sunlight on the body of the fish would have a most profound relationship with the concept of the solar Christ, and would be something akin to the mystical power of the raised host during the Mass. The original effect would have been mystical and profoundly anagogic, being charged with the deeper significance of Piscean arcane symbolism, representing the sudden revelation of the symbolic body of Christ.

The effect is at its most powerful just before 4.50pm when the Sun is in 17 degrees of tropical Pisces. However, the build-up and residual effects for a day before and a day after are almost as impressive. In practical terms for the modern visitor, we should note that the effect when related to the contemporary calendar, may be studied on the:

7th, 8th, 9th March.

40

There is a corresponding effect when the sun reaches the 14th degree of tropical Libra, corresponding at present to the:

6th, 7th, 8th October.

These dates are variable because the actual effect depends on the placing of the Sun in the zodiac, while the calendrical equivalents are determined by the time of the winter solstice, which is variable from year to year.

The sunlight falls on the foot of Christ in the evening when the Sun is in the 4th degree of Virgo and in the 26th Aries, which corresponds to 24/25th of August (1988) and the 15/16th April (1989) respectively. It is best to be present in the church well before 6.00pm to witness the movement of the slab of light as it sweeps across the lower part of the apse mosaic up to the foot. These calendrical dates are variable (within a day or two) for the same reasons adduced above in connexion with the dating of the lighting of the wall-fishes.

When, well over a decade ago, I was first fortunate enough to witness the ray of light illumine the left foot of Christ the experience was without doubt the most profoundly aesthetic and arcane that I had ever had in my life. However, I must regretfully record that in modern times this direct experience is no longer possible within the basilica. Some four years ago (circa 1983) those responsible for the fabric of the church elected to cover five of the 'eastern' upper clerestory windows with a special protective masking. The aim of this protective masking was to cut down the anticipated deleterious effects of the sunlight on the newly restored organ in the 'choir' of the church. Its more profound effect, however, was to cut down the light falling from these windows by about 75 per cent. As a result, while it is still possible to observe the fall of sunlight on the mosaic foot, much of the original intensity is lost, and when the sky is even partly cloudy, the effect is lost entirely. It is this protective masking which has made it very difficult for me to study the precise zodiacal placing of the Sun in relation to the mosaic during the past four years. One trusts that eventually those responsible for this masking will realize that the organ may be protected in a different way – perhaps with an angular screen on the end window, which will permit the sunlight to perform its arcane wonder as of old. Until that time, part of the solar mystery of San Miniato will be diminished.

No covering has been inserted over the two lower windows of the church, which means that the pristine quality of the original flow of light on to the wall-fish is still preserved. However, the Michelozzo cappella now hides this phenomenon as it was designed to be experienced, as a sudden influx of light from the well of the passageway, from below upwards. In spite of this, something of the original wonder of anagogic lighting may be experienced from the steps leading up to the raised choir, or from directly in front of the wall itself. For this reason I would recommend those who wish to experience at first hand something of the original grandure of the San Miniato lighting to visit the church an hour or so

41

before sunset in the early days of March or October.

It is important to note that we must not assume that any of these degrees (or dates) relating to the sunlight effects in modern times were of importance to those who established this solar symbolism in 1207. Precession has naturally changed these degrees with the passage of time, and calendrical changes have also left their effects. However, I hope eventually to establish the relationship between the important zodiacal and stellar equivalents of 1207, and to determine any anagogic relationships which these hold to the ecclesiastical calendar.

The third symbolic element which uses the fall of rays of light is the zodiac itself. In the last week of March, the light of the setting sun falls through the western façade doorway, and cuts a swathe through the body of the church to touch the rim of the zodiac, eventually (with the passage of days) reaching the centre. In modern times the sunlight first touches the rim of the zodiac at about 5.50a.m., when the Sun is in 26 degrees of tropical Pisces. For the next few days the sunlight moves across the zodiac shortly before sunset. Unfortunately, the wooden structure behind this doorway is relatively modern, and it is therefore not possible to gauge by direct observation the dating or zodiacal equivalents of the original apertures (these now being unknown). Additionally, there is now an extensive growth of cypress trees to the west of the churchyard, which occlude the rays of the setting sun during the period under review, and this makes the requisite direct observation difficult. While it is quite clear that there was at one time a significance in the fall of light upon the zodiac (almost certainly linked with the fall of the rays upon the solar centre), it is now difficult to establish exactly how the anagogic symbolism was related to the zodiac or the constellations. For this reason, I point to the fall of light on the wall-fish as representative of the original anagogic symbolism, and I do not place much emphasis on this zodiac lighting. Even so, we may see in it a relict of the obvious fact that it completes the solar symbolism we have already noted in the wall-fish and in the foot of Christ. For those interested in witnessing this fall of light, I would recommend a visit to the church in the last week of March.

Through the power of the Christ Pisces, we have been carried out into the world of stars and zodiac, into the realm of the spiritual, from which we ourselves (as spirits) have descended to the Earth. According to the mediaeval cosmoconception, it is the realm to which we shall ultimately return after death, where we shall find 'life even in death'. We are reminded of this by a symbol in the crypt of San Miniato, in the lowest part of the church, immediately below the mosaic which we have just admired. In that part of the crypt is an altar, in which is contained the ossary of San Miniato himself. On this reliquary box – and no doubt intended to show that San Miniato has returned to Christ and to the spiritual realm – is carved the sigil for Pisces ♓ . The sigil is itself mediaeval (probably thirteenth century) which would suggest that it was carved round about the same time as the school of Benedictine monks from Oliveto rebuilt this church. The symbolism of the Piscean Sun at the top of the church, and the symbolism of the Pisces sigil on the crypt-tomb below, invite us to draw a vertical through the church, from apse mosaic to crypt floor. Previously, we had walked the length of the church nave. Now we draw a vertical in space. In these two psycho-physical gestures we have unwittingly made the sign of the cross. Perhaps it is merely an accident that the sigil for Pisces is found in the crypt, below the most impressively engineered Piscean symbolism in the upper choir of the church? However, it is more likely that when men work so closely in co-operation with spirit there can be no such thing as accident in art.[13]

We have just witnessed the excarnating principle of Pisces at work, and in our thinking we ourselves are carried out into the spiritual realms. Yet, this excarnation is only one part of the Christian doctrine. What makes the new religion of the Logos unique in the face of the ancient mystery wisdom is the account of the Resurrection. The concept of the Resurrection of Christ, and of the eventual resurrection of all men, is the fundamental miracle, or mysterium, upon which Christianity is based. Without the fact of the Resurrection, there could be no inner message in Christianity. Whatever prevarications modern theologians may issue, the fact remains that the essential message of the Christian doctrine is that Christ became man, died, and then returned to life in the Resurrected body, into what is widely believed the early church called the 'Augoeides'.[14] The fact that the nature of this resurrected body was misunderstood relatively early in the history of the Church is of no real concern to us here, though it is perhaps worth noting that it is in the true understanding of the nature of this spiritual body that esotericism and Christianity are likely to find a fruitful meeting point in the future.

Christ descended into the earthly body, and sacrificially gave His blood for the healing of the Earth and man. After His death, He resurrected and returned to live within the Earth until the end of the world itself. It is this central teaching (of the incarnation of a god) which is continued within the framework of the other zodiacal symbol, Taurus. The image of Taurus spreads its symbolism downwards through the church in much the same way that excarnating Pisces spread its symbolism upwards through the church.

In the apse mosaic, recently made redolent with meaning by the magical rays of sunlight, we see Christ in Glory. He is surrounded by the images of the four Evangelists (figure 16). These images, of lion, eagle, winged-human and bull, are of course derived from pre-Christian zodiacal images. The history of this development from a pre-Christian Zervan image, need not detain us here, but we might observe that several of the early Christian writers were aware of the zodiacal origin of these powerful images.[15] The lion of St Mark is the image of Leo. The eagle of St John is the eagle of Scorpio, which sign (alone of all the twelve) has two images, the eagle the symbol of the redeemed and spiritualized Scorpionic nature, the scorpion its fallen, unredeemed and earth-bound nature. The winged human of St Matthew is the waterbearer of Aquarius: the waterpot which poured spiritual sustenance for all humanity has become the life-giving gospel in the hands of the winged human. The bull of St Luke is the animal of Taurus.

These four Christian images are derived from the four fixed signs of the zodiac, each of them representing the four fixed elements of mediaeval astrology. Leo is Fire, Scorpio is Water, Aquarius (for all its name) is Air, whilst Taurus is Earth. The symbolism of San Miniato uses this earthly Bull symbol, the animal of earth, to bring us down from the starry realm of Piscean spirit, back into an earthly state. Through the symbolism of Taurus, we shall see (indeed, experience) Christ descending back to the earth.

The four so-called 'beasts' of the Evangelists, which frame Christ in his Glory, are echoed in the symbolism of the thirteenth-century pulpit to our right (figure 4). The marble lectern upon which the priest rests the Bible, is made up of three figures of the Evangelists. At the bottom is the lion of Mark (Leo of the zodiac); at the top is the Scorpionic eagle of St John. Between these two, with his head lifted by the aspiring eagle, his feet resting on the bestial nature of the lion, stands man, the Aquarian symbol of St Matthew. Missing from the lectern design is all reference to the image of the Taurean bull. At this moment, the 'bull' is invisible.

17 Detail of the 'missing bull' from the tenth-century pulpit in Gropina. The bull's head is the fourth from the left among the top range of decorative motifs.

It is only when the priest mounts the steps of the pulpit, either to preach or to read from the Bible, that his own head completes the lectern triad of marble, turning it into a living symbolic tetrad. His own human head becomes involved in the lectern symbolism, and forms the fourth 'missing' symbol. In this way, his head is transformed into the living image of the bull. To fully grasp this symbolism, we must recall that within the zodiacal tradition Taurus has rule over the throat: symbolically speaking, therefore, this may be linked with the Word or Logos, itself. Here, in this pulpit, we have a living image of a human being reading from the Holy Word of God. The spiritual idea of the Christ, or 'Logos', which was formerly excarnated in the realm of Pisces in the apse, now pours down towards the earth with the Logos, and spreads out as a 'sacrificial sound' in the church nave below.

This triadic symbolism of the lectern appears in other churches of that period, with much the same symbolic intention.[16] In such other churches, however, the 'missing' bull imagery is depicted in some fairly well hidden place upon the

18 *Detail of the lower lion from the triadic lectern of the pulpit in San Miniato al Monte.*

45

decorations of the pulpit. On the eleventh-century pulpit in the pieva at Gropina (Loro Cuiffenna), for example, the bull's head is represented in an obscure part of the decorative motif below the lectern, as one of the series of triangular motifs (figure 17). No such hidden bull is found on the pulpit of San Miniato: a minute search of the entire pulpit reveals no sign of a bull symbol such as is found in Gropina.[17] Where, then, we might ask, is the missing bull of this mediaeval symbolic device?

An indication as to where we may look for the bull may be seen in the glance of the lion which forms the base of the triadic lectern (figure 18). This lion is not looking frontally, like the other two symbols: it is directing its attention towards the zodiac, below, in the nave of the church. This is the clue as to where we should look for the missing bull. If you stand on the centre of the zodiac, your feet on the sun, and look upwards towards the pulpit with binoculars, you will see the eyes of the lion looking directly at you. There may be no doubt that this is where we are being directed in a search for the missing Logos bull.

There is a symbolic connection between this lion-gaze and the zodiac. The eyes of the lion, like the eyes of the other figures in the lectern, appear to be made from lapis lazuli inserts. The lapis lazuli was a semi-precious stone, valued by artists because, when it was ground to a fine powder, it gave an exquisite blue pigment of great permanence. Because the stone looked rather like the night skies, being a dark blue, flecked with silver and gold, it was regarded as being a suitable stone from which to make the blue for the dress of the Virgin, who was visualized as having come down from the skies, and who was linked with the Virgo of the constellations. The lapis lazuli in the eyes of the lion would in itself conjure the idea of the heavens, and readily call to mind the image of the heavens symbolized in the zodiac of the nave below.

Inevitably, therefore, this logic of anagogic forms brings us even further down to earth. It literally incarnates us further, for, if we follow this steady Leonine gaze, we are returned to the marble floor, where the missing bull is seen in the image of zodiacal Taurus. Since it is by means of the symbolic magic of the astrological associations drawn around Taurus that we have descended back to the earth, we must now expect there to be something of especial importance in connection with Taurus which confirms this link with the earth. Just as the excarnating symbol of Pisces was linked with the movement of the sun, so we might expect the excarnating symbol of Taurus also to be linked with the movement of the sun.

One of the most extraordinary things about the basilica of San Miniato is that it breaks all the established rules of Church orientation. It is in no way orientated towards the east. The 'wrong' orientation of San Miniato may be easily seen if one stands outside the basilica and looks into the panoramic view of Florence below, over the trees above San Niccolo, and the mediaeval walls. One observes that all the other churches below – Santa Croce, San Lorenzo, the Duomo, among many

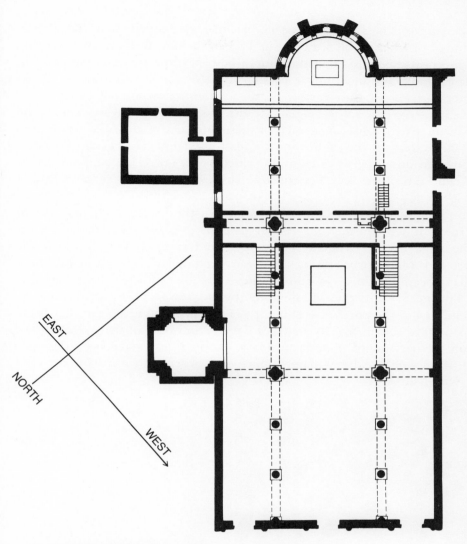

19 Orientation of San Miniato al Monte to the cardinal points.

others – are orientated with their longitudinal axes quite differently directed from that of San Miniato. Without exception, these churches have been orientated with their eastern end (the altar-end) towards sunrise, according to normal ecclesiastical practice.

Of course, the question of church orientation is far from being a simple one. Whilst it was normally the aim of mediaeval church builders to orientate their naves longitudinally towards sunrise, there remains the vexing question of 'which point of sunrise?' An architect instructed to orientate a church on an east–west axis might well ask what precisely this means? If the orientation is to be determined in relation to the sunrise (the symbolic east-point), then one must ask on which day should the line of orientation be drawn? The French theologian Durandus, writing in the twelfth century,[18] insists that the church be orientated towards the point of sunrise at the equinox, and mentions in passing that this is standard practice. Other mediaeval literature points to a variety of such 'orientation points', however. It seems to have been the practice in England to direct the church towards sunrise on the feastday of the patron saint. Yet, each of these different methods of orientation is involved with directing the church on the east–west line of orientation.[19] San Miniato is directed on a line of orientation which bears no relationship to any of these points. The axis of the nave lies approximately on a north-west to south-east axis (figure 19).

There is nothing accidental in this orientation, in the breaking of masonic or theological rules. If we consider the matter carefully, it will soon become clear that, had the nave of San Miniato been orientated towards sunrise, then the magical effect of sunlight proclaiming a Piscean symbolism on the foot of Christ would not have been possible. The sun would set, as it sets for ten thousand other churches in Europe, with its rays illuminating the western front, even with its rays falling through one of the porches as though it were trying to reach the altar itself. This is not at all possible at San Miniato, of course, and one must therefore ask if this deviation from standard ecclesiastical orientation might have been designed precisely to allow for the light-magic which we observed earlier on the apse mosaic and wall-fish?

20 *Detail of Taurus from the San Miniato zodiac.*

In fact, this deviation from the norm of orientation actually allows for a further remarkable strain of occultist symbolism in the church. An examination of the zodiac will show us that the mystery of the incarnating Bull (figure 20) is itself linked in a most significant way with this orientation. The fact is that the zodiac has been so orientated that the daily sunrise takes place in the direction of the segment occupied by Taurus! Since it is this sign of the zodiac, rather than the axis of the church, which is orientated towards the east, it is this 30-degree arc containing the image of Taurus that greets the rising sun each day (figure 21). Just as the sunlight of Pisces is used to point to an annual miracle of light symbolism, so we find that Taurus is used to point to the light of daily sunrise. Here, then, in the zodiac, we find the symbol of the missing bull of Taurus which resurrects into 'incarnate' form, each and every day.

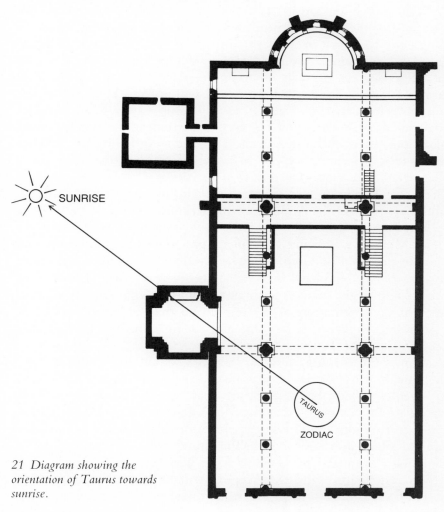

SUNRISE

TAURUS

ZODIAC

21 Diagram showing the orientation of Taurus towards sunrise.

For us to begin to appreciate more fully the significance of this Taurus orientation, we must turn once more to the date of the zodiac. The year of its foundation is clearly marked in the top line of the Latin inscription which we have already examined (figure 1). Since a zodiac is a timeless image, depicting as it does celestial images beyond the confines of time, the conventional mediaeval zodiac is rarely dated. Yet here, in San Miniato, within the marble inscription which refers to the zodiac as the 'numine celesti', a 'divine image of the heavens', we find the Roman numerals for what we must assume to be its date of foundation – 1207. Recent research has shown that there is nothing accidental about the choice of this year to lay down the zodiac, with Taurus orientated towards sunrise.[20]

Ephemerides (planetary tables) for the year 1207 show that on 28 May there was a momentous event in the heavens. On the morning of that day, as the sun rose over Florence, there was a gathering of no fewer than five planets in the constellation Taurus. In mediaeval times such a phenomenon was called a 'satellitium', though the tendency in modern times is to use the word 'stellium' instead. On that day, the Sun, Moon, Mercury, Venus and Saturn were all gathered within a few degrees of each other in the asterism of the Bull. This particular stellium in Taurus is very rare indeed, and will not repeat for thousands of years.[21] We see, therefore, that the orientation of Taurus is more than merely a link with the symbolic daily sunrise over Florence – it is indeed intimately bound up with the foundation date of the zodiac itself. The date recorded by the builders of the church and zodiac refers not only to the year of construction, but to the momentous stellar event which they perceived in the skies.

Foundation charts for buildings were in use even during the twelfth century, derived from similar practices of the Arabian astrologers and architects. In his *Liber Introductorius*, the astrologer Michael Scot, who was writing the text at about the same time that San Miniato was being built in its present form, points out that anyone who wants to put up a building which will remain intact for a long time should do so when there is an emphasis on fixed signs of the zodiac.[22] Taurus is of course the first fixed sign of the zodiac. Such an orientation will certainly remind the modern reader of the orientation of the temple on the ancient Acropolis of Athens, which according to Penrose, was on an axis line directed towards the Pleiades, in the constellation of Taurus.[23]

The whole question of the astrological factors at work within on this day in May 1207 is a complex one, and for the modern mind at least seems to lead mainly to more questions. Are we reasonable to suppose that the mediaeval astrologers would have been aware of this phenomenon of the satellitium? Would they have realized on which day it would occur? Did they have the instruments to record it properly? Is there any other indication within the church that the implications of the stellium would be recognized by the builders? Was this orientation of the zodiac towards the constellation Taurus in keeping with mediaeval practices – in other words, is it 'good theology' to orientate a zodiac to the east point, in a church which itself is not orientated towards the east?

Such questions are important ones, and must be answered if we wish to appreciate the significance of this zodiac orientation in terms of the mediaeval frame of mind. Because of this, I have set aside a whole chapter to examining the nature of mediaeval astrology, specifically in regard to what an early thirteenth-century astrologer would have known about the planets and stars, and how he might have used what he knew within an acceptable framework of theological symbolism (see Chapter 4, pp. 83–96). In that chapter, I shall also take the opportunity to describe in detail the horoscope for the foundation date. Such a detailed treatment will also enable us to form an idea of precisely what an observer in Florence on 28 May 1207 might have experienced. After reading this chapter, it will be evident that as a symbolic device the Taurean orientation is quite momentous.

It was, of course, a normal procedure for late mediaeval buildings to be constructed according to what are now called 'foundation charts', reflecting astrological principles. The evidence for this 1207 chart would suggest, however, that the use of these astrological principles is a little earlier than is generally realized, for all Michael Scot's reference to the art. The builders of the basilica were probably aware that they were making a radical departure in orientating a zodiac, and a whole paraphernalia of church symbolism, towards a specific stellar point. It is probably for this reason that they left behind a secret script which confirms not only the direction of orientation, but the exact day on which the satellitium in Taurus was seen in the skies, as well as the names of the planets involved in this satellitium. The coded inscription is therefore of considerable importance to the study of the history of astrology in this period, for it confirms the nature of the early 'foundation chart'. The implication of this is examined in detail in Chapter 5, pp. 97–117.

Just as we found a Pisces sigil on the San Miniato reliquary, in confirmation of the axis-line of 'excarnation' (the vertical line, from crypt to apse), so we find a Taurus symbol on the Taurus-to-sunrise line. This second axis line appears to have been 'indicated', by means of an extraordinary symbolic touch, by someone anxious to point out (as late as the fifteenth century) that he knew about the mystery of the church zodiac, and its orientation towards Taurus.

When the distinguished architect Antonio Manetti finished his model for the chapel and tomb of the Cardinal Prince of Portugal (who had died whilst passing through Florence in 1459) he might have known about the strange link between Taurus and sunrise. We cannot be sure whether it was Manetti (who died in 1460) or Antonio Rossellino, who sculpted the tomb itself in 1466, who knew about the occult link with the point of sunrise and Taurus. However, it is certainly very clear that someone involved in this tomb project knew about the Taurus orientation.

The building of this chapel tomb really involved a desecration of the church, for a part of the north wall had to be knocked down to accommodate it (see T, figure

14). It is difficult for us now to determine precisely why this part of the wall should have been allocated for the new chapel and tomb. I know of no records which show what the removed part of the wall looked like. In the absence of details of the original wall, and in the absence of literary references to what its structure was like, one is free to speculate if there was some symbol on the wall which pointed to the orientation line from Taurus to sunrise? One wonders if there was an aperture, such as one finds in the numerous mediaeval calendrical horologia[24] of northern Italy to this day. One cannot help asking oneself if, prior to this wall being knocked down, there was a solar-fronted aperture to allow the early beams of sunrise to fall across the zodiac. Such an aperture would be much the same as that still surviving in the mediaeval solar-fronted design in the south wall of the astrological frescoes in the Salone of the Palazzo della Ragione, in Padua. A solar aperture of this kind would have been entirely in keeping with the symbolism of the church as we have so far seen it. Could there have been an image of the Sun, an aperture to permit the sunlight to fall through, or even an image of the bull on this wall, at the point which marked the centre line of the 30-degree arc?

The truth is that although we do not know what was there originally, the symbol which has been left by Rossellino or Manetti is itself quite astonishing. The sculptor (or the tomb designer) so arranged the placing of this tomb that its corner

22 Mithras killing the bull – detail from the lower corner of the tomb of the Cardinal prince of Portugal.

fell on the line between the arc of sunrise and the arc of Taurus. On this exact point, which intersects the sunrise-axis, the sculptor then carved the image of a bull. The image is derived from the Mithraic image of a bull having its throat cut by the knife of a god. This piece of Mithraic imagery is so well hidden on the tomb (with a space of perhaps only a foot between its own surface and that of the retaining wall of the chapel), that it has proved impossible to photograph it, and so a reconstruction of its appearance must be used by way of illustration (figure 22).

This remarkable image is exactly upon the line which connects the centre of the arc of Taurus with the arc of daily sunrise over Florence. Such precision of placing, within such a pregnant framework of symbols, was not accidental – we must presume that Rossellino, or perhaps his patron, knew of the zodiacal orientation. The bull is figured as having its throat cut by Mithras, in an imagery which we now recognize as fairly standard, but which (for all the interest in Roman archaeology and Egyptian symbolism) was not widely known at all in the fifteenth century. Is it not evident that with such a pregnant symbol of 'bull, sun and blood', Rossellino is hinting at something almost beyond the normal Christian symbolism?

Michael Scot, the personal astrologer of Frederick II, and certainly the most intellectual of that period, had mentioned in his astrological *Liber Introductorius* that the symbol for Taurus suggests 'that the Gentiles sacrificed a bull to Jupiter'.[25] In spite of the fact that he refers to the zodiacal images of Taurus, it is possible that Scot had in mind one or other of the Tauroctonies of Mithraic origin, some of which are surrounded by zodiacal imagery, and by initiation symbols which are often taken by laymen to be zodiacal.[26] The reason why I suggest this is because there is nothing inherent in the standard images of Taurus, from Egyptian, Graeco-Roman or Arabic sources, which suggest the idea of either sacrifice or Jupiter. There are, of course, numerous surviving bas-reliefs of Roman design showing the bull being led to sacrifice, and it is quite possible that Scot had either seen, or heard reports of, one of these. However, this in itself does not explain why he should like the idea of the sacrificial bull with Taurus, save through some remembered reference to esoteric lore. On the other hand, it is likely that Scot, or his information source, had noted images similar to the many surviving bas-reliefs which show Mithras killing a bull, within a circle of zodiacal images (figure 7). The fact that Jupiter was in early Christian literature often used as a name synonymous with Christ is probably irrelevant to our own inquiry. Scot's *Liber Introductorius* was really a compilation, a summary of existing astrological lore and knowledge, so that it is likely that his tantalizing reference to Taurus is merely being recorded from some earlier Arabian sources, which he does not name.[27]

In fact, it actually doesn't matter a great deal to our own study of San Miniato if Scot was influenced by Mithraic imagery or not. However, because the symbolism is itself relevant – being so clearly expressed, and being virtually contemporaneous – one should at least try to seek an origin for his curious notion. His own reference to Taurus and the blood sacrifice was written (almost certainly in Italy) only a year or two after the San Miniato zodiac had been constructed, and it is extremely unlikely that such important ideas should have been unknown to other specialists in this field. One notes, in passing, that Scot's observations are a sort of extension of those made by Arnaldus in connection with the manufacture of amuletic devices.

Is it possible that either Rossellino or Manetti read the words of the astrologer Michael Scot about the sacrifice of the bull, and being aware of the Taurean orientation line, used it to add significance to this symbolic construction? I do not for one moment suggest that the architect who put down the 1207 zodiac had Mithras in mind. Even if he had been aware of that cult, which was by then virtually forgotten, it is as likely as not that his view of the significance of the Mithraic image (figure 22) would be as imaginative as his view of ancient history as a whole – which is to say, entirely fanciful. Speculation as to the precise symbolism intended is probably fruitless. Even so, it is evident that whoever planned the orientation of this zodiac, and the rich sequence of symbols in the church and on the façade, had a profound knowledge of both astrology and its arcane symbolism. It is inconceivable that such a man, or such a group of men, should not be familiar with the link made in astrological literature between the sign Taurus, the concept of sacrifice, and the association drawn between this sacrifice and the healing power of the bull's blood.

Meanwhile, to return to the symbolism of the basilica as a whole, we may recapitulate something of the complexity of hermetic symbolism. By now it must be evident to us that there are three distinct (though related) cycles within the basilica, each linked with the zodiac. There is the daily cycle of the sunrise, welcomed or received by the arc of Taurus: this Taurean symbolism points to the daily rebirth or 'incarnation' of the solar Logos. There is also the annual cycle of the perfect meeting of the sunlight with the foot of Christ: this proclaims the Piscean mystery of Christ's sacrifice. Further, there is a much more vast cycle of time, hinted at in the planetary configurations which dominated the year in which the zodiac was laid down. The first cycle I will term the 'Taurean' symbolism; the second I will call the 'Piscean' symbolism; the third cycle, which is perhaps of a contentious nature, I will term the 'epochal' symbolism. Each of these symbolism forms I shall examine further in Chapter 4, pp. 83–96, in which I shall attempt to relate them to the early thirteenth-century theological and astrological tradition. For the moment, however, we may ask 'what is the meaning of the Taurean "epochal symbolism"?'

The significance of this 'epoch' is not known. In modern times some astrologers might be inclined to speak of it marking a subsidiary period of Taurean import. Without doubt the majority of astrologers (for all the different forms of astrology practised in modern times) might be inclined to agree in admitting the stellium as an astrologically important event. The mediaeval astrologers would also view the event in such a way. We know from a large accumulation of surviving astrological documents[28] that the famous satellitium in Pisces was in the early sixteenth century regarded as a presage of a World Flood, and dire omens were always read into such major conjunctions. The Arabian astrologers, whose work formed the basis for mediaeval astrology, had written about similar planetary epochs in connection with both the theory of precession, and that peculiarly Arabian theoretical extension of precession which is now called the 'trepidation theory'. These were linked with the cycles which are now called 'precessional cycles' of 2,160 years periodicity. The mediaeval astrologer did not view the precessional periodicities with modern eyes, and there were available to him several possible periods and cycles by which he might explain or date such periodicities – at least six different theories of this periodicity were in circulation in the first decade of the thirteenth century.[29] Both the precessional epoch and the so-called 'Great Year' offered cycles which might be linked with satellitiums, leading to predictions (dire or otherwise) in the manner of the later Piscean scare, when a similar gathering of planets in Pisces led to predictions of the flooding of Europe. There appears, however, to be no surviving early-thirteenth-century record of such traditions relating to Taurus.

Three hundred years would elapse before the occultist Trithemius set down his text on the Archangelic periods, linked with planetary rule of what he called the 'Secundadeians'.[30] These were the 'intelligencies' who moved the spheres, and whose cycles were linked with historical periodicities. Michael Scot called these beings 'the seven senators', and it is likely that Scot, who was a brilliant translator of many Arabic documents on astrology, was aware of their role as rulers of history.

There is even more certainty that Peter of Abano, the magician who in the fourteenth century so profoundly influenced Giotto in regard to astrological symbolism, was familiar with these Archangelic periods, for Trithemius admits that he took his whole theory of planetary rulerships from him.[31] Peter of Abano in turn took his own records of the planetary rulers of the ages from the Arabs, who presumably had them from Gnostic sources. The idea was therefore around in literature – may we take this as a hint of a literary tradition, with which the initiate-builders of San Miniato were familiar? Was it possible that the initiate school responsible for the building of San Miniato knew of such a tradition of epochs, orally transmitted by initiates, and not set down in writing?

The fact that the periodicities of what Trithemius called the 'Secundadeian Beings' do not link with the zodiacal sequence, but with planetary series, is not really important. What is important is that we should recognize an awareness within the mediaeval world-conception of the idea of cycles or periodicities linked with stellar or planetary configurations. The chapter on mediaeval astrology will throw more light on this question, however.

Perhaps more directly pertinent to the early thirteenth century, however, are the cycles of history promulgated by the influential followers of Joachim of Fiore. We shall examine the possible implications of these cycles later in the present chapter, however, after we have briefly studied the esoteric symbolism of the façade of San Miniato.

55

23 Thirteenth-century marble intarsia of humanoids eating fishes, on the façade of San Miniato al Monte.

The anagogic symbolism which we have seen in this lovely interior is also proclaimed with equal artistry on the façade of the church. Again, it is a symbolism which has somehow evaded the attention of conventional art-historians, who have failed to penetrate the hermetic and astrological lore. We find a recapitulation of the Piscean fishes on the square of intarsia below the large cross which dominates the façade (figure 23). Here we see two semi-humans, or mermen, each holding a fish to his mouth, and presumably about to eat it. This is obviously a reference to the sacramental aspect of the Eucharist – the taking into our own bodies of the Body of Christ. The two fishes are a general reference to Pisces: in this case they are a specific reference to the two parallel fishes which represent Pisces within the interior of the church. We see in this unique mediaeval image the two fishes being taken into the body of man. This is a particularly brilliant reversal of the interior symbolism, in which man was being invited to enter into the space between the two fishes – invited, that is to be received into the body of Christ. This delicate intarsia, scarcely visible in its details from the ground in front of the church, is one of the most esoteric of all basilican symbols, recapitulating a wide range of Piscean themes which seems to have dominated mediaeval astrological symbolism on façades as widely separated in time and space as Chartres in France and San Miniato in Italy.[32]

24 Eagle on the façade of San Miniato al Monte.

The 'missing bull' theme is also expressed in a recapitulation on the outer fabric of San Miniato. We may trace in the ornate figurations of the façade precisely the same triple progression that we observed on the marble lectern of the pulpit – eagle, man and lion. Dominating the church is the symbol of the Lana Guild (or Woolworkers) who contributed to the building of the basilica: an eagle resting upon a bale of wool (figure 24). This is, of course, at the same time the eagle symbol of St John, a parallel to the eagle we found in the apse mosaic, and in the pulpit lectern, and which is also set in the marble intarsia pavement of the nave, in a related sequence of symbols. The eagle itself was not placed on its pinnacle perch until some time after 1207 (see Appendix 2), but it probably replaced an earlier eagle image in marble or bronze.

Below, on either extreme of the eaves, is a human being, in the curious posture which most art-historians call the 'orans' gesture (figure 25). In fact, as occult-historians have convincingly shown, this is the ancient image of the spiritualized human being (a 'postmortem' gesture according to some, an 'etheric gesture' according to others) symbolized in the winged human associated with St

57

25 Orans on one side of the façade of San Miniato al Monte, below the eagle (figure 24), and above the lions (figure 26).

26 Lions on either side of the window on the façade of San Miniato al Monte. The position is anagogic as Leo is linked with the sun, the light of which streams through the window.

Matthew.[33] Below, at the bases of the two pillars which frame the square central window of the façade, we see the heads of two lions (figure 26). These, of course, represent the leonine images of St Mark. The descending sequence of eagle, man, lion, is exactly the same as on the pulpit lectern inside the church.

Nowhere on the façade do we find the image of the bull. And yet, if our interpretation of the secret symbolism of the interior is correct, we are led to see the bull as the hidden symbol of the Christ Logos, who sacrificed His blood for the human world. Such a transformation of the 'missing bull' is in the image of the triumphant cross which dominates the apex of the façade (figure 24), with the Piscean imagery below, and the triumphant St John symbol above. We may take it that the curious 'tears' which are, as it were, being thrown off this cross actually point to the four blood-wounds of Christ. These are the two wounds of the crucified hands, the single nail-wound through the feet, and the lance-wound. This cross is at once the symbol of sacrifice (the blood of the bull) and of resurrection (the excarnating power of Pisces). It is here, on the façade, that the symbol of the Incarnation and Redemption (the Cross) meets with the symbol of spirit, for the cross is raised above the esoteric intarsia image of Pisces, which has the same symbolic intent as the symbol for Pisces that was engraved on the reliquary over the remains of Saint Miniato, in the crypt.

San Miniato reveals itself as a mystery of rhythms. First, we have the daily rhythm, expressed in the 'Taurean' orientation to sunrise. Second, we have the annual 'Piscean' rhythm, expressed in the culmination of the precise lighting of Christ's foot. Third, we have the planetary or 'epochal' rhythms, expressed in the dating of the zodiac, which links with a Taurean stellium. The study of these three rhythms requires the personal involvement and activity of the human being: we ourselves must stand on the zodiacal Sun, we must climb the steps, experience the sunlight-magic, return down the steps at the insistence of the lion's glance, and so forth. There is a perfect co-ordination of movement within the symbolic elements of the church. The zodiac-Sun inside the church, the sunlight which streams into the building, the daily rising and setting of the Sun within our own solar system, are all integrated into this magnificent play of symbols. In our own movement around the church in study of these symbols, we echo the movement of the sun.

The modern esotericist will note with satisfaction that in following the pathway of symbols, from zodiac to wall, from wall to apse, then back round the lectern to the zodiac, one is not only making a movement up and then down, in imitation of Christ – one is actually making a lemniscatory movement (figure 27). The point of interchange in this lemniscate marks the position where one stands, midway between the lay part of the church and that occupied by the religious. This point marks the midpoint of spiritual experience, at which one must make a decision for Christ. This symbolism of lemniscatory movement may merely be a projection of a modern mind, but it proves to be worthy of some further reflection. The lemniscate, which in modern times is a mathematical symbol for 'eternity' (by which the modern mind means 'infinite progression'), is said to be derived from a sigil depicting the meeting of Sun and Moon ⃝⃝. In mediaeval times the Moon was a symbol for the crowd (hence for a congregation), for the 'natural life', for all that fell under the sway of the demonic.[34] The Sun was a symbol of the religious life, of all that which was concerned with the discipline required of the priest. The lemniscate was a fairly popular symbol in mediaeval art, but its form is more often than not used in hidden structures, especially in connection with planetary considerations, or in relation to the spiritual hierarchies. It is interesting to observe that an illustration to one of Scot's astrological texts of the fourteenth century in

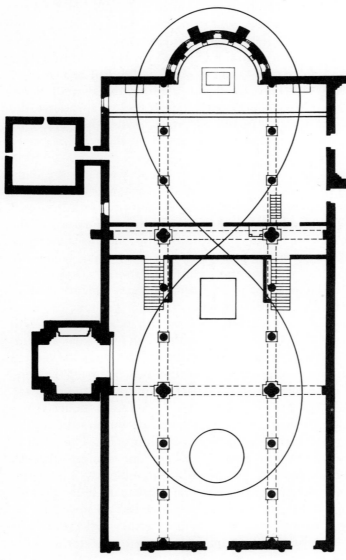

27 *Lemniscatory movement induced by following the symbolism of San Miniato al Monte. The lower part of the lemniscate, originating in the zodiac, is to be visualized as moving upwards (the movement is up the steps), and reaching the double point at the position where the fishes are located on the sides of the doorways. It is at this point that the human being stands, and then visualizes the higher part of the lemniscate, in conceiving of the movement of the sun through the heavens, with the zodiac on the periphery of the cosmos. The movement back down into the church is made by way of the foot of Christ, down through the symbolism of the lectern (to the right), and back to the zodiac through the gaze of the lion.*

the Bodleian Library at Oxford (figure 28) contains just such a lemniscate in its design. I do not refer to the lemniscate made by the two carriage wheels, but to the lemniscate produced by the large aureol within which sits the personification of Sol, touching the circle of planets. There is no mystery in the arrangement of the planetary sequence, for this is merely a reflection of the mediaeval notion of planetary distances from the Sun. In fact, the notion of the lemniscatory movement was widely recognized in mediaeval times, for it was a custom to set down pavement calendars inside buildings, sometimes beneath unwalled arched roofs, to chart out the daily positions of the sun at midday. Several of these horologia or calendrical machines still exist, as, for example, the mediaeval external system in Bergamo, or the more recently constructed internal system in Bologna. As these indicate, the seasonal drift of the Sun traces a lemniscatory pattern on the earth.

In standing at the point of intersection in this San Miniato lemniscate, looking up to the image of Christ in judgment, one is symbolically standing at the inner

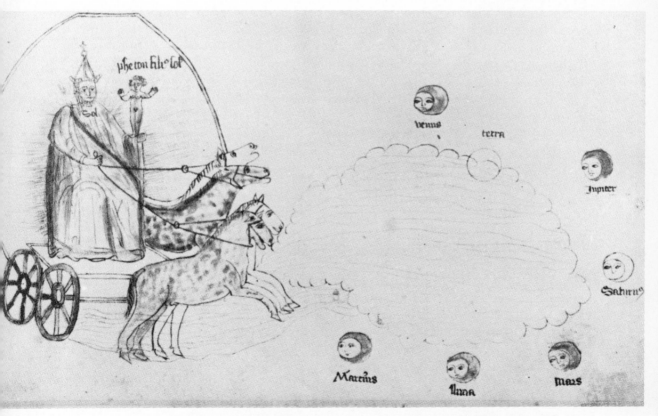

28 *Lemniscatory pattern in an illustration to a fourteenth-century manuscript on astrology by Michael Scot. The facial personifications of the six planets are ranged in order of the mediaeval notion of distances from the Sun.*

space where one may make the decision to leave behind the sphere of the Moon and step into the sphere of the Sun. In the raised apse one has a higher repetition (a modern esotericist might call it a 'higher octave') of this entry from Moon to Sun, at the midpoint of the lemniscatory path which one traces in the church. Perhaps this explains something of the relevance of the left-hand of the three doorways in the San Miniato façade. On the front of the doorstep are carved the words 'Haec est porta coelestis' (This is the gate of heaven).

So far as I know, there is no accepted term for this point of intersection in the lemniscate. Within San Miniato it clearly symbolizes a state of being in which man finds himself poised between two worlds – it may therefore be called a 'doorway' rather than a midpoint. In a different astrological context, George Adams calls this intersection a 'midpoint': this would seem to be a reasonable term were all two-dimensional lemniscates symmetrical.[35] In his interesting study of cosmic models, Davison[36] uses the word 'double-point', which is of course, specifically adapted for Vreede's concept of planetary movements in three-dimensional space. The point I wish to make about the lemniscatory pathway in San Miniato is that it is 'spiritual'. The first circle is traced on the earth, with the 'midpoint' on an axis along the nave. The second circle is 'invisible', being a circle traced from this midpoint by the imaginative faculties as a solar cycle in the skies. In more senses than one, a person who stands before this space between the two lapidary fishes is standing between two worlds, the world material and the world spiritual. It is part of the sheer brilliance of the San Miniato symbolism that it here points to a truth which is absolute in time and space: man by his very nature stands continually poised between these two worlds.

I labour somewhat the importance of this 'midpoint' or 'double point' of the lemniscate because of the significance of the numbers 3 and 2 in the mediaeval mind during the first decade of the thirteenth century. The Joachimist philosophies, which were later to be linked with heresies, were intimately woven into the history of the period by virtue of the rationale given by Joachim for his prophecies, which predicted the coming of the Antichrist and the end of the World, towards the middle of the thirteenth century.

Before glancing at Joachim's view of history, and his prophecy for the end of the World, we must first note the significance he places on the numbers 2 and 3. The approach to graphic symbolism set out by Joachim[37] is involved with a highly personalized view of the sigilic structure of the alpha and omega of Christian art, written in the Byzantine manner in forms corresponding to A and ω respectively. He says that the alpha belongs to the 3, for it is itself triangular. The omega, which would appear to be a 2, consisting of two ω crescents, is actually visualized as a 3, for 'the two proceed from the point' – thus $\smile.\smile$. Now this point is invisible: even though Joachim does not say so, he takes this for granted. He makes this emergence of 3 from 2 link with both history and Trinitarian theology. Both are relevant to our present inquiry.

Joachim of Fiore died in the same decade that the San Miniato zodiac was constructed, yet there is a possible link between the San Miniato zodiac and inscription and Joachim's 'etatulae' or sub-periods. Joachim's personal view of the Trinity was condemned by the Fourth Lateran Council in 1215, but (curiously) not his other more radically dangerous ideas. He had computed the duration of the period from Christ as being 42 generations, with each generation being a nominal 30 years in extent. These numbers, with 42 being derived from $2 \times 3 \times 7$ is derived from magical numerology, of course, as is his insistence that there are three main ages, that of the Father, that of the Son, and the third being that of the Spirit. The relevance of his prediction for the thirteenth century is that, according to his view of history, the years from 1200 to 1260 were to see the culmination of tribulations and the coming of the Antichrist. The appearance of the second Antichrist (named by Joachim 'Gog') in the year 1260 would mark Christ's Second Coming and the End of the World. What was often overlooked in interpretation of this literature was that there was to follow a third age of the Holy Spirit, one of the 'Eternal Gospel', devoid of ecclesiastical subterfuge and machinations. One might see why the Franciscans should find his views congenial, and why they were anathema to the established Church. Certainly his prophecies had a depressing effect on very many people.

In view of the history of the period, it is tempting to confront the security of predictive symbolism in the San Miniato zodiac with the hysterical insecurity of the pessimism attached to the Joachim prophecies. Joachim marks the year 1260 down for the End. In contrast the zodiac inscription gives a specific date (1207), links it with astrological cycles, and then insists that the church (or zodiac) will endure for all time. It is as though a new age of Taurus, of unspecified extent, had just dawned. It is Christ who would reign for all time, not Antichrist.

The 'alpha' and the 'omega' on either side of Christ in Glory in the apse of San Miniato (figure 16) belongs to the ecclesiastical tradition which sees Christ's reign as being from the beginning until the end of time. The alpha is the beginning of the Greek alphabet, and the omega is the last letter. Christ will stay with the world, as He himself promised, until the very last letter. In contrast to the Joachimite pessimism, the imagery and inscriptions are optimistic of futurity. Could it be that the San Miniato inscription and zodiac have been placed down as an authoritative seal on the ancient form of prediction in contrast to the terminal prophecies of Joachim?

One is aware that the apse mosaic was finished almost a century later than the church fabric, and that it has been restored, however slightly, and however well, at least twice since that time. The building of churches and cathedrals did take a relatively long time in the mediaeval world, yet even so, it is possible that the alpha and omega of this design are linked with the Joachimite prophecy. This would account for the insistence with which four groups of three dots have been added as ornamentation to these two sigillic forms of alpha and omega, almost as though they deny the 3 from 2 graphic theory promulgated by Joachim.[38] However, this may be too deep an esotericism to hang upon tesserae which may in fact be restorations. On the other hand, we shall see a similar use of sigillic triad dots being used in a most clever way in the lapidary inscription.

Whatever the significance of this 'invisible midpoint', which makes of the two circles of the lemniscate a three, we may see it as marking a temporary confluence or union of the three-fold man. Above is the spirit, below is the marbled earth, and here, at this invisible point of intersection, stands the questing human, poised between two worlds. One has just traced the beginnings of the 'lunar circle' of the lemniscate with one's body, having walked from the centre of the zodiac, and climbed the steps in search of the fishes. This is the act of the body. One then stands poised between the two halves of the church, in which the emotional life is addressed by the Christ-image of the two fishes. One is standing here without motion. At the same time, one looks up to the apse mosaic, and through its symbolism one's intellect is called into activity, and one traces in the imagination that full circle of the daily sweep of the sun (and that of its annual circuit) in the skies beyond. The body, emotional life and intellectual activity find a union at this point. One stands at a centre, but the real centres of the circles are elsewhere, in circles drawn by body and spirit, beneath the gaze of Christ and the Evangelists.

29 The so-called 'labyrinth' in the nave of Chartres cathedral.

One cannot help thinking of those remarkable words of Michael Scot, which are so rarely understood in modern times – that genuine astrology is concerned with things 'not obvious to the eye, but to the intellect, such as mathematical lines and spirits in the air'.[39]

The Sun itself is used to render anagogic the Byzantine image of the Christ which dominates the interior of the church from his Glory. In following the sun, with all our faculties, with what the ancients would have called our triadic being (body, feeling and mind), we find that we are dancing to the imitating Christ. This dance, in which the inner and the outer find symbolic equivalents, is echoed in the dance-like movement, which is performed by anyone who traces the curvilinear path of the misnamed labyrinth in the nave of Chartres cathedral (figure 29). Anyone who has attempted to follow these 'labyrinthine' lines will confirm that one immediately becomes involved in what is almost a 'floral dance' as though one were edging along a formal pattern of ritual steps, at one moment swaying in towards the centre, at the other moment swaying away from the centre.[40] It is worth noting that there is an extraordinary conflux of meaning in the esoteric symbolism of Pisces which is expressed on the façade of Chartres and that expressed on the façade of San Miniato. Is it possible that the ancient church zodiacs, and the so-called 'labyrinths', found at one time in many of the mediaeval ecclesiastical structures, are related in some symbolic way? Is it possible that the zodiac was seen as an image of the dance of the stars in adoration of the solar God, while the labyrinth symbolized a dance of man in the house of God, beneath the stars? After all, the zodiac is a symbol of the highest heavenly spheres, imprinted here in San Miniato into earthly marble, in adoration of a Taurean-bull Christ. In contrast, the labyrinth of Chartres is a symbol of that prison designed to keep a bull-headed monster within the earth. What is important to both formal patterns is the 'invisible centre', one of which was marked by symbolic figures relating to a great earth-mystery, the other of which is still marked by the Sun.

At Chartres, this earth-prison has been raised to the earth's surface, printed in marble slabs to mark out the formal pattern of a dance. In such a brilliance of symbolism has the demonic in man been tamed that he might dance in adoration. Just so, the god-like which became man in the being of Christ has, in San Miniato, been turned into a symbolic form which describes a dance of adoration which carries one through the church, and upwards, as one participates in what is perhaps the most remarkable of all ancient esoteric sigillic forms. To make this lemniscatory dance of San Miniato is actually to live for a while in a conscious or unconscious imitation of Christ.

'Every astrologer is worthy of praise and honour . . . since by such a doctrine as astrology he probably knows many secrets of God, and things which few know.' So wrote Michael Scot, round about the time that the zodiac of San Miniato al Monte was completed.[41]

3 Astrological considerations

The usual view has been that western Latin learning was not affected by Arabic science until the twelfth or even the thirteenth century.

(L. THORNDIKE, *A History of Magic and Experimental Science*, 1923, vol. 1, p. xxx.)

One cannot spend much time in the vicinity of the San Miniato zodiac without noting the wonder which many modern tourists experience in finding (perhaps for the first time) a large zodiac in a Christian building. 'Surely the zodiac is a pagan thing?' they will mutter to each other, and then, glancing in awe around the lovely interior, they might ask somewhat uneasily, 'Wasn't astrology banned by the church?' Such questions are often posed by visitors to the basilica, who are usually quite unaware of the extent to which astrological symbolism had penetrated into the theology and art of the twelfth and thirteenth centuries.

The innocent-seeming questions of these visitors are not easily answered. In the twelfth century the zodiac was still something of a pagan thing, and it is true that the church had succeeded in discouraging certain aspects of astrology for almost seven hundred years after St Augustine wrote in the fifth century. The ban on astrology had entered the Christian legal codes, under Theodosius, as a relict of earlier pagan political manoeuvring, but it appears to have pleased the ecclesiastical authorities to continue such a ban largely because of the heresies and distinctions drawn by the Gnostics, who made great use of astrological and cosmological lore.

However, in spite of the bans, and in spite of uninformed theological prejudices about the nature of astrology, it is evident that a certain amount of the post-classical astrological lore and literature did survive, and was used during the entire period of the early history of the church. Lynn Thorndike, in the book quoted in the chapter-head above, has well documented the early surviving literature which preceded the flood of astrological lore which came to Europe from Arabian sources in the twelfth and thirteenth centuries. If one may be permitted a wide generalization about the development of astrology prior to the thirteenth century, it is true to say that there were two vast streams of astrological thought which flowed together in the twelfth century, and formed the essential astrological doctrines of the following centuries. The first was the flotsam and jetsam of surviving late classical lore in the popular literature, much of which represented an astrology of a very low order, some of which represented misunderstood notions which could be linked with sophisticated late classical lore and even with the esoteric streams of what has been called 'Neoplatonic' astrology, which is essentially the externalized astrology derived from the mystery wisdom of the late Roman period. The second, and certainly the most influential, stream was that which proceeded from the Arabic learning of the ninth and tenth centuries – a stream which actually penetrated into western thought and symbolism much earlier than is realized by non-specialist historians. Within the academic histories of our modern times, the early development of these Arabic influences appears to have been noted for the first time by Thorndike, when he pointed to early astrological manuscripts connected with Gerbert.[1] This material, written in the eleventh century, makes use of Arabic astrological and astronomical terminologies. Thorndike was reasonably convinced that the Gerbertian texts were representative of the astronomy of the eleventh or early twelfth centuries – a notion, incidentally, which was in conflict with much of the established historical opinion of Thorndike's time. From Thorndike's observations, and from his descriptions of the content of this material, we can see that even at this early date there existed in Europe a sophisticated astrological lore which incorporated much of the classical tradition in connection with planets, signs, constellations, lunar mansions, and many of the sophisticated notions which one finds (albeit in different dress) in many modern textbooks which deal with traditional astrology. The same indefatigable Thorndike points also to the existence of eleventh-century manuscript copies of Firmicus Maternus, who is certainly the most important of the surviving late classical sources for our knowledge of practical astrology – far more important than the more widely known texts of Ptolemy.

Such references as these, while they have not yet been fully incorporated into the academic histories of astrology, and are totally ignored in the potted 'histories' of astrology which more and more fill the shelves of modern bookshops, merely confirm what one may see presented openly (though often with a hidden or esoteric meaning) on the façades and interiors of the twelfth- and thirteenth-century cathedrals and churches of Europe. The fact is that the astrological lore demonstrated in several surviving cathedrals and monasteries – for example in Canterbury cathedral, or in the Sacra di San Michele, in the Val di Susa – points to a knowledge of astrology, and an awareness of the esoteric potential within astrological symbolism, which is not adequately charted or paralleled in contemporaneous literature. We might almost say that the true books of the esoteric astrology of the mediaeval era are not to be found in manuscripts, but in the stone and marble of the mediaeval cathedrals and churches. This dual stream of astrological symbolism might arise from the somewhat uneasy relationship which appears to have existed between the body politic of the twelfth-century theological hierarchies and the creative impulses of the cathedral builders, who were clearly excited by the potential offered to regenerate, redeem and re-state certain Christian truths by way of the newly rediscovered astrological symbolism.

The relationship between mediaeval astrology and theology has never adequately been charted by scholars: this means that it is now difficult, if not actually impossible, for the historian to draw parallels between the surviving literary tradition of mediaeval astrology, symbolism and sigillic esotericism and the symbolic astrological forms used contemporaneously in the cathedrals and churches. If ever the story of that relationship between astrology and theology were to be unearthed and told, then the account of how an art which remained in the statutes as a Theodosian interdict, became 'the supreme science in the thirteenth century' would be a fascinating one.[2] In the present context, however, we may simply observe that it was true, as the questions of the tourists imply, that for many centuries the practice of astrology was contrary to canon law. Yet, in spite of this interdiction, astrology did flourish in literature, theology and art, so that by the beginning of the thirteenth century astrology was probably the most important single philosophical idea permeating ecclesiastical thought and esotericism. The most extraordinary thing about that freedom of thought which was the hallmark of the twelfth and thirteenth centuries is that the church, no doubt pressurized by new concepts of learning and social changes, and certainly steam-rollered by the rapid infiltration of Arabism into Europe, did begin to make a way for the practice of astrology, and one consequence is that the condemned and rejected pagan zodiac was convincingly Christianized.

The zodiac of San Miniato is itself a potent proof of this significant renaissance and redirection of human thought and consciousness which took place in the twelfth century. Even a perfunctory glance at the history of the subject makes it clear that a scholastic orthodox definition of astrology was not formulated until the twelfth century, shortly after which the San Miniato zodiac was designed. Yet this zodiac itself, when seen within the context of its extraordinary esoteric symbolism, points to a knowledge of astrology, and to a use of astrological symbolism, which is far more sophisticated than one may read about in the literature of the preceding mediaeval period. One really has to ask from which source Joseph, who is mentioned by name in the San Miniato inscription (figure 1), received his knowledge of astrology, and how he was led to use the zodiac as an instrument through which to create an esoteric work of art which is a wonder even in our own age?

Perhaps this distinction between the 'knowledge' implicit in San Miniato, and the astrological knowledge available in surviving texts on the subject is merely yet another example of the distinction between what is 'esoteric' and what is 'exoteric'. The true esotericism did not find its way in an explicit form in literature until the nineteenth century, after much disagreement and conflict within esoteric schools.[3] In previous centuries it is found in a hidden form, as a sort of spiritual code-system hidden by a number of what occultists call 'blinds', of which alchemy, Rosicrucianism and astrology are perhaps the most interesting exoteric forms. Because of this, many of the genuine occult streams which have flowed through European history have been misunderstood by scholars, who are accustomed to reading by the word, and are usually ignorant of the esoteric spirit behind the word. This explains why the fundamental esotericism of alchemy, Rosicrucianism and astrology has been misunderstood by so many modern scholars. It is quite possible, for example, for a modern scholar such as Frances Yates to write a book on the Rosicrucians which evinced an extraordinary breadth of knowledge of the literature of Rosicrucianism, and profound knowledge of the sources, but which demonstrates not the slightest knowledge of the esoteric nature of the movement.[4]

Alongside this 'academic lore' which passes for history in modern times, we now have an extensive 'esoteric lore', but the two methods of recording history rarely interpenetrate. In reference to the history of Rosicrucianism, for example, the esoteric stream is perhaps most ably presented by Rudolf Steiner.[5] It is illuminating to observe that although the many texts on esoteric Rosicrucianism, and on the history of the movement, were available whilst Yates worked on her own history of the movement, not a single bibliographical reference to Steiner is made, and not a trace of what Steiner or his many able followers have said is found in her book. This is not meant to be a criticism of either Yates or Steiner – as a matter of fact, I have a profound respect for the two methodologies of which they are such capable representatives – I merely wish to point to the existence, even in modern times, of two quite separate streams of historicism.

Such occult and esoteric sciences as Rosicrucianism and astrology have always been careful to erect a façade of exotericism which has hidden the real work of the practitioners, and at the same time protected their esotericism from misuse. It is this fact – that esotericism has a history of its own, and one which is almost separate from exoteric history – which accounts for the confusion in academic circles about the development of the occult sciences. The situation appears to have been little different in the twelfth century, for many of those ecclesiastics who wrote against astrology knew little about the subject, and were content merely to re-work the entrenched positions of the Church Fathers, who (the mediaeval commentators failed to see) had a vested interest in putting down the exoteric and esoteric astrology of the Gnostics and related sects. Such writers also failed to see the esoteric nature of astrology, being blinded, in the way of scholars, by the surfaces of words. At the same time, the twelfth century was of particular interest to the history of astrology because this century experienced the full impact of a new astrology, replete with esoteric nuances from schools of initiation, from Arabic sources.

There are clear indications that those responsible for esoteric lore in Europe, usually monks and ecclesiastics, were sufficiently aware of the promise of arcane symbolism in this new astrology to make use of it in the new programme of cathedral building which appeared to spring up almost spontaneously throughout Europe, but which was actually controlled by a number of different esoteric groups.

It would be difficult to say precisely which esoteric group was responsible for the astrological lore and symbolism of San Miniato. Tradition holds that San Miniato was built by the Benedictines, but it is not sufficiently realized that the orders were themselves very often the outer form of esoteric movements, the mediators between the arcane schools and the material world. The purpose of the unknown group, however, is a little more evident. By means of a sophisticated symbolism of new astrological devices, they constructed a philosophical machine which could only have a therapeutic effect on those who visited the church, for prayer or contemplation. This arcane device would also, incidentally, radiate hermetic symbolism into the future by means of the newly worked astrological lore and programme of esoteric symbolism, designed as it was to integrate the human being into the system of symbols within the church. Additionally, as will perhaps become clear later on in this study, it is possible that the group of designers was to some extent concerned with mitigating the baneful contemporaneous influence of the Joachim prophecies at the beginning of the century.

Who these people were, we have no idea. Even that single individual whose name is known to us, the 'Ioseph' of the zodiac inscription, who may well have been the leader of this esoteric group, is now lost in history. In a sense, this is only to be expected. It is one of the characteristics of esoteric groups that, whilst they will leave behind works of art, and esoteric symbols in painting, sculpture, music and certain poetic structures or dances, they rarely leave behind traces of their activities in written histories or literature. Esoteric groups are rightly suspicious of the non-poetic use of the written word, which is one reason why so little of the activity of esoteric groups has been perceived by modern historians, who depend mightily upon the written word. The esoteric implications in San Miniato are there for anyone who is prepared to give the place space and time (by which I mean inner space and inner time), and perhaps it is best for me to leave the matter there. Having made this point, and indicated the painful difference between esoteric and exoteric history, it is none the less important that we attempt to establish the situation in twelfth- and thirteenth-century Europe in connection with astrological lore, in the certainty that this will throw some light on San Miniato al Monte, at least from an exoteric point of view.

The practice of astrology – as opposed to the theory of astrology, which by the decline of the Roman Empire was highly systematized and well integrated into social life[6] – was certainly frowned upon by the official bodies of the church prior to the twelfth century. By the fifth century, Saint Augustine had called up all his emotionalized rhetoric against those astrologers who cast horoscopes and read them, condemning them as the unwitting servants of the devils, yet at the same time recognizing that the stars did have an influence over the human being.[7]

Augustine was merely poaching the arguments of the Greek philosopher Carneades, who, in the second century BC, had set out the arguments and emotional attitudes towards astrology which were repeated *ad infinitum* by later writers until well into the sixteenth century. All this was more than merely a question of semantics, however – it was a question of good theology touching on matters of the human will, itself the bugbear of Christian dualism. Yet, more important, it was also a question which reached into the heart of prediction. Few people prior to the eighteenth-century Enlightenment doubted that the future might be known, but the stand of the early church had been that the future could be known only to God – or, ominously, received as a gift from demons, as part of the beguilement of the Devil.

It is almost a commonplace argument in mediaeval texts that anyone who professed knowledge of the future could at best have had that knowledge only from the Devil. This belief, whether it is rooted in truth or not, is naturally reflected in attitudes to astrology, for the majority of people who do not practise the art believe that astrology is ultimately concerned with predicting the future. The fact that this is not true is fairly irrelevant, for the majority of people in the Middle Ages believed it to be true.

It was not until the late twelfth century that men began to distinguish once again (as had the ancients) between the astrology which did pretend to predict the future and the astrology which was concerned with establishing relationships between things in the world, in establishing 'correspondences' with such matters as philosophy, theology and the arts. This was the mark of the new attitude to spiritual matters which laid the foundations for what the later esotericists and magicians called 'Natural Magic'. In effect what was really happening was that the esoteric astrology of Plato, as elaborated by such commentators as Macrobius,[8] linked with the Gnostic tradition that the church had attacked, and the different stream of Aristotelian astronomy, which gave some sort of intellectual justification for an interest in astrology, was beginning to interest men once more. It was in fact at this period of history that the various strands of theology, in the terminologies and concepts of Dionysius, began to merge with the vestiges of astrological mystery wisdom of the Platonic school, so that certain individuals were able to treat astrology for what it really is – a powerful philosophic machine, replete with tremendous power of symbolizing. No mediaeval writer seems to have been more aware of this than Alexander of Neckam, for his texts are really expositions of a brilliant new approach to allegorizing, often within a framework of the new astronomy, astrology and vestigial remains of occult lore. This new attitude to astrology may be sensed as a sort of unconscious rebirth of repressed Gnosticism, yet the church was not to realize the dangers in this for some centuries.

The weaknesses in the anti-astrological emotional attitudes (for they are not arguments) of the early fathers, particularly in the fulminations of Augustine, became evident when the refined disciplines of the schoolmen gave them the intellectual tools for discernment. The theological question was settled once and for all in the middle of the thirteenth century by Aquinas, and arguments based on the nature of divination were relegated to divinatory techniques, from which astrology proper was separated.[9] Astrology was being re-defined as a science worthy of investigation by the highest authority on theological matters. Albertus Magnus, the teacher of Aquinas, is sometimes credited with having divided astrology into a science (mathĕsis) and a practical art (mathēsis), playing almost slyly with the emphasis on the Greek 'e', but the implication in his writings is that one who predicts from mathematical considerations is to be respected, whilst one who makes predictions by any other means is a deceiver. As we have seen, this distinction is older than Albertus Magnus, but his dwelling on it does at least point to the importance which this held for the mediaeval mind. The distinction points more to attitudes than to names: one astrologer might be working at his art as though it were a philosophical machine, whilst another astrologer might well be working at the behest of demons who would certainly give prescience, even though at a price. That single lower-case 'e' took on for the mediaeval mind something of the importance of the single Greek iota in the earlier Byzantine mind. It was an idea to which the astrologer Michael Scot would return, even in the decade when San Miniato was being built in its present form.

However, the voices which disputed the value of astrology in the wake of the invasion of Arabian literature were already talking anachronistically, for by the time that Albertus Magnus and his contemporaries put the seal of acceptance on the subject, it was already being widely used in cathedrals and churches as an important element of ecclesiastical symbolism. Even in the twelfth century astrological symbolism was regarded as being sufficiently important for it to form the basic leitmotif in places so far separated in distance as the pavement (circa 1175) dedicated to the murder of Thomas Becket at Canterbury, and the so-called zodiacal arch in Sacra di San Michele, in Italy (early twelfth century). The two histories of the zodiac which may be traced in theology and art appear to be quite different. The imagery of astrology, and the secret symbolism inherent in its forms, appealed to the artists and the symbol-makers of the twelfth century, while the theory inherent in the vast philosophical machine of astrology perplexed and worried the great thinkers, who essentially failed to grasp its importance as a summary of the ancient mystery lore. As is so often the case in all periods, the artists and symbol-makers of the mediaeval period displayed greater wisdom than the contemporary thinkers and professional philosophers. Whether it was used or not used, whether it was understood or misunderstood, if we wish to grasp the essence of thirteenth-century art, we must look into the roots of the new flowering of astrology which has its ramifications deep in the soil of the twelfth century. What was the background to this new interest in astrological imagery?

'The greatest astronomical event in Latin Christendom was the translation of

Ptolemy's "Almagest",' writes Sarton.[10] The Greek manuscript which had been brought to the court of Sicily in the twelfth century, and almost certainly taken from the library of the Comnenes, was translated (anonymously) in Sicily in the middle of the twelfth century. This was almost a symbol of that great one-way importation which the west has enjoyed from the Byzantine courts, for almost all important esoteric lore seemed to drift into Europe from the east. Also from Sicily, but in the early part of the next century, came one of the most beautiful western astronomical manuscripts, a Latin version of an Arabic book of fixed stars, the arabianized drawings translated into the hierarchic Romanesque style with great fidelity and verve.[11] In the course of the twelfth century, however, the direction was not from pure Graeco-Byzantine sources, but from Greece and Rome by way of the highly sophisticated Arabian astrology, which began to percolate into the west at about that time from both Jewish cabbalistic sources and from Arabic texts. Thus, the most important idea which was to fructify in the symbolism of the cathedral builders came by way of Europe's back-door, which was Spain.

It is important to distinguish between the view of astrology which was discussed by the scholastics of the eleventh century as a sort of 'classical idea', as a system of beliefs and a predictive method ultimately linked with the ecclesiastical notion of demonology, and the practical and theoretical form of astrology which developed after the injection of Arabic learning into the west. The non-Arabic notion of astrology is deeply involved with the morality of the art – that is, the morality of what is believed to be the astrological art, as perceived through the known texts of such classical writers as Firmicus Maternus. This important Roman astrologer was apparently known in the influential School of Chartres (the cathedral fabric of which, in the late twelfth century, incorporated much esoteric astrological symbolism). Pope Sylvester II is said to have studied Firmicus in Spain as early as 1000, but even if this is scholastic imagination, traces of the Firmican literature are found in many twelfth-century documents. Marbodus, cleverly changing the objective fairness of Firmicus Maternus into an attack on astrology, criticizes the fatalistic influence of such beliefs on ethics and social orders.[12] As the modern historian Wedel suggests, there are indications that Bernard Silvestris was seduced by the astrological notions of Firmicus, and that he had knowledge of the esoteric notions linked with astrology – for example, with the spherical descent of the soul – in the Neoplatonic commentators such as Chalcidius and Macrobius. One gets the feeling from a reading of Bernard Silvestris that he was attempting to lay the foundations for a new approach to a paganized-Christianity (which is essentially what humanism is) almost three hundred years before Europe was ready for it. To what extent he was responsible through his writings for the new esotericism which permeated the design of cathedrals is a matter I leave to other historians.

Usually, however, in the mediaeval theological literature, the astrologer and his art get short shrift – a sure sign that the writer is merely quoting (usually without acknowledgment) from the curious *Etymologiae* of Isidore, or from Augustine. Canon law, so much influenced by Augustine, had conveniently classified astrology among the diabolical arts.[13] This might well have been an accident, but it does at least show two things, that the church tended to see only that side of astrology which was concerned with prediction, as it was usually held that the Devil and his hordes were the only sources of knowledge of futurity available to ordinary men. A modern reader is often puzzled to find astrology heaped in with those divinatory methods which were little short of necromantic or sciomantic. The influential John of Salisbury threw all his authority behind this commonplace view of astrology. Yet, one wonders what John of Salisbury really knew about astrology, for he seems only to have been interested in the diabolical implications of the predictive side of the art, and everything he says in the second part of his *Polycraticus* of 1159 appears to rest on Firmicus Maternus, and actually contains several errors in the use of astrological terminology. He does, however, repeat the distinction between mathĕsis and mathēsis, which he almost certainly has from Hugh of St Victor, but which has much older beginnings. This was a distinction which echoed through mediaeval literature for some three centuries, until such time as the differences between astrology and astronomy were much clearer. It is a fact that John of Salisbury's attitude is merely 'that of the Church Fathers in mediaeval dress', as Wedel put it.[14] It is also a fact that one may quote John in support of the rationale for the canon law interdiction of the art. Living at a time when Arabic science was already filtering into western Europe through Latin translations, he was still unaware of its presence. It is clear from a reading of John of Salisbury that, although Firmicus Maternus is quoted freely, the pagan sophistication behind the theory of astrology was no longer appreciated: the stream of hellenistic astrology, with its source in the ancient mystery centres, had almost run dry by the twelfth century. This certainly had its consequences in the twelfth and thirteenth centuries, when the church and the cathedral builders, began to integrate into their work the thrilling new symbols, the esoteric reworkings of the ancient astrological quarries of astrology, which had been reintroduced to Europe by way of translations of the Arabic lore. In some cases, the forms were more Arabian than they were classical.

Whilst John of Salisbury was writing from the few surviving Roman astrological documents, Adelard of Bath had travelled as far as the Arabian lands, and some of his learning in astrology was introduced into the School of Chartres, which was perhaps the centre for the promulgation of the esoteric aspect of astrology in the twelfth century. Some of the twelfth-century zodiacal and planetary symbols used on church fabric during that century already betray Saracen origins, rather than classical ones. For example, one may observe a very obvious line of iconographic development in the image of Taurus from the narthex portal at Vezelay (figure 8), for this semi-bull with a fish-like termination is not from a classical manuscript but from an Arabian source, similar to the one in figure 30. The fact that the fish-tail

30 Detail of Taurus, with a fish-tail, from an Arabic astrological manuscript of the twelfth century.

termination points directly to initiate lore should not detain us here, but it should serve to remind us that it is difficult for the modern mind to perceive many of the hidden nuances of astrological symbolism because it is so used to the modern exoteric forms of astrology. The impact of the Arabian astrological literature was of an iconographic as much as an intellectual kind, and a detailed study of this iconography would probably necessitate the re-writing of twelfth-century history *vis-à-vis* the influence of Chartres on astrological lore. It was the astrology of new Euro-Arabism which dealt the *coup de grâce* to the ecclesiastical view of astrology as represented by such men as John of Salisbury, even though traces of these entrenched outlooks and prejudices reappear for some centuries afterwards.

Perhaps the most important translation from the Arabic into Latin during that century was the work of John of Spain, who for the first time presents in the Latin tongue the 'Rudiments' of Alfraganus, who was a century and a half later to be the source for almost all the astrological ideas used by Dante. In 1142 John of Spain wrote – or rather compiled – his own text, sometimes called 'the Epitome of the Art of Astrology', in which he brought together a few of his own observations, alongside the traditional streams from classical times – streams which are generally called 'Ptolemaic' and 'Dorothean', along with concepts developed by the Arabian specialists such as Messahala and Alchindus.[15] Next in importance was probably the strangely named Plato of Tivoli, who round about 1138 had given us a translation (again from the Arabic) of Ptolemy's *Quadripartitium*, as well as a text usually entitled the *Judicia* of Alkindi.[16] Daniel de Merlai, or Daniel of Morley, as he is usually called, attempts to relate astrology to Christian thought,[17] and appears to have found it necessary to leave England for Spain to do so: his own astrological writings greatly influenced twelfth-century thought.

There were much earlier strains of astrological lore already in pre-thirteenth-century literature, however. Hildegarde of Bingen, in both her visionary and remarkably original *Liber Divinorum* and in her more opaque *Causae et Curae*, had incorporated a strange and even personal astrology into some of her ideas. For example, in the latter text[18] she treats the signs and the zodiacal asterisms as though they were virtually the same thing – which is far from being the truth. William of Conches, popular among the theologians of the next century, divided astrology in three areas, and linked what he called 'the fabulous' with the star-lore fables of such writers as Hyginus, the 'astrological' (which is what we would probably now call the 'astronomical') with Martius Capella, and the 'astronomical' (our 'astrological') with Ptolemy and Firmicus Maternus. It is a curious classification, and betrays as much ignorance of astrology as his own quaint commentary on the zodiac and the planets. When he wishes to give an explanation of the zodiac to his readers, he advises them to consult the ninth-century author Helpericus of Auxerre, whose astrological writings appear to be lost, though the reference permits us a tantalizing glimpse into the existence of early forms of astrology. We see from such references that there was not only a new Arabic astrology descending upon an unsuspecting Europe in the twelfth century, but that there were already weak currents from classical Roman and Greek sources carrying a flotsam and jetsam of astrological lore, some of it more or less strange, most of it no longer understood, and all of it pointing to the ancient tenet that man is a microcosm, and mirror of the macrocosm.

This was soon to change, for a new astrology was to sweep through Europe on a tide of Arabian manuscripts and fragments of classical lore. So fundamental were the changes in astrological lore, so rooted were they in the ecclesiastical stream of esotericism, that when Michael Scot left an introductory text for would-be astrologers, almost *en passant* he said that anyone who learned from this book would have learned the 'new astrology'. Needless to say, this text, which betrays considerable esoteric lore, is steeped in the arabism with which Scot had a first-hand acquaintance.

The changes took place at the end of the twelfth century, before Scot had produced his own important text. Alexander of Neckam and the Italian Gerardus of Cremona both helped to inject into the European stream of culture the quintessence of the Arabian astrology. In doing this they were to start a revolution which changed our western view of the celestial realms. Neckam's approach was very different from that of the Italian, however, for, whilst he leaned heavily on the Arabian astrologer Albumasar in his own work, he seems to have been more interested in establishing a relationship between theology and astrology than in accurately representing, through direct translation, the astrology of the Arab.[19] The debt of the San Miniato zodiac to Neckam's thought is probably considerable, for what he in fact achieved was virtually a renaissance in astrological thought and church symbolism.

Almost all of Michael Scot's surviving writings are dated shortly after the completion of San Miniato, but it is clear from contemporaneous records that he was influential as an astrologer and occultist during the first decade of the century. It was Scot who appears to have established the difference between natural magic and ordinary magic (though seemingly not actually using either of these terms), in order to resolve the theological difficulties of the period. Natural magic was concerned with using the virtues inherent in the material (natural) world, such as those in stones, plants, and stars, as opposed to the necromantic magic of the grimoires and other spirit-raising techniques, which were largely demonic, and openly made use of 'spiritual' powers instead of natural virtues. One observes that Scot was involved with more than a play with words – as man turned his attention from the wonders of the demonic and angelic realms, to the wonders of the material realm, he began to forge those attitudes of soul which later developed into modern science, which tends to negate (at its own cost) not only the demonic, but also the spiritual. Scot does not show the modern liberation himself – he believed in the hierarchies of demons, and in their power in human life. However, this does not prevent him from establishing certain lines of inquiry which led to the so-called Natural Magic of the later occultists such as Trithemius and Agrippa. A similar distinction, and for similar theological reasons, was drawn between predictive astrology and 'natural astrology' – Scot distinguishes between 'superstitious astronomy' and 'Ymaginaria astronomia', the latter of which 'concerns things not plain to the eye but to the intellect'.[20] It is this latter form of astrology which most profoundly influenced the development of zodiacal and planetary symbols in ecclesiastical architecture.

If one wished to point to one astrological document which summarizes the astrology of the early thirteenth century most completely, then it would be to the manuscript which Michael Scot wrote for his patron Frederick II. His translations of the Arabic lore had made him intimately familiar with the astrology of a 'classical' kind, and it is evident from his survey of 'case histories' (still largely of the electional kind) that he practises a form of astrology which is a subtle combination of Arabian, classical and personal. One might even say that this text, *Liber Introductorius*, perhaps written c.1228, is the first astrological text of a personal kind, the first of a long series of proliferating texts which degenerate into the fissiparous and turgid streams of modern personal astrology.

While it is fairly certain that Scot was in Italy at about the same time that the San Miniato zodiac was being put in place, there is no evidence of his being connected with Florence, and most of his written works are dated to a few years after its completion. Therefore, tempting as it is to quote Scot at length about the nature of astrology, and about the esoteric quality of zodiacal and planetary symbolism, we shall have merely to note his influential literary presence, and leave him out of this general sketch of the historical situation which surrounded the building of the San Miniato zodiac.

As we have observed, the interesting thing is that even while the arguments about the validity or morality of astrology echoed through the new universities, and flowed into the bloodstream of the newly awakening Europe, astrological and constellational symbolism was already being used in a sophisticated way in the fabric of the cathedrals and abbey churches which were springing up throughout Europe, in such places as Canterbury, Paris, Chartres and Vezelay. The exoteric academic realm which interested itself in such matters seemed to have little or no contact with the artistic life around them, and as the scholars said one thing, the artists (no doubt working under the instruction of esoteric schools) did another. Some years after the San Miniato zodiac had been laid in place, Alexander of Hales was still following in the footsteps of Augustine, for in his own *Summa* of 1245[21] he described the casting of horoscopes (by which he almost certainly meant the 'reading' of horoscopes) as mere superstition. He simply must have been blind, for the casting of horoscopes, and the use of astrological symbolism, was being practised by the greatest men of his age – the cathedral builders. As is so often the case, scholarship lagged behind art.

What then were the seminal works which encouraged this growth in the study and practice of the art? Besides Roger of Hereford and John of Spain, whom we have already mentioned, there was another important English source and a slightly less important Italian source. Perhaps the most easily available text for one seeking to learn astrology would have been the recent translation by Gerardus of Cremona of the Arabian astrologer Alfraganus, who, in the ninth century, translated the astrological masterpiece of Ptolemy. This Gerardus had made his own translation from the Arabic available prior to 1187,[22] and had also been the first to translate, directly into Latin from Greek, substantial parts of the *Almagest* itself. We sense from this achievement that if the characteristic spread of astrological symbolism in the following century may be attributed to one man, then it is to Gerardus. Certainly, through his translation of Alfraganus, he was the undeniable primal influence on Dante's view of astrology,[23] at the end of the thirteenth century. The second influence of great importance was the encyclopaedic allegorical writings of Alexander of Neckam, a most remarkable English monk, and his translations of some Arabian astrological texts – most notably a paraphrase of Albumasar. If Gerardus began the popularization of astrology, then Neckam began to tie it into theology: these two great men stand as sentinels to a new age of inquiry.

The astrology of Ptolemy which Gerardus portrayed was far from being the sophisticated thing which it became in the following centuries. A beginner would have been able to cast a simple natal chart according to the principles set out by Ptolemy, but he would have found it difficult to interpret that chart according to the rules given by Ptolemy by way of Alfraganus. Those modern writers who claim that there is little difference in the astrology of Ptolemy and the astrology of (say) the English seventeenth century, simply do not know what they are talking about: the difference in methods, in outlook, in astrological rules, even in chart symbolism and the forms of sigils, is very profound. It is significant that a whole batch of horoscope figures which have survived from the twelfth century, and which are drawn up in a contemporaneous hand, are rarely natal figures at all[24] -- not strictly horoscopes in the modern sense of the word at all, but 'elections' relating to the horary branch of astrology. As we have seen already, one textbook on astrology which most profoundly influenced the thirteenth century was that written (derived mainly from his reading and translating of Arabic sources) by Michael Scot,[25] but even this is concerned in the main with such elections and 'questions'.

We tend to project our own prejudices into the past, and this represents a hidden danger in regard to a study of astrological lore. When we are confronted by mediaeval astrological symbolism there is a tendency for us to assume that astrological images are intended to point to the zodiac and zodiacal lore with which we are familiar. In modern times, most astrologers use the tropical zodiac for their work, and this is the one which has been favoured as the base for astrological symbolism in the west for many centuries. However, the astrology of the early thirteenth century was not exclusively concerned with tropical symbolism. The tropical zodiac does not become the main concern of symbolists until later, as the rules of astrology were codified to meet the needs of the new consciousness, and as interest in personal horoscopy became more widespread. One result of this is that the tropical zodiac has generally been an instrument for the study of personal horoscopes, and was also used for the important 'elections', while the constellational asterisms were in ancient times the source of a rich mythology and symbolism. This distinction must be borne in mind by all those who approach the symbolism of mediaeval architecture. All too frequently the non-specialist historian tends to confuse the asterisms and signs, and appears sometimes to assume that they are the same, with similar histories, symbolic natures and significance in astrological contexts.

There is ample iconographic evidence to show that the images of what are nowadays called the 'zodiacal signs' in cathedral architecture of the twelfth and thirteenth centuries are not zodiacal but constellational. We have already noted the Taurus of Vezelay (figure 8) as an example of an image derived from a constellational text (figure 30), yet almost all the guidebooks and histories of the fabric write of it as being zodiacal. Another outstanding example of this sort of confusion is the misnamed 'zodiacal arch' in Sacra di San Michele, in the Val di Susa, since all the symbols in this arch (including the so-called zodiacal ones) are derived not from zodiacal traditions at all, but from the constellational lore.[26]

This general truth is in itself of great significance in our study of San Miniato al Monte. As will gradually emerge, it is my conviction that the zodiacal orientation and the related horoscope data of what has been called the 'foundation chart' are specifically related not to the tropical zodiac (as a modern astrologer might easily assume) but to the constellational zodiac. Any non-specialist reader who is not sure what is meant by the last sentences will find a clear exposition of the difference between the tropical zodiac and its constellational counterpart at a later point (pp. 100–101), as well as in the glossary in Appendix 1. At this point it is merely my aim to challenge the basic assumption of a general reader that the methods of the thirteenth-century astrologer will be similar to those of a modern astrologer – or even to those of an astrologer of the fifteenth century. This is far from being the case. The associations attributed to the twelve signs differ greatly from those attributed to the twelve related asterisms, and this simple fact must be borne in mind by anyone who seeks to interpret the twelfth- and thirteenth-century astrological symbolism. It must also be noted that in mediaeval symbolism there was a tendency to merge these two different traditions, thereby evoking the anagogic associations particular to the two separate streams.

What in fact may we derive from the astrological writings of the late mediaeval period which are relevant in a further sense to our study of the symbolism – esoteric or otherwise – of San Miniato al Monte? The most satisfactory answer to this question is set out in the astrological writings of Michael Scot. However, in passing we may note that each of the authorities (Ptolemy, Firmicus, Neckam, Gerard and so on) gives the rulership of Venus over Taurus, and similar traditional material (Taurus is the 'domus' of Venus, the 'occasus' or fall of Mars, for example). Taurus is portrayed in the constellational texts as a bull – or more accurately as the top half of a bull, the 'Sectio Tauri' as it was sometimes called (figure 8). A number of stars, including Aldebaran, the Hyades and Pleiades, are usually drawn into the Taurean manuscript images, and sometimes these stars are named and described. In the early thirteenth century it is already standard practice to relate the tropical and the constellational to the extent of considering the symbolic significance not only of the degree of Ascendant (tropical) but also the fixed star in or in conjunction with that degree, constellationally considered. Michael Scot deals with this at great length. In some of the twelfth- and thirteenth-century astrological manuscripts the sign (and not the constellation, which has its corresponding image, and even its own sigil) is accorded a sigil which is different from the one used in modern times.[27] It is possible that the modern sigils used to denote the twelve signs were originated in the School of Chartres, only partly derived from hellenistic sigils.

The important chorographies and melothesic images of the mediaeval astrological renaissance are dredged up from hellenistic and Roman times, largely from Ptolemy by way of such sources as Alfraganus. The fact that Ptolemy derived the rulerships of places from a particular application of long-archaic 'trigons' was ignored, and only his conclusions were noted. Thus, in the mediaeval tradition, England is ruled by Aries, Scotland by Cancer, Italy is ruled by Leo, Florence is ruled by Aries, and so on.[28] As we shall see, such rulerships have relevance to the San Miniato symbolism.

Perhaps for the first time in early mediaeval literature, the melothesic man, which was to proliferate in endless variations on a theme in the shepherds' calendars of coming centuries, is described in words. Almost every nuance of these associations was carried from the astrological texts of the Roman period. A few images of the melothesic man (in popular terminology the 'zodiacal man') begin to emerge in astrological texts at about this time, though not always in the familiar form of the human figure overlaid with zodiacal images or sigils.[29] The traditional melothesic listings link Aries with the head, Taurus with the throat, through to the rulership of Pisces over the feet (figure 5). As we have seen, such associations built around the 'melothesic images' are of profound importance to the symbolism of San Miniato. We find in parallel literature of a more directly theological kind a similar tendency of the mediaeval mind to allegorize and to draw anagogic connections between apparently unconnected elements in the world. It is a realm of allegorizing which reaches its perfection in Dante, and, within a specifically astrological context, in the frescoes of the pseudo-Giotto of the Salone at Padua. In the century preceding the San Miniato zodiac, Alexander Neckam had linked the planets with the seven gifts of the Holy Spirit.[30] In doing this, he was extending a method at least as old as that of Martianus Capella,[31] who appears to have given the first human personifications of the arts, and which found its complete expression in the septenaries (actually uneasy octets) on the Florentine campanile, almost a symbol of the flowering of Florence at the beginning of our modern world. The link established in the (now moved, and partly reconstructed) zodiacal floor in Canterbury cathedral reflects this tradition, for this points to a system of relationships between the virtues and vices and astrological lore which is clothed in a sequence of symbols derived from hermetic lore.

Chance survivals of the earlier astrological traditions occasionally bob to the surface of this river. Some of the ideas recorded by Neckam hint at types of astrology which really belong to the Gnostic streams, as for example a reference to what can only be taken as a version of the so-called Trutine of Hermes, which links the conception chart with the natal chart. The literature of Michael Scot, while ostensibly astrological, is even more replete with esoteric references and astrological truths, pointing to methods and outlooks which are now lost to the modern world. As we have seen, such writers as Arnaldus and Michael Scot were openly interested in the deeper pagan and Christian significance of the images for zodiac, constellations and planets.

A complex star-lore, developed by the Arabian astrologers, but founded in Ptolemaic astrology, is preserved in mediaeval astrology. Sometimes this is contained in a separate stream of literature, in which the stars are named, their influences given, and in certain cases their sigils preserved. In other cases, it is intimately linked with ordinary astrological lore – as, for example, in the writings of Michael Scot. The manuscript stream of star-interpretation is different from the literature of star-lore of the Aratus kind, and these are both different from the literature of the astrological-astronomical kind. An astrologer of that period would obviously make himself familiar with each of these streams of literature, and symbolizing, as the astrological text of Michael Scot indicates. Scot preserves from the Arabian tradition a series of 'personality' readings for the constellational non-zodiacal star-groups, pointing to an interesting astrological method which is no longer used in astrology, for all that some of the notions survive in popular star-lore texts.

I draw attention to this now-disused constellational material mainly because it is my conviction that the foundation chart of San Miniato al Monte is linked with the star-lore attached to individual stars in Taurus, a lore derived from Arabian sources. However, it is not a point I would wish to labour here. It is sufficient here for me to indicate my convictions that the Taurus of San Miniato is constellational rather than zodiacal. In demonstrating this, by way of an analysis of the astrological factors involved in the foundation chart, we not only encourage a new view of mediaeval astrology – we also show that the San Miniato zodiac is itself orientated to the constellations, rather than to the zodiac.

One result of the mediaeval emphasis on the interpretation of fixed stars, and upon the non-zodiacal constellations, is that mediaeval astrology is now foreign to modern astrologers, and radically misunderstood by modern historians. This calls for some adjustment of our view of mediaeval astrology, which is not merely a version of Ptolemaic astrology, no more than it is a recognizable form of astrology to the eyes of practising modern astrologers. Michael Scot, who, I must repeat, was practising while the San Miniato zodiac was being put down, often writes of the importance of the stars and non-zodiacal constellations, and indeed leaves a detailed list of associations and interpretations accorded the main asterisms.

4 Sunlight, Bull and Fish as secret symbols

And he . . . became one of the priests and shared in their philosophy – which for the most part was hidden in myths and words, containing dim reflections and transparencies of truth, as, doubtless, they themselves make indirectly plain by fitly setting sphinxes up before the temples, as though their reasoning about the Gods possessed a wisdom wrapped in riddle.

(PLUTARCH, *The Mysteries of Isis and Osiris*, IX, i.)

There is no sphinx set up before the basilica of San Miniato, but the curious image of the humanoids eating fish, set on the marble façade (figure 23) is just about as near to the ancient mystery wisdom as a Christian symbolist might go in pointing to a teaching 'wrapped in a riddle'. It is no accident that the phrase 'myths and words' in the quotation from Plutarch incorporates the Greek mystery word 'logoi' (words), for the Christian mystery is itself the mystery of the Logos (the Word), partly taken over from the esoteric wisdom which permeated the ancient world. In the passages preceding the above quotation, Plutarch's survey of the mysteries of Isis and Osiris leads him to examine the drinking of the wine, and the nature of initiation, in terms which no successor to the claimed Apostolic Succession would challenge. There were spiritual rituals and disciplines within the ancient mystery wisdom which the early Christians found conducive to their own purposes, and a whole plethora of symbols which they could adopt and adapt for the new religion. It is therefore hardly surprising that the mediaeval church should have inherited a living symbolism which was derived from the ancient mysteries, and which reflected the hermetic strains within the Christian religion. Among these hermetic Christian symbols are several which are relevant to our own researches, such as the sun, the bull, the fish and the zodiac.

In noting the presence of such ancient mystery symbols in Christian art, we should not fall into the error of believing that the Christian mysteries themselves were little more than a continuation of the ancient mysteries: there can be no doubt that something profound – something so profound that it would change the nature of the mysteries and indeed the nature of the earth itself – occurred when Christ died upon the cross. The humanoids on the façade of San Miniato are doing more than merely eating the symbolic body of a fish-god in the manner of some long-forgotten pagan rite – rather, they are participating in the transformation of their inner being, preparing the future body of Resurrection, by uniting themselves with the Christ, whom many saw as fulfilling the promise of the older pagan mysteries.

The full complexity of the ancient mystery symbolism cannot be dealt with here, or perhaps in any single book. Even so, it is evident even to a casual observer that when we stand on the centre of the San Miniato zodiac, and participate in the diurnal and annual solar mysteries, and our benumbed conceiving stops short on the edge of the mystery of the Logos era of Taurus, then we are surrounded by ancient mystery symbols, and we perceive a wisdom wrapped in riddles. One of the commentators on the Plutarch passage quoted above points to an interesting connection between the word 'riddle', and the mediaeval Latin 'ridellus', which (like the modern French 'rideau') means 'curtain' or 'veil'.[1] Is this the veil or riddle which clothed the form of Isis, which no mortal has ever lifted? The question is not one directed merely at the feminine mystery of an ancient Egyptian tradition, at the goddess Isis, but has relevance for the Christian world, since there is much evidence to show that aspects of Isis (including the symbolic content of her clothing) was incorporated into the late Christian feminine mystery of the Virgin Mary.

The Virgin Mary, as a development of Isis, the Egyptian goddess, is portrayed as carrying the Christ child in her arms. Just so does Isis carry the child Horus. Yet, as we have seen (figure 3) in the Christian symbolism, the Virgin is linked with the stellar Virgo, and the Christ child is linked with the fishes of the heavens, Pisces. Virgo and Pisces are on opposite sides of the zodiac, looking eternally towards each other, in adoration and joy. This symbolism is the basis for many hermetic commentaries in paintings and sculpture during the mediaeval era, yet there is something most strange about its use in San Miniato al Monte.

If one stands on the periphery of the San Miniato zodiac with one's feet touching the centre of the arc containing the image of Virgo, and then looks across the centre of the zodiac, over the sun-symbol, one sees the image of the Piscean fishes. Virgo and Pisces, Virgin and Child, are united by your gaze, as by the central sun. If one continues this gaze beyond the confines of the zodiac, yet still along the axis of the Virgo-Sun-Pisces line, one sees upon the continuation of this line a painted image of the Mother and Child. In a single line the 'pagan' images of Virgo and Pisces unite with the Christian image of Virgin and Christ.

This fresco of Virgin and Child is probably early fifteenth century, and it is not my argument that the picture was painted in order that it might play a part in this magical anagogic symbolism. On the contrary, it is known that the painting was once fixed to the wall a few yards further towards the altar, towards the nominal east, where it played no part in this symbolic orientation. The entire fresco was moved to this new position during the late nineteenth century. We may presume therefore that whosoever caused it to be moved was aware of the nature of the

84

anagogic significance of the zodiacal orientation which this new position demonstrates: at the very least he must have been aware of the ancient symbolism which unites Virgo with Pisces within the wholesome framework of the Christian symbolic lore? I do not wish to claim that this axis symbolism is an integral part of the esoteric content of San Miniato – all I wish to point to is that there is a continuity of living symbolism in the church. Such is the power of San Miniato al Monte, so efficacious its guardian spirits or angels, that in the nineteenth century, at the very time when officious 'restorations' were effacing and materializing the great cultural heritage of the past in other parts of Florence and Italy, alterations in San Miniato were somehow involved with demonstrating even further the hermetic stream of thought of which the church is Europe's greatest representative.

This Virgo-Pisces symbolism is again astrological in content. However, such symbols as the humanoid on the façade and the dragons on the four corners of the zodiac itself (figure 2) should warn us that our concern with the anagogic astrological principles within the church might easily blind us to the relevance of those other symbols which are peripheral to astrology. As we have seen, these include the use of sunlight symbolism, the image of the fish, the Mithraic imagery, and so on. While these examples are easily treated in connexion with astrology (the Sun being a planet in the mediaeval cosmology, the fish being linked with Pisces, Mithras with the Taurean bull), it may be as well to glance at this symbolism from a different view from that afforded by astrology. There are many other symbols in the church which may be traced to the hermetic streams of mystery wisdom, but it is not our purpose here to make a thorough study of all these symbolic devices: our aim is rather to investigate only the deeper meaning of the zodiacal imagery in relation to thirteenth-century mysticism and theology. However, it is worth pointing out that the dragon-forms on the corners of the nave zodiac, almost all the formal patterns and theriomorphic forms on the nave pavement, many of the marble devices on the walls, and the (restored) paintings on the ceiling and beams (which include images of the Sun and Moon, along with several demon symbols), as well as the rich collection of symbols and demonic forms on the wall below the pulpit, are derived from the secret tradition of hermetic initiation symbolism. We can easily appreciate why Dante, who was perhaps the greatest literary representative of the initiation wisdom of the thirteenth century, should have found this church such an inspiration, and why he should have mentioned it, within a framework of initiation symbolism, near the beginning of his greatest poetic work.

One special area of mediaeval symbolism which has particular relevance to the San Miniato zodiac, is that anagogic literature which visualizes a link between the Sun and Christ. This idea, perhaps first set down in the Christian literature associated with Clemens, suggests that the solar Christ may be visualized as standing in the centre of the 'twelve zodiacal signs' as so many disciples. St

Ambrose of Milan had issued a seal of approval to the idea of the solar Christ, when he wrote, 'What the sun is for the Universe, Christ is for the spiritual structure of the world'.[2] Certainly more relevant to our theme of the early thirteenth century, however, is the fact that Neckam himself also drew a famous connection between Christ and the sun, in which he says that Christ (the 'verus sol justitiae' – the true sun of justice) gives His light to the Church and to the faithful in the same way that the Sun gives its light to the Moon.

So far as I can see, the particular symbolism of the light-effect of the annual solar cycle, in which a shaft of sunlight falls with such anagogic power on the foot of Christ, stands in isolation in western art. As we have noted, there is, however, a well-established literary and liturgical tradition which links Christ with the light of the Sun, and with the solar rays, and there was a similar anagogic use of light rays in the Egyptian and Roman tradition.[3] In a much wider sense, there was also a well-established technique of directing light-beams inside and outside religious buildings, though mainly for calendrical purposes, or in connection with zodiacal effects: indeed, as the mediaevalist Davy says, 'the importance of light in the Romanesque period will form the subject of a great book'.[4] The magical use of light in Byzantine churches has been noted in the writings of the scholar Otto Demus,[5] and it has been argued for certain of the buildings in the heretical areas of southern France, built to serve the Cathars and Albigensians, that heresy so much feared by the Papacy was contemporaneous with the San Miniato symbolism.[6] Was not the Logos itself called 'Light of Light' in the Bible, and were there not a large number of hymns of praise which figured Christ in solar terms? One twelfth-century hymn runs:

Sol de stella,
Sol occasum nesciens,
Stella semper rutilans,
Semper clare.
Sicut sidus radium,
Profert Virgo filium,
Pari forma;
Neque sidus radio,
Neque mater filio,
Fit corrupta.

This hymn[7] is replete with cosmological significance, and it is difficult to convey the layers of meaning in a simple translation. However, it may be translated approximately as 'Sun of the star, Sun which never sets, glowing red star, always clear. Just as the star throws down a ray, just so, in the same way, has the Virgin produced a son: and neither the star by the ray, nor the Virgin by the Son, will become blemished.' One of the ideas in the hymn is that the Sun and the Virgin belong to the incorruptible spheres beyond the lunar sphere. This would be taken for granted in the mediaeval period, for it was believed that the stars were composed of the incorruptible fifth essence, but the notion requires a gloss in present times, otherwise the symbolic significance of the hymn is likely to be missed. The esoteric symbolism of this short verse may be understood fully only in the light of the thirteenth-century view of church symbolism, however. The sacristy was seen as a symbol of the 'womb of the Blessed Mary', wherein Christ puts on his robes of humanity. According to Hugo de St Victoire, the nave pavement, upon which the dressed priest (symbol of the 'human Christ') stood during the officiation, was a symbol of humility and the body of Christ, in which the worshippers would gather, as in an ark.[8] The piercing of such a pavement, or nave, with a ray of light was therefore analogous to the fecundation of the womb of Mary by the Holy Ghost. There is surely no accident in the fact that the ray of light which performs its Piscean magic in the nave of San Miniato falls through a window above the sacristy, for it is redolent of symbolism, rendered chaste by its association with the solar Christ.

The surprising thing is that there appears to be no literary reference in mediaeval scripts to this remarkable and unique light-effect in San Miniato. On the other hand, nor are there contemporaneous references to the heretical and anagogic symbolism in any of the mediaeval cathedrals – this conspiracy of silence may well be a result of the oaths which initiates were required to make – oaths which survived in the apprentice documents well into the sixteenth century, and which are still formally sworn in the various grade initiations of masonic lodges. The light-effect and its Piscean connotations may have been observed and noted in earlier times, of course, but I have so far been unable to find any reference to this. However, I was fortunate enough to experience this anagogic use of light personally for the first time, by what is generally called 'accident', about ten years ago.

Perhaps more puzzling than the scarcity of literary reference to the solar lighting of the apse in mediaeval manuscripts is the fact that there does not appear to be reference to this sunlight-effect even in the marble inscription. Ultimately, therefore, the symbolism of the extraordinary light-effect must be taken on trust, without the support of contemporaneous literature. This aesthetic experience is of course firmly rooted in trust based on direct experience, and is supported by the fact that it plays such an important role in the integral design of the whole anagogic structure of the basilica. Having watched the miracles of light on several occasions, I am not prepared to countenance contra-arguments about their anagogic significance, as they light the Piscean foot of Christ, the wall-fish and zodiac, from anyone who has not personally witnessed it. My conclusions relating to this light may be questioned, but the fact of its aesthetic splendour, and its connection with the symbolism of Pisces may not be doubted. The anagogic lighting leads to an inner experience which neither brooks nor seeks an argument. The experience of this light-effect is all in all, and consequently my argument for its validity, and for its connection with the Piscean mysteries rests entirely upon that experience itself. Such an experience, like any experience edging on the miraculous interpenetration of the spiritual with the material, has no need of documentation, or even of explanation within the framework of zodiacal imagery.

We may be reasonably certain that the visitor is not being carried by the flow of Piscean symbolism from the lower part of the front nave of the basilica, up to the raised 'choir' end of the basilica, merely to study the two intarsia fishes on the wall. The vertical fishes invite one to continue further, both to enter into that religious space and to look upwards, towards the apse, in anticipation of another Piscean symbolism. The Piscean light-effect is an essential part of this experience of excarnation, of liberation from the marble, and from the lower confines of the church. The end-product of this flow of anagogic experience is that the human being who 'lives' within this symbolism is identified first with the microcosm, is transformed by the anagogic symbols into the image of the melothesic man, and then, in turn, is transmuted into a macrocosmic image. He becomes the living macrocosmic image of Christ.

It is not difficult for a modern scholar to draw literary-based connections between Christ and the fish-symbol, Christ and the Pisces image, and hence, by way of the melothesic man, to Christ and the feet. However, such an exercise is scarcely necessary. The literary or documentary evidence for what I claim about San Miniato al Monte is really a side issue, an exercise in scholarship, and all discussion must start from the primal experience, from what Goethe in his wisdom would probably call the 'Urphaenomenon' of this mysterious and mystic solar light on the foot of Christ.[9] Fortunately, the restorations of the fourteenth century and the nineteenth century do not appear to have dislodged the tesserae on Christ's feet from the important place in the curve of the apse dome: indeed, the restorations appear to have done less damage than is usual in such works of art. However, what has been almost entirely lost is the Latin inscription which once ran along the base of this huge mosaic. Of this only such slight vestiges remain as to make even conjecture as to its original Latin fruitless. Perhaps this inscription, at the feet of Christ, would have afforded a direct clue to the Piscean symbolism, and satisfied the modern craving for intellectual explanation?

The great temples of classical Greece were built to contain mysteries within, and yet to be admired from without: they were precisely balanced on stellar orientation lines linked with the solar motion. There is more than a similarity of orientation, but even a similarity of direction, in the axis line claimed by Penrose for the earliest temples of the Athenian acropolis – which was directed towards the Pleiades, in Taurus. The basilica of San Miniato contains mysteries within, and reaches outwards towards the Sun itself, not in mere orientation, but in mystic alchemy of symbolic directions. One thinks back to the temple of Apollo at Bassae which broke all the rules of classical orientation, and required the architects to build a special door to the east to allow the light of the rising sun to fall on the sacred image of Apollo within the adytum. The orientation of San Miniato is of a similar order of rationalization: norms and rules are broken, and the result is a work of art.

From such typical mediaeval analogies, we may see that the solar image at the centre of the marble zodiac of San Miniato (figure 11) is not a prescience of Copernicus, but rather a symbolic link with a theologically sound literature, pointing to Christ as a solar being, as King of the Cosmos. One is of course reminded of the other solar-centred zodiac in Florence, in the Baptistry. The Latin alchemical or anagogic scripts around the zodiac and the solar centre of the thirteenth-century zodiac in the Baptistry in Florence (figure 12) are more alchemical than theological, however, and there is no accident in this, for Christ was the great healer, the great alchemist, the eye of the world. The twelve-rayed Sun of San Miniato is just as much a symbol of Christ in Glory as is the thirteenth-century apse mosaic to the eastern end of the basilica.

Again, Christ as the fish has also an ancient lineage – it was old even when St Augustine attempted to trace in the symbolism an acrostic which has in modern times been reproduced *ad nauseam* by symbolists. In his *City of God*, Augustine had copied an extract from what he presumed to be an ancient Sibylline book, showing how the name of Christ was linked with the acrostic for 'fish'. That the Christ-fish should be linked with Pisces was almost taken for granted in the allegorizing mind of the mediaeval artist, and is attested to in remarkable esoteric imagery in such places as Chartres, where the two fishes of Pisces are transmuted into a single and unique anagogic image of the single fish of Christ.[10]

Christ figured in early Christian literature as a 'sacrificial bull', but for one reason or another this imagery seems not to have entered the mainstream of Christian symbolism. Perhaps the conflicts in the early centuries of our era between Christianity and Mithraism had been too intense: the Logos bull was suppressed in the face of this challenge from the ancient mysteries, rejected with the same vehemence as were Gnostic extremes in cosmic symbolism (and incidentally zodiacal and planetary symbolism). There was a narrow iconoclasm in the west long before the iconoclast controversies hit the east. I therefore cannot point to any early mediaeval manuscript tradition which links Christ directly with the Taurean bull. The exception here – a most notable one which appears to have evaded the academic historians – is the use of the Bull image, nominally linked with the evangelist St Luke, though of definite oriental and zodiacal imagery, with the Logos, such as we have seen in San Miniato. There are too many lecterns, and too many references to the Logos bull in mediaeval art, for the symbolism not to have been quite conscious on the part of the sculptors. It may be observed that the richly esoteric and anagogic symbolism in the eleventh-century pulpit of Gropina, near Loro Cuiffenna, depends almost exclusively on the reading of the missing bull, and its annexed symbol, as a Logos image, linked with Taurus. It is surely no accident that one finds such an iconographic antecedent to the San Miniato lectern only some thirty miles from Florence. Shortly after the symbolism of San Miniato had been completed, we find Michael Scot established in Bologna (circa 1220). In his *Liber Introductorius*, which, even though intended for beginners in astrology, is complex, replete with Arabic lore, he makes an interesting reference to the symbolism of Taurus. Whilst discussing the sign Taurus, Scot records that the Gentiles sacrificed a bull to Jupiter, that its gall is helpful in 'colliria', an illness probably much the same as colic.[11] To the modern mind such a reference may look like a digression, but to the esotericist the implications are considerable. The mention of the Gentiles and sacrifice calls to mind by anagogic completion the sacrifice made by the Jews – in this case the 'bull of Taurus' would be Christ. Again, a reference to the gall which is helpful as a specific against illness might be taken as a parallel to the 'Book of Tobit', in which the gall of the fish was so regarded (and indeed used, by Tobias). This fish, which was originally not a fish, but a sort of crocodile, was by the twelfth century well established as a type of Christ, a symbol of the healing force in the body of Christ. Again, I do not wish to labour this point, or to force anagogic correspondence too far – perhaps it is sufficient to note that the mediaeval manner of reading glosses into digressions is not at all like the modern manner.

In spite of the paucity of literary supports for my claims relating to Taurus and the Logos, I feel that out of fairness to the symbolism within San Miniato, I should point out that within the stream of esotericism (in which, as I have already indicated, the historical principles and methods are very different from the academic principles and methods) there are many scholars who insist quite openly on a connection between Taurus and Christ. The fact that the letter 'Aleph' of the Hebraic alphabet is linked with the constellation Taurus, at a time when this was the first asterism of the zodiacal constellations, has been taken by some occultists as a direct link with the idea of the 'First Born', to whom the letter was sacred. The 'First Born' of the Lord was of course Christ. Blavatsky,[12] after recording these and other associations, says quite definitively that Taurus (both in sign and constellation) was linked with Christ. In passing, she notes that this is why St Augustine (who almost certainly had the Logos symbolism in mind) called Taurus 'the great City of God', and that the Egyptians deemed it 'the interpreter of the divine voice' (in its aspect of Apis-Pacis). Such esoteric asides need not detain us, however, especially as the occult literature of such writers as Blavatsky has never received the attention or respect it deserves from academics, and, on the whole, it is really only the academics who have to be persuaded of the truth of a connection between Taurus and the Logos.

In the face of this lack of academic evidence for the Taurus-Christos pact, it is however quite clear from the compelling visual logic of such sculpted lecterns as those on the pulpits of Gropina and in San Miniato, that the Christ-Logos was associated with the bull, and therefore with Taurus, through the Luke symbolism I have developed in a previous chapter. There is even some evidence of a manuscript tradition which parallels this symbolism in connection with the idea of incarnation of the Word, as for example in the Harding Bible of circa 1110, which preserves in an initial to the 'In Principio' of St John (figure 31), a similar arrangement of zodio-evangelistic forms as on the San Miniato lectern. In this figure the triad is worked into a floriated initial I for the opening 'In principio . . .', and is therefore an excellent literary setting for a symbolic play with the idea of incarnation, since

31 *'In Principio' initial from the Harding Bible of circa AD 1110.*

91

the first verses of this first chapter of St John's Gospel deal precisely with this subject. The eagle grasps in its beak a banderolle with the opening words of the gospel. The talons of its right foot are gripped into the human figure below, piercing the ears, eyes and mouths, to become somewhat unconventional symbols of the total overshadowing of the Holy Spirit – an indication that the text he is writing is literally 'inspired', the word of God passing through the being of the human without impediment. This human figure is John himself, dressed in the robes of a Cistercian. The banderolle, emerging as though from his sexual parts (ruled by Scorpio in the melothesic image of man), continues the Scorpionic text. The lion at the base of the floriated letter is swallowing a bird-like creature. Perhaps it is significant of the Logos, the missing Bull, that each of the three creatures has something in its mouth?

The extraordinary detail of Mithraic sacrifice on the tomb of the Cardinal Prince of Portugal (figure 22), and its placing on the Taurean–sunrise axis, is all the more remarkable for emerging into the San Miniato symbolism as though from nowhere. In a sense, however, we may regard this chapel and tomb as being almost a summary of Renaissance artistic thought, for whilst it appears to have been the brain-child of a single artist, Antonio Manetti (who was Brunelleschi's most talented pupil), the painters, sculptors and architects worked together in a unison which is rare in Italian studios and workshops of that period. Although a distinctly humanist version of the Mithraic tauroctony, this bull on the Cardinal's tomb is probably derived from one of the many ancient symbolic forms which was being spewed up during the great new interest in Roman archaeology, but its use in this particular context is quite extraordinary. Why was this humanistic tauroctony hidden from the gaze of anyone who examines the tomb from the normal position? Why was it located on the Taurus-axis line? Is there any significance in the fact that when one stands in this corner, looking down at the bull, the Child above, in the arms of Mary high on the tomb, looks directly down upon one? Was the connection between Taurus and the astrological conceptions of the Mithraic cult recognized by Manetti or Rossellino? Indeed, how was the esotericism of the Medici, who so influenced the internal structure of San Miniato, and who also so influenced the growth of our own western culture, related to the esotericism of the original builders? So far as I am aware, there are no sure answers to these questions, but we may not doubt that a relationship between the bas-relief and the zodiac was intended. One indeed wonders to what extent the connection between the ancient cult of Mithras and the zodiac was understood by Manetti or his fellow artists?

In the presence of the rich esoteric symbolism of San Miniato, the modern reader is tempted to read depths of symbolism and symbolic intent which might not be proper to the period. However, it would not be fair to the art of the thirteenth century to impose too many of our own prejudices, our own richly striated astrological lore and associations, upon the zodiacal symbolism of San

Miniato. Indeed, if we do this, we stand in danger of losing the subtle meaning of this achievement. If, for example, we assume (in the face of contemporaneous twelfth-century art and documentation) that the foundation chart of the horoscope for 28 May 1207 is tropical, by applying the standard modern methods of astrology, then we might finish up with a quite meaningless reference to Gemini, which would have no relevance to the symbolism within San Miniato, no relationship to the inscription, and no esoteric content. With such an interpretation, we would be tempted to misread the acrostical data in the inscription, and therefore miss the basic symbolism of the Taurean 'incarnation' cycle in relation to the Logos. Again, if we fail to be impressed by the novelty of the mediaeval melothesic man, and the multi-layer level upon which mediaeval symbolism works its lateral thinking, then we fail to appreciate the full significance of the Piscean element of the 'excarnation' cycle in relation to Christ. In failing in this respect, we may also miss much of the subtle symbolism of Pisces which permeates the church, alongside the more obvious Taurean symbolism. For example, we would not be able to make sense of the fish-men on the façade (figure 23), and we would miss many of the esoteric nuances of the later additions of artwork within the fabric of the church. We might be armed with sufficient knowledge of modern esoteric lore to recognize that the fish-men of classical lore were the initiates – that Annedotus and Ichthon were ranks of initiation in the Babylonian and later mysteries – but we would be foolish to attempt to apply this modern knowledge to the mediaeval lore inscribed in San Miniato al Monte. The fish and the fish-men may be references to esoteric lore, and were later carried from Christian symbolism into alchemical symbolism, yet, for the sake of safety, we must presume only a reference to Christ and to the Eucharist, on the grounds that Piscean symbolism is time and time again used in mediaeval and proto-Renaissance art in reference to both Christ and the body of Christ.

Before turning to a more detailed analysis of the astrology involved in the study of the mysteries of San Miniato al Monte, it might be as well for us to glance briefly at the question of orientation. The orientation of ancient zodiacs is on the whole fairly standard. As Gundel shows, ancient zodiacs in ring-forms are normally aligned with Aries at the top of the circle, and Cancer to either left or right. [13] Some zodiacs are presented clockwise, others widdershins – the direction actually appears to be linked with whether or not the spectator is visualized as looking up at the stars, or (as it were) down through the spheres, as though he were standing outside space and time, beyond the Empyrean, examining the stars from the outside. In the case of the San Miniato zodiac the circle is presented as being clockwise. That is to say that whilst we are actually looking down at the zodiac, we as spectators are imagined to be looking up directly at the skies above us. The symbolism of this will be evident when we bear in mind the fact that the individual symbols within the zodiac eventually lead us to conceive of the sun itself moving through the skies, when we ourselves are looking up towards the apse mosaic.

93

The orientation of the ancient zodiacs has received some attention of late in connection with the zodiacal symbolism of the Mithraeums, especially in relation to the so-called 'zodiac' in the Mithraeum on the island of Ponza.[14] The general orientation of the Mithraic zodiacs is reasonably linked with a passage in Porphyry's *De antro nympharum*, which explains that the northernmost sign is Cancer, the southernmost Capricorn: however, the zodiac at Ponza gives the Cancer–Capricorn axis on the west–east line. Interestingly, it is on this axis that our San Miniato zodiac lies, though with Cancer directed towards the nominal east-end of the Church (in fact more to the south). However, the Ponza zodiac is a ceiling-zodiac, and in any case the orientation of the pagan temples was different to the general rule of the orientation of post-sixth-century Christian basilicas: the cult centres were to the west, and not to the east. From this we may derive the interesting fact that, just as the Ponza zodiac of the Mithraeum has Cancer directed towards the cult niche end of the chamber, so the San Miniato zodiac also has Cancer directed towards the 'cult end' of the basilica, regardless of the actual direction in terms of the cardinal points.

There would be several possible ways of 'explaining' away this orientation towards Cancer in terms of Christian theological notions. For example, the Cancer–Capricorn axis is linked with the two extremes of the spheres, for the Moon (ruled by Cancer) is the sphere nearest the Earth, whilst Saturn (ruled by Capricorn) is the sphere on the edge of time itself, the furthest planetary sphere from the earth. As one walks down the nave towards the altar, one may be seen as progressing from the outer periphery of the zodiac towards the earth itself – one would, by such a progression, be following in imitation of Christ his descent through the spheres as a prelude to the redemption of the earth. There are in fact several convincing rationales which might be offered for a Cancer–Capricorn axis along the nave of a basilica (especially if that basilica were orientated on the east–west line). However, the truth is that it would be possible to give a convincing rationale for virtually any of the six possible orientations. Aries–Libra would link with the seasonal orientation, and the beginning of springtime, possibly also with the symbolism of the Lamb (linked in mediaeval astrological lore with Aries, with the Lamb of God).

The argument for the Taurus–Scorpio orientation need hardly be set down here, in view of what has already been said on behalf of Taurus: I have purposely avoided discussing the significance of Scorpio in relation to its demonological associations, on the grounds that the dichotomy of Christ–Devil must be evident enough to anyone interested in mediaeval symbolism. The Gemini–Sagittarius orientation might be argued convincingly in terms of the two natures of Jesus Christ (as God and Man, as King and Priest), for Gemini has been linked in more than one source with such theological arguments. The Virgo–Pisces orientation would perhaps be the most convincing of all, and it might even be the orientation which one would naturally expect in a church or cathedral given over to zodiacal symbolism: indeed it is curious that, while Virgoan and Piscean symbolism abound in many churches and cathedrals of the mediaeval period, there appears to be no attempt to orientate symbolism along such an axis, or to make use of such an axis in a significant way.

The conclusion which one is forced to is that the orientation of the zodiac in San Miniato is directed towards the arc of sunrise over Florence, and that everything, save for the exigencies of geometric order in the nave, has been sacrificed to that orientation. The fact that the Cancer–Capricorn axis is along the nominal east–west axis is itself remarkable, and perhaps more of an occult blind than anything deeply significant. The additional fact that the so-called east-end of the earliest part of the basilica (which is the crypt) is itself orientated to the nominal east–west axis, would imply that there has been no significant change in the orientation of the basilica since 1000, when the crypt was built more or less in its present form. I can offer no explanation for this fact of orientation. Obviously the zodiac had to be laid out according to some convincingly hierarchical arrangement to satisfy the geometrical aesthetics of the nave. Had any other axis than the Cancer–Capricorn axis been adopted, then Taurus would not have been directed towards sunrise, nor towards that stellium of 1207. That is perhaps itself a sufficient argument for the orientation of the zodiac on the Cancer–Capricorn axis along the axis of the basilica.

One possible conclusion – which I myself will not draw – is that the basilica was orientated in such a way as to combine the light-effect of the Piscean symbolism (which would in fact allow considerable latitude, provided that a specific day was not required for such a symbolism) and the Taurean orientation. The only possible alternative argument is that a basilica already orientated in a bizarre way was later 'adapted' to meet certain conditions of lighting and marble tessellations. Given the need to fix the two specific directions in space (and perhaps in time), it was a relatively simple matter to orientate the church to meet these requirements, even though such an orientation would break all the rules known to the mediaeval builders. The breaking of such rules is the most certain fact that we have in the midst of all this speculation about orientation. On the other hand, far more logistic brilliance, and far more thought, was required to fit the symbols we have so far studied into an already constructed church.

Of course, I have scarcely touched upon the question which must be asked by anyone who makes himself familiar with the esotericism of San Miniato al Monte. Who built the church, and for what reason? It is my conviction that the designers of San Miniato were involved in Christian esotericism, almost to the same extent as were the Albigensians and the Templars, both organizations which were destined to a bloody end within a century of San Miniato being built. I am further convinced that, being the outer periphery of an esoteric school, with full access to the mediaeval equivalent of the Secret Doctrine, they were well aware of the role which Florence would play in the destiny of Europe. There is a brilliant use of hidden symbolism in the choice of the two 'hermetic' images of Taurean bull and Pisces fish as the fiducial symbols for this church. The fact is that the only sign which falls between Taurus and Pisces, as though protected by them, is Aries, which in all the chorographies is the ruler of Florence. In this chorographic symbolism we see the city of Florence, which was to mark indelibly the future development of western culture, caught between the poetic sensitivity of Pisces and the delight in the physical realm associated with Taurus the bull. It is no accident that the esoteric group, which did its work throughout Europe mainly under the guise of the new banking centred in Medici Florence, Bruges and England, had Florentine origins. Surely it is no accident that these people chose as their symbol the Golden Fleece, one of the esoteric symbols of the pendant golden ram?

It is a tradition in esoteric history that whenever a new culture is embryonic in the womb of an older one, or when an esoteric school recognizes that a culture has served its purposes and is coming to an end, then a major work of art is created in dedication, as an outer sign for future ages. The work of art may be a remarkable piece of music, a poem, a garden or a building – but whatever its external artistic form, it encapsulates, in entirely esoteric principles, a summary of what has gone before, and what is to come. All great esoteric artists, from Dante to Shakespeare, from Milton to Blake, have recognized this primal function of their art. The interesting thing is that all too often it is the exoteric aspects of their products which attract the attention of those who follow, and the esoteric contents remain hidden, save perhaps for the seeing few, who are themselves alive to the esoteric background to human history. I suspect that this has been until now the destiny of San Miniato al Monte.

5 Astrological considerations in relation to San Miniato

Look, how the floor of heaven
Is thick inlaid with patines of bright gold:
There's not the smallest orb which though behold'st
But in his motion like an angel sings,
Still quiring to the young-ey'd cherubins, –
Such harmony is in immortal souls;
But whilst this muddy vesture of decay
Doth grossly close it in, we cannot hear it.

(WILLIAM SHAKESPEARE, *The Merchant of Venice*, V, i.)

What then is the true nature of the San Miniato zodiac? Is it a figure related to the tropical zodiac beyond the periphery of mediaeval space, or is it a figure related to the sphere of fixed stars on the rim of heaven itself? The mediaeval astrologer would have framed the question in a different terminology, of course. For example, he might have asked, 'Is the zodiac of San Miniato to be orientated to the Zodiacus, or is it rather to be related to the eternal Stellatum, ruled by the eighth hierarchy of the Cherubim?'[1] He would have put the question in such a manner because, when he looked up into the heavens, he did not see the mechanical model of our modern vision, but the very operations of the celestial hierarchies (the 'young-ey'd cherubins'), who were themselves intimately concerned with the life of man.[2] The quotation from *The Merchant of Venice* at the head of this chapter is rooted in ancient hermeticism. William Shakespeare lived in the age which saw the dying of the live model of the cosmos, but it had not yet been replaced by the mechanical model beloved by modern man. Shakespeare did not know it then, but he would make us moderns dizzy by referring to the heavens as a 'floor', for our model of the universe is somehow more fixed than the ancient one, and we now usually think of the heavens as being above our heads, as a sort of canopy rather than a star-studded pavement. Yet Shakespeare had no doubt that when he gazed up at the stars he was also looking down at them, down through the long shadow-finger of the earth, which scribed a circuit through the inferior spheres, almost brushing the opposite side of the sphere of the Sun itself. In the centuries which were to follow Shakespeare's genius, man would almost joyfully don an even thicker muddy vesture of decay, and, in so doing, would shut out more completely the living music of the spheres, and that concept of the heavens as a living being.

Did the mediaeval monk Joseph, named as constructor of the zodiac, use a tropical zodiac as the basis for this orientation of San Miniato, or did he use a constellation asterism? Before we examine this question in some depth, we must observe that the mediaeval astrologer did not confuse the constellations with the zodiac. He did not assume that the constellational figures were, like the zodiacal signs, to be divided into equal arcs of 30 degrees. Direct observation of the night skies revealed to him in a most dramatic way that the asterisms were of greatly different sizes, and that their 'beginnings' and 'ends' were far from being defined. It would have been inconceivable for a mediaeval astrologer to think of the constellations as being 'zodiacal', in the way a modern astrologer so often does.

The star catalogues available to the mediaeval astrologer usually list about 48 constellations, which are described in terms of their most important stars. Even by the thirteenth century, however, one finds 'readings' for the supposed influences of many of these asterisms, even if one is not clear as to how most of these are related to the ecliptically derived chart. Indeed, in the Arabic astrological tradition which so influenced mediaeval astrology, great emphasis is laid on the interpretation of fixed stars in the interpretation of personal horoscopes: this tradition was gradually almost lost to western astrology, though it remains within the manuscripts concerned with the making of amulets relating to what are sometimes called the 'Behenian' stars, for which even the sigils have survived in many of the modern textbooks (which usually fail to understand their significance). In the mediaeval texts, the fixed stars which lay behind the constellation images are denoted sometimes by location – which presumes an ability to translate the asterisms into images – and sometimes by name. This presumes some knowledge of the stars, as well as a fair ability as an observing astronomer.

So far as I know, not a single mediaeval star-list delineates exactly the confines of the asterisms: where an individual asterism ends, and where it begins, did not seem to concern the mediaeval astronomer. In this imprecision they were merely following the direction set by Ptolemy, who no doubt felt that his readers would be sufficiently versed in star-lore to be able to recognize an asterism when they saw one, and would know for all practical purposes where it began and ended. In fact, this imprecision, which might infuriate the modern astronomer, seems to have been quite intentional – most certainly the ancients had the geometric tool by which they could have defined some arbitrary beginning and an end to their asterisms if they had chosen to do so. All the 'beginnings' and 'ends' of the asterisms so minutely described by the modern astronomers[3] are fundamentally conventions of a mathematically or spherical-geometric type, if not of a methodology, which could have been used by the ancients, had they regarded such definition as necessary.

Yet, while there is no precise way in which one might define the 'boundaries' of the mediaeval constellational figures, there is a residue of a closer definition of the asterisms in the ancient lunar mansion lists.[4] These 28 divisions, which measure the daily movement of the Moon through the constellations, relate to fixed-star fiducials within the stellar sphere (figure 32). It is certain that such lists were used by mediaeval astrologers who wished to make calculations in regard to constellational charts.

The mediaeval textbooks on astrology place far more importance on star-lore, and constellational lore, than do most modern astrologers. In this they were largely following the additions made to the Ptolemaic tradition by the codifications and imaginative interpretations of the Arabian astrologers who, so to speak, made the reading of individual stars their own speciality. Michael Scot writes of the influence of constellations on humans, in much the same way as a modern astrologer might write of the influence of the zodiacal signs. In doing this, he refers to asterisms which are too far from the ecliptic for the sun alone to be the transporter of the supposed influences. It is one thing to convert a star placing, itself remote from the ecliptic, to zodiacal co-ordinates, and from this conversion suppose an influence from that star – it is quite a different matter to convert a whole asterism in such a way, in the supposition that this may somehow supplant the zodiacal influence, or that of the relevant asterism. We see in such methods a kind of astrology which is different from that used today, even though the mediaeval lore derived from these early methods still survives to some extent in the modern star-lore used by astrologers. The modern astrological star-lists, with their absurd spatial and temporal conversions for ecliptic readings, are the degenerate atavistic survivals of this ancient tradition.[5]

It is clear, then, that the stars, and the asterisms into which they were grouped, were much more important to the mediaeval astrologer, than they are to the modern astrologer. We should therefore not be surprised to find great emphasis on the stars, the asterisms and the stellar mythology in mediaeval literature, art and astrology. This point must be made because it has been ignored by most writers and art-historians in modern times. As I have already pointed out, much of the symbolism which is noted as being 'zodiacal' on ecclesiastical buildings and cathedrals of the mediaeval era is actually 'constellational'. Because of this, it belongs to a different tradition, with a different set of meanings, both for their creators and for those for whom they were designed.

In view of this, we must accept that in the mediaeval period the zodiacal asterisms derived from the stellatum were regarded by twelfth- and thirteenth-century astrologers as being quite different from the signs of the Zodiacus. This does not preclude the fact that in the popular tradition the Zodiacus and the Stellatum are often confused in the mediaeval world, just as they are today. One wonders indeed to what extent even relatively learned people were aware of the implications of the steady changes in co-ordinates arising from the phenomenon of precession. Hildegarde of Bingen often wrote[6] about the zodiac in a way which showed that she confused the tropical zodiac with the asterisms. This confusion, which in modern times has been called the 'homonymous error',[7] is one of the fundamental mistakes made by those who are not specialists in astrological terminology or practice.

The use of constellational and fixed-star readings went well beyond the confines of ascendant-conversions, and asterism readings which are to be found in great number in the astrology of Michael Scot. There is much evidence that even in such a realm as amulet-making, which shows a great dependence upon signs of the zodiac, and the so-called planetary hours, the constellations were also used. In the *Liber Veneni*, a set of instructions for the construction of Venusian gamalei or amulets, we learn, for example, that we should await the conjunction with Venus with the Pleiades before making certain magical stones.[8]

The signs of the zodiac were of course intellectual constructions and could not be seen by the human eye. In contrast, the stars in the asterism were not only visible, but were the nightly companions of the mediaeval astrologers, who probably had a more profound first-hand knowledge of the stars than most moderns.

When the mediaeval astrologer attempted to trace the positions of the stars from a reading of a classical text available to him – for example, from an Aratus – then he could not fail to observe great differences between the arc containing an asterism such as Taurus, and that containing an asterism such as Libra. The differences in arc would be very similar to those noted in a modern popular textbook on star-lore,[9] which gives Taurus an extent along the equator of 36 degrees, and Libra 21 degrees.

Some texts permit an even greater latitude for the extent of Taurus. If we examine the structure of the constellations from the point of view of a mediaeval lunar-mansions chart (figure 32), we find that while there are two clearly defined

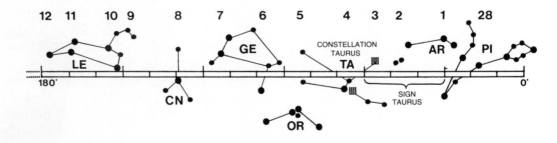

32 Segment of the lunar zodiac from a mediaeval lunar-mansions list, incorporating the section of the heavens including the asterism of Taurus.

fiducial groups related to Taurus ('Caput Tauri', of which the fiducial is the Pleiades (3 in fig. 32, and 'Cor Tauri', of which the fiducial is the Hyades, with Aldebaran the brightest star – 4 in fig. 32), there is a gap of over 40 degrees between the beginning of Taurus and the first fiducial for the next zodiacal constellation Gemini, marked by 'Sidus parvum lucis magnae' (small star with great light) (6 in fig. 32). Interestingly enough, this corresponds fairly closely to the extent of Taurus in the so-called 'Modern Zodiac' of Delporte (figure 33). It is true that in the lunar lists, between the Hyades and the first Gemini fiducial star, we find a fiducial for the 5th mansion, 'Caput canis validi' (Head of the great dog – 5 in fig. 32), but this relates only to Orion, which is not near enough to the ecliptic to warrant its being regarded as zodiacal. We may deduce from this that while the mediaeval astrologer disdained to say exactly where his Taurus asterism began and ended, it was of greater expanse than that visualized by modern authorities.

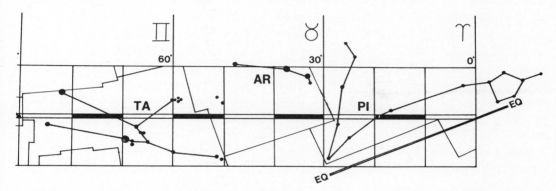

33 Detail of the modern constellational zodiac (the IAU zodiac) showing the relationship between the constellational zodiac and the tropical zodiac. The tropical zodiac is indicated by sigils, while the asterism, or constellation, zodiac is indicated by means of abbreviations. The asterism of Taurus is much larger than the 30 degree arc of tropical Taurus.

It is perhaps worth pointing out that the latitudinal variations are even more remarkable. In the mediaeval system, the band of the zodiac was only 16 degrees (8 degrees on either side of the ecliptic), yet the constellation Taurus extended from at least 2 degrees south of the equator to 34 degrees north, a span of 36 degrees at its widest point. Libra had a widest span of about 17 degrees, to the south of the equator. A diagram of the difference between the Stellatum and the Zodiacus sets out the differences of these extents (figure 33) with particular reference to the area of Taurus. In this diagram, the Zodiacus is indicated by the convention of equal-arcs representing 30 degrees (divided into threes, the traditional 'decanates'). The constellations are presented in the convention of line-joined dots, which represent the main stars of the asterism.

Aratus, who was one of the primal sources for mediaeval star-imagery (as opposed to star-lore used in astrology, which was derived ultimately, though by circuitous routes, from Ptolemy), makes the observation that the stars of Taurus do really mark out the head of the ox. For Aratus, the Hyades is 'in the forehead of the bull', and one star marks the tip of the left horn, as well as the right foot of the Charioteer. Indeed, he says 'not by other signs would one mark the head of an ox . . . and . . . in such wise these very stars, wheeling on either side, fashion the image'.[10] This tantalizing reference to a supposed similarity between the pattern of the stars, and the image of the asterism to which they belong, is fascinating. In the eighteenth and nineteenth centuries it was widely assumed that the names of the asterisms and their supposed influences were derived from images suggested by the patterns of the stars: this idea is even now widely accepted in popular circles. However, in the esoteric lore the relationship between the patterns of the stars and the images they represent is explained in quite a different way. It is suggested that the areas of sky marked out by certain star groups were first experienced as areas of spiritual influence. It is likely that such 'experience' would not be available to all men, but would be available to those initiates who had endured the disciplines and spiritual enlightenments of those teachers in the mystery schools who were the mentors of the pre-Christian cultures. By more or less clairvoyant vision, such men would experience the stellar areas, and then choose names and images which would encapsulate the qualities of the stellar influences which they sensed as streaming from these areas. Thus, it is maintained by the esoteric tradition that there was nothing arbitrary about either the name (actually, the 'sound') or the image ascribed to particular areas of the sky. Such names and images only became arbitrary when, after the fifteenth-century Renaissance in Europe, astronomers began to create new pictures from the stars.[11] Once the ancient name for an area was determined, a corresponding image fitting to the name was then projected on to that specific stellar area. This explains why the ancient images of the constellations seem to the modern mind to be so arbitrary – we have inherited the images, but we have lost the ancient feeling for the different qualities of being within certain boundaries marked out in the skies. Because we no longer see the images as representative of numinous influences beyond the stars, but as 'random patterns' organized into a Gestalt, we fail to understand the reason why they are there at all. No amount of Gestalt theory will explain how the image of a woman holding corn is traced against the skies which mark out our Virgo. As a purely intellectual exercise, one might as well trace out the image of a railway train, and designate the fiducial star Spica as the single headlight!

Aratus was of course aware of this difficulty of tracing images against the backdrop of the skies, which is why he remarks the fact that the image of Taurus actually may be traced with ease into the chief stars of the asterism. The ancient mystery centres from which our constellational imagery was originally derived did not work in the modern way – these teachers did not trace images over the stars, in the way a child might trace the forms of dragons in the clouds. On the contrary,

34 The constellation of the Cetus, from the twelfth-century arch at Sacra di San Michele, Val di Susa.

the esoteric stellar tradition insists that they marshalled the positions of the stars so that they symbolized the stellar influences experienced in the relevant areas of the skies.[12] The ancients were convinced that the stars were made from the quintessence, and were living beings. This idea is remembered now, if at all, only through the personalized names which are given to groups of stars, or to the ruling daemons or planets, or to the intelligencies of the spheres. For the mediaeval astrologer, the sky at night was a living reminder of the realm of gods. It is this notion, or reality, which they seem to express in their symbolic forms for the constellations, and it is this living reality which we fail to sense in modern times, when we look at these long-discarded images.[13]

If we wish to examine further the importance of the constellational zodiac in the thirteenth century, we do not have to envince documentary evidence, or to study the theory or methods of such thirteenth-century astrologers as Scot. We may turn with a sense of relief to mediaeval art itself, for the differences were adequately set out in the symbolic devices of mediaeval sculpture. A striking and beautiful example of this is the so-called 'zodiacal arch' at Sacra di San Michele, in the Val di Susa, which we have already noted in a different context. This was probably constructed originally (in the early twelfth century) around a portal of the baptistry built by the Benedictines in the main approach to their monastery. It is not a 'zodiacal arch' at all, but rather a constellational arch. Its imagery is sufficiently important to our theme to warrant special treatment in Appendix 4. Here we shall merely note the fact of its zodiacal series being constellational rather than tropical.

On what is now the left-hand pillar there is a series of eighteen pictures of the constellations, bound into a floral chain of squares (figure 34). The images are Christianized equivalents of those with which the mediaeval artists would have been familiar from the star-lore of Aratus or Manilius. What is now the right-hand pillar gives a series of eleven roundels of the zodiacal constellations (figure 35), also derived from model books or zodiacal manuscripts. There is no pretence that this latter is a zodiac at all. Following the established classical tradition, Scorpius is sculpted as a scorpion grasping in its claws the image of Libra. Now the fact is that while in the tropical zodiac Libra has of necessity occupied the same 30 degree arc as every other sign, in the constellational zodiac it was in classical times not accorded an independent place at all. Libra was at one time called 'Chelae' (the Claws), and was viewed merely as a continuation into the stellar space of Scorpius. The image of the balance in the claws of Scorpius is an atavistic throw-back to this earlier constellational image, and is found with remarkable frequency in mediaeval star-lore imagery. Again, in the mediaeval lore the name 'Scorpius' refers to the constellation, while 'Scorpio' refers to the sign. It is indeed this distinction which gives us the curious pair of genitives, 'Scorpii' and 'Scorpionis'. On the San Michele portal, the name alongside this double-constellation image is 'Scorpius'. The arch is not zodiacal at all, but constellational. Other similar instances of the twelfth century might be given as examples, but this one is sufficient for our purpose, which is to show in mediaeval art a familiarity with the asterism, and a tendency to favour the zodiacal asterisms in contrast to the tropical zodiac.

Let us assume for the moment, then, that the orientation of the San Miniato zodiac is also involved with such a constellational symbolism, rather than with the expected tropical symbolism. Let us work on the assumption that the nave zodiac is directed towards an asterism, or a stellar fiducial, rather than towards a tropical point. Where does such an assumption lead us?

Now, the moment one begins to talk about 'constellational zodiacs' one is usually faced with the problem of relating these to a contemporaneous 'tropical

35 *Three twelfth-century zodiacal roundels (Sagittarius, Scorpius and Virgo) from the constellational arch at Sacra di San Michele, Val di Susa.*

zodiac'. What is the equivalence in the year 1207 between a degree given in terms of a tropical zodiac and the asterisms? The conversion of tropical data to constellational data calls into play what is nowadays called the 'Precession of the Equinoxes', the question of ayanamsa, and several other vexing questions, and we must therefore (however reluctantly) touch upon these matters here.

The gradual drift of the Sun's position against the background of the stars, due to the phenomenon called 'precession' was recognized by mediaeval astrologers, even though its nature was understood in a radically different way from that proposed by the modern astronomer. However, since in mediaeval astrology there are several different theories about the rate of precession, about what precession was, and whether it was a cyclic phenomenon or an oscillatory 'trepidation', the matter is a complex one for the modern historian to deal with. Without specific documentation, or without access to actual calculations involved in a particular operation, it is rarely possible to determine which theory of precession is being adopted by a particular astrologer.

Due to the translation made by Gerardus, the work of Alfraganus was especially influential during the thirteenth century, so that his precessional theory was widely adopted. Alfraganus gives the round figures of 1 degree in 100 years. It is, indeed, this Alfraganian rate which Dante adopts in his symbolic model of the *Commedia*, as a result of which (in the popular mind at least) the Alfraganian rate was more and more believed to have been the only one used in the mediaeval world.[14] Alfraganus had his statistics, if not his theory, from Ptolemy, who had abstracted his figures from a latitude of possibility given by the great Hipparchus.

Prior to Dante, however, at least three other systems were considered viable, any one of which might have been used by the astrologers at San Miniato. Gerardus mentions the oscillatory system of Albumasar[15] which gives a precessional rate of 7 degrees in 900 years, a motion which was by its very nature seen as being reversible: a special motion of a sphere had been added to the Ptolemaic model to account for this slow motion, called a 'trepidation' – which is a regression and progression of the vernal point. Albategni, the Arabian astrologer, gives a rate of 1 degree every 60 years and 4 months.[16]

Some Arabian astrologers accounted for precession not in terms of 'nutation' of the poles, but in terms of a steady, non-oscillatory, movement of the spheres. Even if the phenomenon of this retrogression is not yet fully understood in modern times, it is widely accepted that its rate is approximately 1 degree in 72 years. We see, therefore, that each of the rates of precession available to the mediaeval astrologer would result in inaccurate calculations in regard to the movement of the vernal point against the backcloth of stars.

The mediaeval astrologer was aware of the spatial and temporal differences between the asterism zodiac and the tropical zodiac (even if his view of what was the reason for these differences was not accurate). However, whenever he wished to convert one to the other, he was not of necessity faced with the mathematical co-ordinate required for accurate conversion, which in modern astrology is called 'ayanamsa'. This, in simple terms, is the question of when the first point of tropical Aries corresponded with the first point of constellational Aries, which must be assumed as a starting point for calculating later differences due to precession. Mediaeval astrologers did have a number of different ayanamsas available, but it is unlikely that they relied upon them in their practical work. The interesting thing is that with such inaccurate systems, and with an inbuilt error of Julian reckoning, the solar tables for tropical patterns remained accurate within a degree or so for very long periods of time.

There was really no need for the mediaeval astrologer to 'reconcile' the Zodiacus and the Stellatum since they each belonged to different parts of the mediaeval cosmic model. Direct observation was all that was required, for by looking at the skies on a particular date it was possible to determine which part of a constellation was rising. All the evidence of the star-gazing involved in navigation shows that it was the fixed stars and constellations which were the fiducials.

From more or less accurate solar co-ordinates, an astrologer was generally under the impression that he could accurately determine the corresponding tropical ascendant. The technical difficulties involved in this conversion are pointed to by Scot, who lists it as one of the likely sources of error which every astrologer faces. The modern astrologer, accustomed as he is to using tables, will almost certainly work in the opposite direction – that is, he will determine the ascendant in terms of tropical co-ordinates, and then, if he wishes to study the corresponding asterisms, he will convert from the tropical to the constellational. . . . The modern astrologer has virtually no need to observe the sky. This is no doubt a considerable loss to his soul-life, but the fact is that he can make all his calculations from ephemerides, tables of houses, gazetteers, and a whole batch of tables of time-place co-ordinates related to calendrical and local time schedules. In truth, he need never consult the skies at all. It was different for the mediaeval astrologer, who had few tables, and who knew that he could not entirely trust even these. We see then that observation was an absolute necessity for the mediaeval astrologer, not only for casting horoscopes for either tropical or constellational reasons, but as a means of checking upon and correcting almost all his tables.

It is very hard for the modern reader to grasp just how difficult it was for a twelfth- or thirteenth-century astrologer to cast a horoscope chart. The problem was that while the stars might be nominally fixed, little else was. Many of the things which astrologers now take for granted had simply not been established in those centuries. There were of course theories relating to the complex series of spheres which accounted for just about all cosmic phenomena, from precession to the erratic movements of the Moon, and from these theories tables of planetary and stellar co-ordinates were produced, but the system itself was too unwieldy to produce consistently accurate tables. There were difficulties with calendars, difficulties with the few available planetary lists (we might hardly call them ephemerides in any modern sense), there were problems in dating, and there were problems even in calculating and recording the time of day.

In the twelfth and thirteenth centuries there were major differences between calendrical systems. In Italy alone there were three different systems (all naturally woven into the ancient Roman system of dating), each with different methods of determining the beginning of the year. In thirteenth-century Florence, the year would be held to begin on 25 March, a date linked in the ecclesiastical calendar with the Annunciation and the Crucifixion. A few miles to the west was the so-called Pisan Calendar, which began on the 25 December, the revised putative date of Christ's birth. It is fortunate for our own studies that the date under question (28 May) does not fall into one of the time-spans which might give a variation on the year – May is the third month of the Florentine system, and the fifth of the Pisan, which means that our date belongs to the common year.

By the thirteenth century some dates were expressed in the Roman system, concerned with the ancient lunar Kalendae,[17] and some were expressed in the equivalent of the modern Arabian-derived system, with the series of days to a month, though of course following the Julian calendar. A number of twelfth-century horoscopes survive for dates given according to the Arabian system (for example, cast for a given moment in the year 529, which is the equivalent of the Christian AD 1135), almost certainly because the tabular date was Arabian, even though the matters relating to the casting of the charts was distinctly European.[18] Whilst by the following century all horoscope data appears to be expressed in terms of the Kalendae system, some computation tables used in astrology and in the ecclesiastical 'Compotus' calendars were expressed in modern calendrical form, and many of the tables were given according to a European system, as for example in the manuscript tables attributed to the astrologer Roger of Hereford, calculated for his native city.[19]

In addition to calendrical problems, there were also questions arising from the recognized differences (sometimes amounting to days) between the real moon placing and the calendrical moon placing. In the mediaeval era the latter was calculated according to a theory of adjustments linked with the Metonic cycle, which did not normally accommodate lunar fluctuations. Methods of computing the lunar positions did circulate (again, these were derived from Arabic sources), and these prove to be reasonably accurate as theoretical bases, but once again the astrologer would of necessity have to check by direct observation to ascertain a lunar position with certainty.

Additionally, we must also remember that the mediaeval system of measuring the time of day was far from simple. It worked quite well in everyday matters of commerce, but it was extremely complicated when it came to making records, or projecting planetary positions into different temporal co-ordinates. For a start, the hours of the mediaeval day were of unequal length: the twelve so-called temporal hours were based on 'sundial time', in which periods of daylight were divided into twelve equal periods or 'hours', with astrological tables erected accordingly. This is why time in the monasteries and churches was not given in hours, but in divisions of the day linked with liturgy. These appear to be derived ultimately from the Roman 16-part day of 1½ (modern) hours, starting at midnight. The hour of sunrise (dawn) was the fifth hour, called 'diluculum'. On the other hand, the theory of a 24-hour day was also used, as for example in time co-ordinates for the rising times of the signs in different climata (approximately the modern latitudes).[20]

Clocks were still very rare in the thirteenth century. There is an interesting note from the astrologer Walcher, who was the Prior of Malvern, to the effect that while in Italy he had been present during an eclipse, in 1091, but had been unable to record it because he had no clock to determine the time.[21] Because of the lack of horologia, or clocks, in establishments such as monasteries, where there was a need for night-hours (again of unequal length) to be recorded for liturgical and disciplinary reasons, it was quite usual for a monk (sometimes called the 'officium horarum', or 'significator horarum') to be appointed for the special duty of observing and noting the passage of time, either with the aid of simple clepshydra or through the saying of prayers in rhythms which gave known periodicity. It is perhaps no accident that one of the names for a simple astrolabium, an instrument used for determining time by the stars (and hence the equivalent signs on the Ascendant and Medium Coeli) was 'horoscopos'.[22]

It is clear, then, that the mediaeval astrologer would be painfully aware that only the things which could be seen, as phenomena in the skies, might be relied upon with any certainty, and that the whole basis of mediaeval astrology was observational. It is a commonplace for modern historians of astrology to say that the Ptolemaic model of the universe worked pretty accurately so far as the forecasting of planetary positions is concerned, but this is far from being the case. Horoscopes cast with the Ptolemaic-based tables were often inaccurate, and this in an art where a degree or so can make a fundamental difference to the interpretation of a chart. The mediaeval astrologer was forced at times to look up from his books and tables to examine the stellar and planetary framework above his head: he could not afford to lose contact with the reality of the stars. If we consider sympathetically the difficulties which any astrologer would have experienced in those days, then we should begin to realize the danger of interpreting their own experience in the light of our easily available tables. Michael Scot emphasizes several times the difficulties which arise in connection with determining the accurate data for a chart.

In view of these difficulties, rather than asking ourselves what astrological information Joseph and his workers might have had from their own tables, we should ask what would they have observed on that morning of 28 May, and in the days preceding the stellium?

In Florence, the coming stellium in Taurus would have been very evident towards the end of May 1207 (always assuming good weather conditions, of course). Indeed, it would have been recognized as an important astrological event for some days prior to the event. Any tables for the tropical zodiac would have shown the planets gathering in tropical Gemini, but direct observation would have shown them passing through the asterism of Taurus, unfolding their patterns against a backdrop of the Pleiades and the Hyades.

Which part of Taurus would these planets have been in? Here again, if we are to approach the question in any depth we must face up to the matter of precession, for we can only calculate retrospectively the position of the sun (for example) in a previous century relevant to a fixed star fiducial if we use a precessional rate. If we do this from a strictly mediaeval point of view, then we face considerable problems, for we may not be sure which of the available ayanamsas an unknown mediaeval astrologer might use, which rate of precession he would favour, and which calendrical fiducial he would take for granted. The majority of astrological commentators appear to place the beginning of the spring equinox in the middle of March, that being the precessional point reached due to a recognized error in the Julian calendar. It is likely that in the thirteenth century the true reckoning should have been 12 March, though it is normal for astrological and calendrical texts to give 15 March. Several different systems of ayanamsa survived into mediaeval astronomy from classical times, the two important ones being Babylonian in origin.[23] However, none of the systems designed to allow for precession known to the mediaeval astrologers were accurate, which means the extrapolation from early calendrical material would always be off the mark – surviving mediaeval lists of solar positions confirm this.

Whether the mediaeval figures were accurate (in terms of co-ordinating fiducials which were later correctly identified) is a question hard to answer. For sure, one of them at least had to be wrong, and in any case all the known methods of precessional adjustment were wrong. Yet, from our point of view, these facts are not of very great importance within the present context. We have to recognize that the mediaeval astrologer, by the very nature of his tables, and by the very fact that he felt free to work with constellational material, would be constantly thrown back into direct observation of the stars. He would be accustomed to rectification of this kind: he would know from his experience of inaccurate lunar tables, of conflicting calendrical systems, of the diurnal struggle to calibrate the passage of time, that in the last resort the only dependable measure would be the passage of the fixed stars which were then held to be immutable, and indeed eternal. It is this which induces Michael Scot to advise his readers that the astrologer should arrange to have a house from which he might observe the horoscopos, the position of the sun, and so on.[24]

If we knew our astronomy as well as the mediaeval astrologers knew theirs, we would not have to make play with ayanamsas and precession to prove a solar rising on Taurus on 28 May. The very name Hyades was believed by some mediaeval writers (though wrongly) to have been derived from the Greek word meaning 'to rain', in reference to the wet periods which were supposed to accompany the morning rising and evening setting of this asterism in late May and November. It was for this reason that, as Allen reminds us, Spenser called them the 'Moist Daughters', even though Allen was for once wrong in his mythology.[25] In modern times, we find the unconventional astrologer Ebertin still calling them the 'rain stars' (Regen-Gestirn), locating them, in 1971, in 4 to 6 degrees of tropical Gemini.[26] The fixed star called 'Primum Hyadum', which is the gamma of the asterism, is in the beginning of this arc, of course, while the powerful star Aldebaran is located towards the further end of the cluster.

In fact, from data supplied in modern times by Powell[27] we observe that Aldebaran is in 10 degrees of tropical Gemini. Applying the known rate of precession of 1 degree in 72 years we find that the tropical position of this star in 1207 would have been in 29 degrees of tropical Taurus, give or take a degree. On 28 May 1207, Tuckerman's five-day intervals[28] gives the Sun in 74 degrees, which is the zodiacal equivalent of 14 degrees of Gemini. The Sun position on the all-important date was 14 degrees of tropical Gemini, which corresponds within a couple of degrees to known tables for the beginning of the thirteenth century, which locate the Sun in 13 degrees of Gemini.

This means that an observer in Florence on that day would have watched the Pleiades in Taurus rising over the horizon, followed by the Hyades clustered around Aldebaran, followed a short time later by the Sun and Moon. The computer-based data for these important days is given in Appendix 3.

To what extent might we say that the Sun, some 16 degrees below Aldebaran, was still in the asterism of Taurus? In a sense, we can only speculate, because we do not really know where the mediaeval astrologer believed Taurus (or any other sign, for that matter) began or ended. We do know, however, from extant mediaeval lunar mansion charts that after Aldebaran there were still well over 20 degrees' space before the next zodiacal asterism (Gemini, marked by the 'Sidus Parvum Lucis Magnae' – figure 32) was reached. We know also for sure that the asterism of the Pleiades must more or less mark the beginning of constellation Taurus, for it is named 'Caput Taurus' as the first of the lunar mansions, and it follows closely on 'Venter Arietis', a group of stars set in the asterism of Aries. Some 5 degrees separate 'Venter Aries' from 'Caput Tauri', which means that if we assume the end of one constellation and the beginning of the other some halfway between these points, then Pleiades is within 5 or 6 degrees of the first part of Taurus. Measuring along the ecliptic, the centre of the Pleiades is only about 10 degrees from the centre of the Hyades. Thus, assuming that Aldebaran (on the edge of the Hyades) is as much as 18 to 20 degrees into Taurus (a considerable exaggeration in terms of the mediaeval charts available), then we may assume at least another 15 degrees of constellation Taurus stretching below Aldebaran. There is no way that the Sun might be described in zodiacal terms as being 'in Orion', as the Sun will certainly not have reached the beginning of constellation Gemini (itself a relatively short-arc asterism), as figure 32 makes clear.

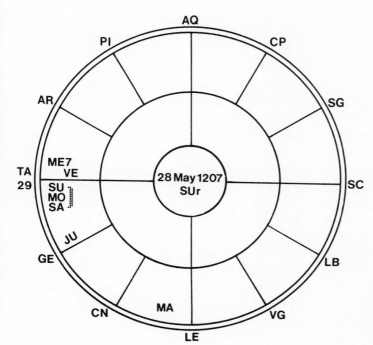

36 The foundation horoscope for 28 May 1207, showing the gathering of planets in the constellation Taurus.

We may be certain that the Sun of the 1207 horoscope (figure 36) is somewhere in the last third of Taurus. Note that I choose these unscientific and unastrological formulations with care, for I am trying to work out what a mediaeval astrologer would have seen, using an approach which is only partly based on scientific method, in that it is an attempt to reconstruct a 'lost' method of observation. I do not speak about the last 'decanate' of the Taurus asterism, for only a sign may have a decanate: the zodiacal asterisms are of unequal length, and may not be converted into 'signs' as so many uninformed astrologers assume. Nor do I speak about the last 10 degrees, for such terminologies apply only to the signs of the zodiac, and not to the constellations in mediaeval star-maps. As we do not know over how wide an arc mediaeval Taurus spanned, so we do not know what a third-arc of that length will be. In sum, we may be only sure that the Sun was located towards the end of constellation Taurus, somewhere in the last third of that asterism.

While I feel that it is sufficient for us to establish that the Sun (and hence the entire stellium of 1207, which extends backwards towards Aries over an arc of 22 degrees) is in the asterism of Taurus, it may be interesting to speculate on the more precise relationship of this sun position to the fixed stars. At the same time, we might link this with the all-important conjunction with the Moon. If indeed we assume the position to be 'in the last third of constellation Taurus', then imposing this on contemporaneous constellation drawings we find that the Sun is to the east of the Hyades, an asterism rightly described by Allen as 'the most beautiful constellation in the skies'.[29]

Ovid had called them 'Thyone', and Pliny had named them 'Parilicium', the Arabian astrologers had dubbed them 'Al Dabaran' (a name meaning 'the Follower', later given to the alpha of Taurus, as follower of the Pleiades), but the Greek word 'Yades', used by Aratus, was the one which the mediaeval astrologers inherited, recognizing five stars of the group, at least according to one late-twelfth-century manuscript.[30] The observer in Florence might watch the Pleiades rising, and then the Hyades, but by the time these had passed over the horizon the morning sunlight would have dissolved the light of the stars. The crescent of the Moon, visible on the previous day, would also be lost, swallowed up in the light of the Sun. In fact, whether the Sun was in the constellation of Taurus or not, it would certainly not have been 'seen' to be in that constellation: the Sun is never actually seen in any constellation at all because its own light scatters that of the stars. On the other hand, it would have been only too evident that Taurus was passing over the horizon on that morning, with the planets Venus and Mercury carried in their spheres against this backdrop of beautiful stars.

Having laboured somewhat the mediaeval 'experience' of the stellium, specifically against constellation Taurus, we have to point out that it would actually look more impressive on paper than it would appear in reality on that morning. The only planet visible would be Mercury.

We are fortunate that a seventeenth-century astrologer who worked from direct observation of the skies left a record of (approximate) heliacal visibility of planets for a latitude not far removed from that of Florence. His researches were actually geared to establishing a new theory of what are called 'orbs', relating to the important branch of astrological aspects, but we may abstract from his figures useful information relating to our own study. From his direction-observation records we find that Venus would not become heliacally visible until it is over 7 degrees from the Sun, while for the Moon to become visible it would have to be over 6 degrees from the Sun.[31] We may be sure that such figures are derived from direct observation, and we may be reasonably safe in assuming such heliacal visibility for Florence itself.

In the San Miniato chart, Venus is 5 degrees from the Sun, while the Moon is just in conjunction, which means that neither would be visible. Only Mercury would be seen in the skies, some 22 degrees distance from the Sun: it would be what the mediaeval astrologers called the 'nunciator', remaining visible for about just over a quarter of an hour before the visibility of the stars faded to the matutine sun.

The effect might have been more remarkable on the previous day, when the Moon, some 12 degrees further back in the zodiac, would have hung in delicate crescent between Mercury and Venus (which might just have been visible). Tuckerman's tables give the Moon on the 27 May as just in the 5th degree of tropical Gemini, which places it well in the asterism of Taurus (see, however, Appendix 3). It was in the course of the next day that it reached precise conjunction with the Sun – though in the early morning the conjunction would not yet have been partile.

Saturn would have remained hidden in the light of the Sun, due to the exactness of its conjunction, but for some days previously the astrologers would have noted the Sun gradually approaching this conjunction, followed by the quick-moving Moon and her train of lesser planets. The effect of the slow build-up of the stellium would have lasted for several days, then, and the recorded date of the 28 May is probably set down in record of the final conjunction between Sun, Moon and Saturn, with the lesser planets in weak conjunction within the same asterism.

Such a gathering of planets in one asterism or sign is very rare, of course. Although he would certainly realize this from 'experience', the mediaeval astrologer did have the means at his disposal to calculate the likelihood of this stellium repeating itself, even if this method would not reflect that used by a modern astronomer. The fact that his calculations would lead to inaccurate results is irrelevant to our argument. He could make such calculations in a relatively simple way, by studying the relationships between what were called the 'peculiar' motions of the planets involved. The non-synodical revolution of the Sun was recognized as being 1 year, that of the Moon 1 month: Mercury was 88 days, Venus 225 days and Saturn 29 years. These figures which are given in the classical texts, including that of Alfraganus, are reasonably accurate, and they indicate that

113

the mediaeval astrologer could not fail to have realized that this stellium was something very special, an effect which would not repeat itself at least in his own lifetime, and probably not for many centuries. Probably he would also have in the back of his mind the (curious) figure given by William of Conches for the so-called 'Great Year', at the end of which all the planets would return to their original relationship.[32] This 'period' was 49,000 years, though the figure given by Conches is much shorter than those recorded by more reliable sources.

The mathematical tools for calculating the repeat of this satellitium were available to the mediaeval astrologer, but as the model is so different from the modern one, and so inaccurate in terms of the modern one, there seems to be little point in attempting to extrapolate from this model. However, I know of no mediaeval documents which calculate similar repetitions, though it is of course possible that such astrological documents do exist. We may be sure, however, that there would be no repeats of a similar satellitium in Taurus in any of the tables available to the mediaeval astrologer.

We should not be surprised that the mediaeval builder of San Miniato should have chosen such a special astrological phenomenon as the basis for his orientation of the zodiac. Given the established link between the bull and the Logos (as evidenced in the lectern of the pulpit, within the church), then he was exercising a brilliant intuition in awaiting this stellium to lay down the marble zodiac, and to emphasize that all-important eastern orientation which the church itself did not have. He may appear to have been breaking all the rules of ecclesiastical architecture in orientating the church to obtain that wonderful ray of sunlight on the foot of Christ and on the wall-fish, but he was showing a deeper respect for those rules with this marvel of zodiacal orientation. Whilst the 'miracle' of the gathering of the planets on the horizon would probably be sufficient reason for laying down a zodiac, and extending its zodiacal symbolism to incorporate reference to Taurus, we might also assume that the chart as a whole might well indicate excellent and propitious conditions for the building of a church.[33]

Whatever Joseph had in mind in regard to the significance of the horoscope as a foundation chart, he did orientate the zodiac towards Taurus on that day in May. This, however, was more than merely an orientation towards the east – and therefore by definition towards sunrise – it was an orientation towards a stellium in a given space and time. This is almost certainly the reason why Joseph (as we shall see in the next chapter) took the trouble to record the date in the Latin inscription set in the marble close to the zodiac, albeit in a cryptogrammatic form. The depth of symbolism implied within the use of such a constellational zodiac goes well beyond considerations of time and space, however, for the best mediaeval symbolism is always rooted in concepts of spirituality. The point recognized by the mediaeval masons who set down this zodiac was that their symbolism should be entirely in accord with the deepest theological conceptions of the nature of the cosmos. After all, it is almost certain that the director of works was a monk, and was concerned with the basilica primarily as a building for worship. Let us try to look at such 'theological conceptions' through his eyes.

The sphere of the fixed stars, the Eighth Heaven of the mediaeval Ptolemaic model, did not mark the 'end' of the cosmos. It was the previous sphere, that of Saturn, which ended the cosmos as far as human experience was concerned, for it was in Saturn that time itself came to an end.[34] This was almost certainly the reason why the name Kronos was given to the Sphere, for the word is Greek for 'time'. There is no accident that the early images for Saturn show him carrying in his hand the encircled snake, the Ouroboros, biting its own tail, as this was an ancient symbol of time, derived ultimately from pagan alchemical sources. Beyond the sphere of Saturn, and his rulers the Thrones, even higher spiritual beings and powers were at work, but these dwelled within the eternal realm, where there was 'time no more'. Saturn, in his identification with Chronos, merely set his seal on the outermost planetary sphere. The human soul might never progress further than Saturn, as the schemas of Macrobius and the Egyptians[35] demonstrated. It took the poetic imagination of Dante to carry a man beyond the realm of time itself.

Beyond the fixed stars, bathed in the 'eternal' (that is, in the correct use of the term, 'out of time'), were at least two other spheres, one required by reasons of Ptolemaic theory, and one required by reasons of theology. The next sphere to that of Saturn, usually called the 'Primum Mobile', gave the motion of the diurnal revolution of all the other spheres from east to west; this was also called the Crystalline heaven. To this series of concentrics was added the Tenth Sphere, the so-called 'Empyrean', which was the calm and motionless abode of God and his ministering angels. This Tenth Heaven is absolutely motionless, but the stellatum, the sphere of the fixed stars, did have a proper motion. In this proper motion it was the slowest of all the spheres, used to account for the precession of the equinoxes. The sphere itself had a proper motion, therefore, but the stars were embedded or fixed in the sphere itself, and (unlike the planets) had no motion. They were at once eternal and motionless, rapt in imitation of God!

In addition to all this, as the pagan Alfraganus himself was not slow to point out, the motion of the stellar sphere was itself quite different from that of the others. Those spheres below 'turn backwards with a motion contrary to that of the heaven', but the stellatum opposed that direction. In the symbolizing tendency of the mediaeval vision, this forged yet another link between the fixed stars and the numinous Empyrean. The interesting fact is that for once Alfraganus is not leaning on Ptolemy – he is rather touching upon the non-Platonic stream of Grecian philosophy, in almost quoting Aristotle himself. Here for once the two great streams which have nourished our western civilization for over 2,000 years appear to merge.

Aristotle had said that the motions of the heavens were twofold, and therefore had a twofold effect on the earth.[36] The motions of the planets from west to east in their respective spheres governed the principle of earthly change, while the perfect

115

sweep of the stellatum from east to west constituted the principle of permanence and growth. 'Permanence', that great longing within the mediaeval soul, and perhaps of the modern – in this word we find how the stars might be found to correspond in moral purity to the Empyrean beyond their sphere. The stars were godlike, moving even in that direction which would emulate the heavens. Are we tempted to read into this Aristotelianism – so fundamental to mediaeval astronomy and astrology – a clue to why a constellation zodiac should be described in the curious Latin words 'celesti numine'?

It is a measure of how indefinite the ancient asterisms were that the Pleiades, an indistinct yet exceedingly beautiful asterism, had several different positions on the old image of the stellar Bull. Most often they were placed in the shoulder of the animal, but Hyginus located them on the hind parts. Aratos located them in neighbouring Perseus. The Arabian astrologer Al Biruni[37] locates them in the Bull, however, and records an ancient tradition from hermetic sources that they once marked the equinoctial point, some 3,000 years before Alexander. It is this tradition, no doubt based on fact, which gave us the 'Great Year of the Pleiades' as a name for the precessional cycle. The classical writers Nicander, Columella, Vitruvius and Pliny loated them in the tail, and record that the last is supposed also to have formed them into a separate constellation.

The above notes may be regarded as being almost irrelevant, until they are tentatively related to the San Miniato symbolism. More than once I have found myself wondering if the doves, which are used to such effect in the pavement design beyond the marble zodiac, are a reference also to the skies at the beginning of mediaeval June, for in ancient times the doves were linked both with Taurus and with the month of May.

The Greek origin of the Pleiades has been variously explained as being from the word meaning 'to sail', in reference to the heliacal rising of the group in May (the group of seven stars being called 'Maiae' by Virgil), and from the word meaning approximately 'many', as well more reasonably from the name of the mother of the seven, Pleione. However, one of the poetic views, indulged in by Homer in his *Odyssey*, linked them with birds, and in some myths they are the seven doves which carried ambrosia to the infant Zeus, the Greek counterpart of Jupiter.[38] Doves were linked with Venus, and thus with Taurus, as ruler. I am of course aware that the many pairs of doves in the pavement have been convincingly traced to Christianized Indian legends,[39] but I have not yet found any satisfactory explanation for the single doves in the original intarsias on the walls and on the façade of the basilica (a few of these are nineteenth-century restoration, of course). It is unlikely that these doves are reference to the Holy Spirit, devoid of other context. My intention in making these references to the doves is not to construct a new theory, but merely to suggest another approach to the symbolism of San Miniato. My words may be regarded as so many literary footnotes or asides, for I place upon them no weight of further hypothesizing.

No matter how we approach the symbolism of San Miniato, whether by way of marble doves, or by way of the stars, we are indeed looking through a great distance of time, and a great confusion of intellect, towards a 'discarded image'. A great effort of imagination must be called into play to correct the distortions inherent in such attempts at long-focus. To obtain a clear image at this distance it is essential that we attempt to catch something of the feeling for anagogic symbolizing which was so characteristic of the mediaeval frame of mind, so much woven into his rich symbolizing tendency. This anagogic method of looking at the spiritual structure of the cosmos is somewhat foreign to the modern mind, yet it was certainly an intrinsic element of mediaeval vision, as the writings of Neckam, and the later poem of Dante proves. It is clear, therefore, that the mediaeval astrologer would see one thing with his eyes (for example, the proximity of Venus to a fixed star), and learn another thing from his tables, or from his calculations with instruments. Above all, however, he would be conditioned in what he thought, in what he pictured in his faculty of imagination, by his allegorizing and lateral thinking, which enabled him to see all things in the world as the material form of something higher. He would see the created world, as Michael Scot said, as being 'only images of the greater world'.

It is my feeling, born out by the astrological literature of the time and from such survivals as the Sacra di San Michele arch and the zodiac of San Miniato, that the astrologers of those heady days of the twelfth and thirteenth centuries would have had recourse to the constellations when laying down a zodiac. This, I would maintain, is demonstrated in the marble zodiac of San Miniato al Monte, which has shown itself to be much more than a complex foundation chart, and more than merely the spiritual hub of a sophisticated wheel of symbols. It really belongs to that special category which has been termed by a modern astrologer 'astrosophic geography', the art of establishing on earth a pattern corresponding to the heavens.[40] The zodiac is really a sculpted marble bridge, replete with Christianized pagan symbols, pitched between heaven and earth. The remarkable achievement of San Miniato is that its builders, perhaps under the direction of the unknown 'prosodian and judge' Joseph, were able to construct a union of theology and astrology which has given us the most sophisticated esoteric mechanism to have survived from the mediaeval world.

6 *The secrets of the Latin inscription*

. . . he was considered to have carried his grammatical subtleties beyond reasonable
bounds.

(THOMAS WRIGHT, quoting Roger Bacon on the thirteenth-century scholar,
Alexander of Neckam in *Rerrum Britannicarum Medii Aevi Scriptores (De Naturis
Rerum)*, London, 1863.

A few yards into the nave of San Miniato, between the central doors and the
marble zodiac, and nearer to the zodiac, is a curious inscription (figure 1). In a
thirteenth-century lapidary form, are the following words:

HIC UALUIS ANTE . CELESTI NVMINE DANTE .,. M.CCVII.RE
METRICUS ET IUDEX . HOC FECIT CONDERE IOSEPH .,. TINENTDE
ERGO ROGO CRISTUM . QUOD SEMPER UIVAT IN IPSUM .,. TĒPOREM̄TĒ

As we shall see, it is an inscription which certainly refers to the zodiac a few feet
further into the nave. Since it contains the date of a year in Roman numerals
(M.CCVII) we may reasonably take this as referring to the year on which the
zodiac, and the nave pavement of which the zodiac is part, were laid down.
Perhaps this year also refers to the foundation (actually the re-foundation – see
chronology in Appendix 2) of the basilica itself, which is of a style
contemporaneous with this date.

Our purpose now is to see what light this inscription throws on the zodiac and
its extensive symbolism within the church. To what extent do its words relate to
the zodiac, to the constellation Taurus in particular, and to the horoscope of
foundation of the present basilica and/or zodiac in 1207? In other words, we must
now determine if there is anything in this inscription which supports the various
far-reaching claims about the planetary configurations which I have made in the
preceding chapters of this book.

The inscription has been noted by several scholars, but the interesting thing is
that many of them appear to copy the guidebook of Berti, who wisely refrained
from offering a translation, and who in fact recorded the inscription wrongly.[1]
Berti's mistakes seem to have been carried into several texts dealing with the
basilica – the tendency being for scholars often merely to follow other scholars.

118

The thorough and almost encyclopaedic writers Paatz scarcely mention either zodiac or inscription, but deal fairly exhaustively with almost every other aspect of the basilica.[2]

If we wish to deal with the inscription and the zodiac in the manner which these deserve, we must be prepared to examine them with fresh eyes, and with some awareness of the historical background. In particular, we should be prepared to consider the astrological and occultist lore which permeated the minds of the cathedral- and church-builders of the early thirteenth century.

First of all, we must observe that if the lines of the inscription are read in a normal linear scan they make very little sense. To bring the inscription to order, one must take into account the curious punctuation (.,.), which then permits the Latin to be read as three lines of Leonine hexameters, and three short lines with visual end-rhymes:

HIC UALUIS ANTE . CELESTI NVMINE DANTE .,.
METRICUS ET IUDEX . HOC FECIT CONDERE IOSEPH .,.
ERGO ROGO CRISTUM . QUOD SEMPER UIVAT IN IPSUM .,.

    ★

M.CCVII.RE
TINENTDE
TĒPOREN̄TĒ

However, even when so presented, the Latin is not easy to interpret. It is far from being 'good' Latin in the classical sense, and indeed it is far from simple to interpret in terms of mediaeval Latin. There is little or no connection of sense or meaning between the half-lines, or between the three hexameters, so that one gets the impression that the poet was intent merely on constructing six sentences, strung together not so much by sense as by their end rhymes. The inscription is sometimes ambiguous in its use of cases and terminations: in addition it is also at times awkward or unconventional in its choice of words. These factors would suggest that the entire inscription is really what occultists call a 'blind' – a mere front disguising some hidden meaning or meanings.

The incorporation of hidden meanings into texts of prose and poetry has been practised from classical times, especially in one or other of the techniques of acrostic. It is maintained that many of the sacred Sibylline books incorporated acrostics and hidden letters, and as we have already seen (page 89), in the fifth century AD Augustine himself, eager to show why Christ was linked with the symbol of a fish, recorded the Tertullian account of how the Greek for fish (ICHTHUS) might be derived from a single Grecian statement about Christ the Saviour.[3] Many secret systems of writing, such as the so-called 'Melachim' and the 'Transitus Fluvii' were developed in mediaeval times,[4] several of them derived from the cabbalistic strains of thought which were already permeating the west, and a few of them derived from Arabian sources. However, the first systematic account of secret writing involving acrostic forms in Latin was not presented until the late fifteenth century, when, under the name 'steganography', a number of such systems were published by the esotericist Trithemius, the Benedictine abbot of Spandheim.[5] Trithemius was not inventing anything new, but merely recording an ancient tradition: his esoteric writings betray a profound interest in the esoteric literature, however, and it is to him that we owe the survival of several esoteric and occult notions preserved in an amended form by the Arabs.

His treatment of Latin texts as the vehicle for acrostic or secret script is far too complex to summarize here, but a relatively simple example will be found pertinent to our study of the 1207 inscription in San Miniato. This example is the secret code 'Penador aneual olmeniel plianu savear cashanti liernoti maduran'. According to Trithemius, the first word of such a phrase is designed to designate the code being used, and once this has been noted the first word may be dispensed with. In similar fashion, the last of the coded words is also ignored. Following the indications of the code, we then take the letters in pairs, rejecting the first and every alternative, and then regrouping the sequence of words in alternatives:

aNeUaL pLiAnU cAsChAnTi – OlMeNiEl SaVeAr LiErNoTi

In this way we abstract the Latin NULLA VACAT OMNES VALENT, which means approximately 'Nothing is without meaning, all things have value'.

Now the interesting thing about this technique is that it demonstrates that there was a continued interest in the ancient technique of acrostics, and that at least one method had been rendered so complex that there was seemingly no longer any need to provide an original text (that is, a blind) with a surface meaning. The phrase 'Penador aneual . . .' is just about meaningless: there seems to have been no attempt to disguise the fact that this primal text is actually a code.

In contrast to this, the San Miniato text, in its role as a lapidary inscription, is an occult blind. It does give a convincing impression of being a meaningful text in its own right. In fact, so convincing is this text (in spite of its disjointed and difficult form) that its secret nature, and the messages it hides, have remained intact for centuries. There was no opportunity for Joseph, the presumed author of this text, to make a nonsense inscription, in the manner of Trithemius, and he was therefore compelled to work to a very tight script-code indeed. Trithemius could choose virtually any Latin message, and then apply to it the rules of steganography, from which he could create a more or less meaningless pattern of words, which might indeed be cracked by any relatively bright reader familiar with the methods, even given that the 'code' was not available to him. The San Miniato cryptographer could work in no such way. He was required to produce a blind – a Latin inscription which conveyed some sort of meaning – and yet, at the same time, he was required to incorporate into this a series of clues which would indicate letters which would reassemble to make secret words or phrases. Additionally, he had to so construct his inscription that it would provide a numerological basis which would have some significance in terms of the religious or heretical interests of his contemporaries. The blind and the coded message it was designed to hide had to work on at least two levels, and on each of these levels there had to be a message for those capable of reading it. The San Miniato cryptographer therefore had aspirations and intensions far more complex than any steganographic system such as Trithemius had in mind.

Although there appear to have been few methods of stenography used in the late twelfth century, a method was recorded in a theological context by Alexander of Neckam. As we have already noted, Neckam was one of the primary influences contributing to the growth of interest in astrology during that century, through his translations of, and commentaries on, the chief works of Arabian astrologers. He was also one of the primal sources for many new iconographic devices in architecture. Perhaps more relevant to our inquiry here, he was also one of the first to reveal a Judaic method of secret script wordplay.

In his most important book[6] he discusses the first word of the biblical 'Genesis', and shows that he was familiar with the Jewish cabbalistic method of Temura, by which letters were interchanged according to certain rules, in order to give rise to new words and ideas. By a simplistic application of such temuric wordplay he attempts to show that the first word of the first book of the Bible contained the three names of the Persons of the Trinity. It is worth noting the method in application to the Hebraic text, if only to show a loose connection with the San Miniato inscription. This is perhaps best done by paraphrasing Neckam.

> Moses was led by the Holy Spirit to give these words at the opening of his work:
>> BE RESIZ bara Eloym . . .
>
> BE means 'in'.
> RESIZ meaning 'the beginning'.
> Now, because of the peculiar structure of the vowellic element in the language, the two words BE RESIZ consist in the Hebraic tongue of only six letters. These six letters are:
>> BEZ, REHS, ALEF, SIN, JOZ, THAVE
>
> The last letter we call TAU.
> We find therefore the first letter to be BEZ, the second letter REHS. Together these give the Hebraic word 'Bar', which means in English 'Son'. We see therefore that the word of two letters represents the Word itself which so condensed on our behalf, as to fit within the small space of the womb of our most blessed Virgin.

In similar fashion Neckam (spuriously) derives from the same opening words the Hebraic words for 'Father' and 'Fire', the latter being the symbol of the Holy Ghost.

Behind such wordplay manipulation, not to say misreading of Hebrew terms, lay Neckam's wish to demonstrate the theologically acceptable tenet that the Old Testament was a prefiguring of the New Testament – that the New Order was known to Moses through the wisdom of the Holy Spirit, for whom he was amanuensis as the writer of 'Genesis'. His theory of temura, and his specific application of this theory to the Hebraic words was wildly inaccurate, but this should not disguise the fact that his mediaeval readers would not realize this, and would at least be familiarized with this temuric method which Neckam applied to many other words in the Bible. Few twelfth-century northern scholars could read Hebrew well, and even fewer appear to have been familiar with such cabbalistic techniques as temura. This attitude towards such a code (whether it be a code or not) is important in regard to our approach to the San Miniato inscription, for Neckam's book was widely read in the thirteenth century, and we may suppose that the general theme of his ideas, if not the specific example, would be known to those involved with the construction of codes.

Of course, in the twelfth and thirteenth centuries, Hebraic etymology was not understood at all in the modern sense of the word, and even the etymological approach to Latin was coloured by the mediaeval penchant for moralizing. Thus Neckam in all seriousness traced the simple word CADAVER (dead body) to 'CAro DAta VERmibus' ('flesh given to worms'). As one modern scholar says of Neckam, 'he was considered to have carried his grammatical subtleties beyond reasonable bounds.' Roger Bacon may have been of this opinion, but few other twelfth- and thirteenth-century scholars were. Neckam's writings, and his moralizing approach to symbolism, were very popular throughout Europe towards the end of the twelfth century, and during most of the following century, and we may assume from this that such principles (however garbled) of the wordplay involved in both Hebraic cabbalistic temura, and the random use of letters within words to give other words, were at least known to theologians, if not actually used by them.

The 'classical' methods of acrostic did survive in the twelfth century, if only in the oft-quoted Sibylline verses of Augustine. However, an example of another acrostic code is found in a manuscript safely attributed to the astrologer Roger of Hereford, dated 1176. This manuscript is a 'Compotos', a mediaeval ecclesiastical calendar, and the initial letters of the table of contents form an acrostic which reads GILLEBERTO ROGERUS SALUTES H.D. This Gilbert was none other than the Bishop of London. Similar acrostic verses have been recorded by J. J. Alexander for an eighth-century Gospel Book, in interlaced pages, giving dedicatory phrases.[7]

The Abbot Trithemius worked from a nonsensical Latin to make a code which was transformed by the application of acrostic rules to make perfect sense. Alexander of Neckam started out with good and sound Hebraic words, and made of them what was in effect a nonsensical interpretation: in his etymology he makes use of sounds to give birth to new words – a method of almost random play with letters. Roger of Hereford used a standard form of acrostic. Our San Miniato scribe, whom we shall presume to be Joseph, used none of these three methods.

The San Miniato method of coding appears to be unique in its time. Joseph, the probable steganographer, produced a Latin 'blind' text which has a surface meaning, no matter how curious the Latin or how obscure its sense: this is the inscription under examination, which has survived almost without blemish for nearly eight hundred years. Within each of the seven sentences of this 'blind' Joseph incorporated a number of distinctive clues, by which an alert reader is led to reassemble the letters of each sentence in order to derive the name of a planet and other data, the letters for which had been included in that sentence. As if this were not enough, Joseph constructed the inscription in such a way as to establish a meaningful numerological pattern which had profound significance both in relation to certain important beliefs of his day, and in relation to the significance of the zodiac. The method of coding is therefore complex, and in order to appreciate it fully we shall have to examine each of the sentences within the inscription in some detail. After such an examination, we cannot fail to sense that the verse is probably one of the most remarkable examples of steganographic writing on record.

Leonine hexametric inscriptions, especially relating to zodiacal imagery, symbolism and sigils, were fairly common in the eleventh and twelfth centuries. They consist of lines divided into two by a metrically central caesura: the word prior to the caesura forms an assonance with the word at the end of the line. Related examples may be noted in the five lines of Leonine hexameters on the zodiacal portal at Sacra di San Michele in the Val di Susa (noted in Appendix 4) or in the single astro-theological line (which actually incorporates an acrostic zodiacal sigil) on the tympanum of the Duomo in Verona. This latter is interesting if only for the incredible simplicity of its sigillic code device. It runs:

+HIC DOMINUS *ol* AGNUS LEO CRISTUS CERNITUR AGNUS

The sigil *ol* naturally stands in place of the M of MAGNUS. Now this sigil itself is one of the standard mediaeval forms for the zodiacal sign Leo, and is indeed the one from which our modern sigil for Leo ♌ is derived.[8] Leo is of course the 'Lion', so the sigillic M *ol* joins the lion with the AGNUS, which is the Latin for 'Lamb'. One therefore finds in this single word of the inscription an assonantal and graphic play on the idea of the 'Lion lying down with the Lamb', linked with the name of the 'Great Lord Christ' (DOMINUS MAGNUS CRISTUS), and with the zodiacal sign Leo. The use of the + in front of the HIC is a fairly normal mediaeval device, the cross representing Christ: it is often carved on foundation stones, or upon important stones within the fabric of buildings, sometimes as a demonifuge, and sometimes as an indication that the stone has been consecrated. In this particular inscription, however, the fact that it is part of the

HIC means that it has a hidden significance for it means 'Christ in his place', a notion which is also expressed in the magical connotation of a word with 3 letters, relating (in accordance with mediaeval symbolism) with the Trinity, of which Christ is a member.

It is of course no accident that this inscription should use such an 'open secret' as the Leo sigil in reference to a hidden meaning within the hexameter, and that it should also make use of zodiacal symbolism to point to this hidden meaning. It will be shown that the Leonine hexameters of San Miniato refer both explicitly and implicitly to a hidden meaning, and that this hidden meaning is related to zodiacal material of profound importance to the symbolism of the whole basilica. The love for 'hidden meanings' and for esoteric reference was endemic in the mediaeval mind – the interest in the 'new' astrology provided an excellent vehicle for the incorporation of such hidden esotericism into literature and art.

Before we examine the San Miniato inscription in relation to the decoding which I propose, we must note the obvious – that it was written in Latin during the thirteenth century. The Latin used in mediaeval scriptoria was very different from classical Latin, and the Latin terminology used in astrological contexts is almost in a world of its own. The reasons for this are perhaps not far to seek – the Latin language was more and more subject to fissiparous influences due to the collapse of Roman influences during those periods which are so often called the 'dark ages': languages which are codified appear to die, while languages which are not codified change. The Latin of the first millennium of our era was not codified from any central source, other than the obvious theological centres, which in any case soon began to require specialist terminologies and syntax. As a result, the Latin language changed over a period of a thousand years in very many ways, and these changes were subject to regional variations and mutations of remarkable complexity. Although he is writing of a more limited (and indeed less volatile) mediaeval Latin than the continental forms with which we deal here, Latham hits the nail on the head when he writes 'If it is hard to decide how much of Mediaeval Latin is really Mediaeval, it is no less hard to decide how much is Latin.'[9] Astrological terminologies, which were introduced into the twelfth- and thirteenth-century literature, did not always come directly from Rome or from pure Latin manuscripts – indeed, most specialist mediaeval Latin terms used in astrological contexts were largely derived by way of the Arabs. This explains why so many of the words used in astrology and astronomy even to this day are essentially of Arabic origin, and why many astrological terms appear foreign to classicists. Although some Latin astrological texts did survive into the later mediaeval world, these were often corrupt, and there is much evidence to show that many of those who read them, and even commented upon them, failed both to understand some of the basic terminologies, and to transmit them accurately. The use of inflexions and orthographies in connexion with astrological texts was regionalized, personalized and linguistically loose, to say the least, and it is very evident that many of the original uses of astrological terminologies – themselves expressive of very precise ideas – were quickly forgotten or confused. For example, there was not even a single mediaeval form for such a term as zodiac. By the thirteenth century, the 'Zodiacus' of the Romans had taken on several different forms and non-classical terminations, the latter often hidden in manuscripts behind abbreviation symbols designed to show contractions. How the classical 'Zodiacus', with its misunderstood Greek etymology, became Zodaicus, Zoacus or Zodiacius (in the genitive), is perhaps a thesis in its own right. The word, which had a very precise application in Roman literature, was often misunderstood, and applied to the Constellations, to the stellatum, or sphere of stars, even though the Ptolemaic model of the universe (which was that inherited and developed by the mediaeval astrologers) made a clear distinction between the two.

Even within the limits of the terms used to denote the signs of the zodiac itself, we find similar confusions. In many mediaeval astrological documents there is much confusion of terminology, sigils, symbols and orthographies until well into the fifteenth century – indeed the confusion of this Babel was only forced into some kind of architectonic order by the conventionalizing power of the printing press.

At the time when the San Miniato inscription was composed, there was a confusion of spellings and case-endings, in astrological contexts which would horrify a classical scholar. It might be argued that the two words used for the sign Scorpio in mediaeval Latin – that is, Scorpius and Scorpio – were perhaps originated to distinguish between the zodiacal sign Scorpio and the constellational asterism Scorpio, though in fact the former reveals a Latin origin, the latter a Greek. However, even those who would argue for the original distinction between Scorpius and Scorpion would agree that by the thirteenth century there were at least three different ways of writing the genitive derivation from these two words – Scorpii, Scorpionis and Scorpiacea, and that (in most cases, at least) all sense of the original distinction between constellation and sign had been lost. For example, the mediaeval scribes often write of the fixed star Antares as 'Cor Scorpionis', 'Heart of the Scorpion', when the original sense should properly have been expressed in the term 'Cor Scorpii'. In the mediaeval manuscripts one finds for this star such variations as the Greek 'Antares' derived from Ptolemy, a number of words from the Arabian 'Cabalatrab' (almost certainly from 'Kalb al'Akrab', 'Scorpion's Heart'), the Latin 'Cor Scorpii', the less classical 'Cor Scorpionis' or 'Scorpiacea Cauda', and so on. The same problems arise in connexion with other zodiacal terms, such as Capricorn, Taurus, Libra, and others.

Now, whatever the classical scholar might think of this hotch-potch Latin, it is one of the linguistic facts of the thirteenth century, so that even specialists in the subject are loath to give opinions about the precise meanings of many of the astrological texts which have survived from that period. The astrological and astronomical terminologies are so interlinked with Arabian concepts, with Byzantine-Greek concepts, with regionalized Latinisms, and with special contractions, that such texts often provide difficulties even for specialists in mediaeval palaeography.

I mention these difficulties here, by way of preface to an analysis of a Latin text, merely to point out some of the issues which we face in attempting to translate accurately a text which is of a hermetic content. In deriving, from a thirteenth-century inscription, a Latin text supposed to be encoded within it, we may not always be sure precisely how this derived Latin would be intended to read. Only a specialist in Florentine astrological lore of the first decade of the thirteenth century might be able to give a reasonably secure opinion about the code-interpretation I have proposed. My method is obviously charged with difficulties, and I lay myself open to much criticism from those who feel confident that they know something about mediaeval Latin and mediaeval astrology. Therefore, almost out of a prescience that a defence will be called for, and on the wise suggestion of my editor, I have attempted to relate the derived-Latin in this study to a form which would be reasonably acceptable to a modern reader, without doing a moral or linguistic injustice to the Latin of the thirteenth century. For example, while it is quite possible that a thirteenth-century astrologer might have used the term 'Tauris' for the Genitive of 'Taurus', I shall give only the word 'Tauri', with which we might feel more comfortable. The fact is (as we shall see) that the two words might be derived from the code with the same ease, yet this is perhaps irrelevant. There are one or two specialist terms which I will derive from the inscription that may appear to be questionable, and so I shall take a particular note of these as they arise. This method, tedious as it may sound, would appear the only way to deal adequately with a subject which is beset with pitfalls.

No doubt a specialist in thirteenth-century palaeography, who has studied astrological and hermetic lore, will be able to criticize my interpretation of this code, or even find himself prepared to offer another way of looking at this strange inscription. However, I doubt that any one – no matter how specialized – will deny that it is indeed a most curious text; that its numerological structure is undeniable (even if not linked with the particular heresy I name), and that the inscription as a whole was surely intended to convey some hidden meaning. Whether this is the occult and secret meaning which I have uncovered in the following analysis is for the reader alone to decide.

Now that we have considered something of the background to codes in the thirteenth century, we may attempt to translate and analyse the San Miniato inscription, in order to see how this relates to the zodiac. As we do this, we shall discover that each of the half-lines of the inscription has been written as a sort of letter-puzzle acrostic. However, they are not acrostics in the classical sense of the word: they are more like ingenious linguistic puzzles. They contain no telestic or mesostic clues, as does a genuine acrostic. Rather, each sentence expresses a sort of conundrum in which hints of curious Latin (even by mediaeval standards, and written, one notes, by a person perfectly familiar with the Latin language) is designed to lend a clue to an important letter or group of letters. As we shall see, one of the themal clues is connected with the use of the letter U, which in Latin epigraphy is regarded as the equivalent of V. Another clue is the use of individual words which appear out of context in the main surface meaning of the inscription, but which become redolent with significance within the framework of the hidden meaning. The groups of letters are unconnected in sequence but are easily assembled to form a word pertinent to the larger context of the zodiac and horoscope.

Another characteristic of this secret writing is that the whole inscription has a distinctive and important numerological basis. The fact that the inscription is presented in three lines of verse is of considerable importance, as is the fact that it is only two of these lines which may be subjected usefully to cryptographic analysis for each of the two main divisions of secret text which we may derive from the inscription. Even more remarkably, we shall find that not only is this 'two from three' important to the esoteric purpose of this inscription, but so indeed is the exact number of letters within the inscription as a whole.

Before we look more closely at the code system, it would be as well for us to examine the first part of the first line, in order to get some idea of the nature of the issues it raises.

HIC UALUIS ANTE

We must take it that the UALUIS is intended to read VALVIS, as the first word does not exist in Latin. However, the three words of Latin are themselves something of a problem. The singular nominative HIC cannot and does not refer to the plural ablative VALVIS. If it is read as relating to the zodiac (i.e. Hic zodiacus), then the rest of the hexameter would not make sense, and the Latin would be remarkably inaccurate, even within a mediaeval text. It is likely that we should read the word in the same sense as the Verona inscription above – as meaning 'in this place'.

Again, the correct Latin for 'doors' is VALVAE, not UALUAE or VALUAE: in fact, the word 'Valvae' refers to 'folding doors'. As we shall see, in mediaeval Latin there is a specialist use of the word 'Valua' (see note 20 below), but undoubtedly the intention here is to refer to doors, for which the more usual Latin is 'Ianuae' or 'portae'.[10] There is actually a lapidary inscription on the outer step of the so-called 'northern' door of the façade of San Miniato, which refers to the doors – 'Haec est porta coeli' in which the Latin used for 'door' is 'porta'. It is reasonable to assume that there must be some ulterior motive in the choice of this word VALVIS, and its variant, UALUIS.

The word VALVIS is in an interesting orthography, for while the Latin word is spelled with Vs, the letter form as it is set out in the marble is actually in the form of a U, yet further on in the same line a U is presented as a V. It is normal for the Latin epigraphists to write the U as a V (for example, on the twelfth-century inscription on the zodiac portal of Sacra di San Michele, where the letter U forms are presented as V) but there is rarely the inconsistency we note in this San Miniato inscription – why, then, these inconsistent deviations? In the word NVMINE, further along the same line, the second letter is given as a V, when it is clearly meant to sound as U. On the other hand, in the line below the penultimate letter of METRICUS is given as a U, whilst the second letter of IUDEX is also given as a U, even though this is exactly the same form as the two Vs of VALVIS. We may take it that there is some significance in this orthographic deviance. The fact is that if we abstract and reassemble a few of the letters from the first line of the sentence we may obtain the Latin word for the Moon:

hic vaLUis ANte = LUNA

Had the word been set out as VALVIS, then we would have obtained the word LVNA. This would have been technically correct, but it is likely that the orthographic form was adopted in order to point to the idea of the V being read as a U. In fact, the repetition of the U in this word (instead of the variant such as VALUIS) also serves a function, for 'were the inscription something like HIC VALUIS ANTE, then it would have been possible to construct from it the word for another planet:

hic ValUiS aNtE = VENUS

It is likely that the orthography was adopted not merely to give the word LUNA, but also to exclude the word VENUS. The sounds of the letters were being respected for good reason.

The phrase 'Valvis ante' may be loosely translated as meaning 'before the doors'. However, there must also be an ulterior motive in the choice of the word ANTE, for the zodiac itself does not lie in front of the doors, no more than we stand in front of the doors when we examine the inscription. It might be argued that the phrase refers to the entire nave pavement, which stretches along the length of the nave from the central door, in which case the HIC refers not specifically to the zodiac, but to the entire floor: the word ANTE would still not be exact, since the nave pavement is behind the doors, rather than in front of them. However, it is part of my argument (as we shall see) that the inscription refers specifically to the zodiac, and the word is therefore called even further into question. We shall discover later that this word ANTE is of paramount importance in regard to a second level of secret messages in the script, so for the moment we need disregard it, save for noting that it is not exact or accurate. Meanwhile, bearing in mind these qualifications, this Latin may be construed tentatively as:

'Here before the doors' or, 'In this place before the doors'.

Actually, this sentence is not what it appears to be. In mediaeval astrology there was a most important notion relating to doors, and it is possible that it is to these doors, rather than to the doors of the basilica, to which the esoteric level of the inscription applies. In mediaeval astrology there are the two doors of the Moon and Saturn. The doors of the Moon are esoterically linked with birth, while the doors of Saturn are linked with death. The fact that the Moon has rule over Cancer, while Saturn has rule over Capricorn, is linked with this notion of the doors. Since Cancer and Capricorn are opposite each other in the zodiac, the axes of Moon and Saturn lie in a straight line, representing the direction of life and death. This has long been recognized as one of the anagogic symbolic devices in mediaeval buildings which are enhanced by zodiacal or planetary symbolism.[11]

An examination of the orientation of the zodiac in relation to the church nave (figure 19) will indicate that this Cancer–Capricorn axis lies exactly on the orientation down the centre of the aisle. This itself means that the symbolism of the Moon and Saturn (the two 'doors') could be the doors mentioned in the inscription. In fact, the depth of the symbolism is linked with the notion of progression down the aisle, for in following this axis, from Capricorn diametrically towards Cancer, the pilgrim moves away from death towards life, from the darkness of Saturn, to the creative realm of Cancer. It is no accident that many of the mediaeval horoscopes for the beginning of the world – the so-called 'Thema Mundi' – give the important ascendant degree in Cancer, which is associated through its ruler with the life-forces. Within the context of mediaeval astrology, it is not at all far-fetched to interpret the first section of the inscription as relating to the Saturn–Moon axis, to the 'doors of birth and death'. This would help us understand why the monks inserted into this curious phrase the name of the planet Moon, the word LUNA.

We may sense a hermetic meaning emerging from these first three words of the inscription. Seen from an esoteric Christian point of view, they point to that idea of incarnation (birth) and descent through the spheres which is a part of the idea of the Incarnation of Christ, figured in the Taurean symbolism.

In passing we should note that the second half of this line is not used to derive the name of a planet. Had the NVMINE been NUMINE, then it would have been possible to derive the word LUNA from:

CELESTI NUMINE DANTE
ceLesti NUmine dAnte

Important as this V is in the present context, we shall discover later that the use of the V in NVMINE is of great importance to the code when it is interpreted in relation to the hidden date. It would also have been possible to derive MARS from

129

the second half of this line, provided that one were prepared to bring over the R from the colophon:

CELESTI NVMINE DANTE . M.CCVII RE
celeSti nvMine dAnte . m.ccvii Re

However, Mars is not one of the planets in the stellium, nor is the nature of Mars reflected in the meaning of the Latin sentence.

This is a most convenient point for us to stop to consider once more the nature of this code, which, I repeat, is not an ordinary code at all, but something quite extraordinary.

Although I use such words as 'code' and 'acrostic' in connexion with this inscription of San Miniato, I do not claim that the Latin is either a code or an inscription in the ordinary sense of the word. Certainly, it is a method of secret or esoteric communication, but not one which may be 'broken' according to the ordinary methods of decipherment. One has to be an occultist, or at least familiar with mediaeval astrology, to read the secret writing convincingly. So far as I know, there was not a recognized system of alphabetical coding in the thirteenth century, though the classical methods of acrostics were understood and sometimes used. The San Miniato inscription is unique, however, and works on a different principle to the ones with which we are familiar in modern times. In essence, the secret communication rests upon the formulation of short sentences, of between three and six words, each denoting a sense, but not necessarily connected together. The interpretation of certain of these sentences suggests the notion of one – and only one – planet. The Latin name for this planet is contained within the letters of the sentence, and may be reassembled from the sentence.

This must be spelled out in some detail, as it might be argued that it is possible to pick out a wide number of different words from the random combination of letters in a sentence. The fact is that without reference to the notion of 'meaning', it is possible to pick out several names of planets, both in Greek and Latin terminology from the sentences: however, the code is not so random as to permit this. The code works in terms of meanings. What I claim is that the sense within the sentence is itself the pointer to the identity of the 'hidden' planet, the Latin name for which is hidden within the sentence. The truth is that only one word will adequately summarize the esoteric message contained within the sentence. We have already noted as example of this, in seeing how the sense of the phrase HIC UALUIS ANTE gives LUNA. Were the orthography not carefully set out, the sentence might also give VENUS. But of course, Venus has nothing to do with the gates of birth or death.

In just such a way, the four sentences in the half lines of the inscription point quite distinctly to four planets. Each of these four planets may be traced in the letters of the relevant sentences. Each of these four planets are those which conjunct the Sun in the 1207 horoscope. This itself is the rationale of the 'code' of

130

San Miniato al Monte, and this is the standard which must be applied to it, rather than any conventional secret writing and coding to which we have become accustomed.

As the following analysis will show, there are one or two other conditions which appear to have determined the structure of this secret message. For example, there is a recurrent distinction made between the U and the V, in the 'lapidary orthography'. This almost certainly arises from the fact that in the mediaeval Latin the U and the V are the only letters common to each of the names of the planets – Luna, Venus, Mercurius and Saturnus. These conditions relevant to the San Miniato code must be set out in this simple way to counter any argument that the code is not 'normal'. We must not argue the nature of mediaeval codes from the insights afforded us by a span of eight hundred years.

The full brilliance of the San Miniato inscription will only emerge at a later point. Eventually, it will become quite clear that even the number of letters within the inscription is of profound symbolic importance – a point which will be developed on page 144ff. Not only is the number of letters in the entire inscription important, but so are the numbers of letters in each line. Within this numerological structure, we have three lines, each consisting of two halves, marked by caesura, plus a small part, the 'colophon', which is itself divided into three. Each line is therefore divided into three, yet what is of importance is the two halves of the hexameter within this line. This notion of the 'two from three' is reflected in the structure of the first line of the code, for the letters making up the word LUNA are all abstracted from only two of the words from the three which make up that phrase:

hic vaLUis ANte = LUNA

This 'two from three' structure is of importance to the interpretation of the inscription as a whole. We note then that the structure of the code, while it does not resemble any method of modern coding (no more than does the Verona zodiacal code we have already examined), is not quite so random as it might appear to be on a perfunctory examination.

Let us turn our attention to the three-word phrase which completes this first line of the inscription.

CELESTI NVMINE DANTE

Why is the word NVMINE the only word in the entire inscription which prints U as a V? In every other case the U-sound is printed as a U. Sometimes the V is printed as a U (as for example in VIVAT, which is given as UIVAT), but the orthography of the U is respected throughout the inscription. As we shall see, this is almost certainly intended to permit the second letter of the NUMINE to read as both a U and a V. This Latin may be construed as an ablative absolute, which gives a meaning something like:

'The divine image of the heavens manifesting'.

One notes that there is none of the expected continuity of thought between this half of the hexameter and the preceding part – there is no grammatical link, and no continuation of meaning. Each of the code-pairs within the triad of each line leads its own individual life of idea. If we are prepared to regard the V of this inscription as one of the simple code-keys, then we might permit the letter to mean both V and U, repeating itself in order to give the name for VENUS. However, this half line is not to be analysed in this way – its importance lies with the second part of the coding, which is concerned with the date.

We may also interpret the V as a U and derive a second LUNA from this half sentence:

ceLesti nVmiNe dAnte = LVNA

However, there is little point in straining the interpretation of the code merely to give the name of a planet already obtained from the previous line. Additionally, were we to do this, we would find two planetary names which were not expressed within the sense of the sentence – which, I maintain, is the underlying theme of the secret coding.

CELESTI is one of the words to be carried almost exactly from classical Latin, though with a slight variation (and with one or two curiosities of case endings) into a change of emphasis in meaning. The original word was 'coelesti', which in the mediaeval ablative form may be 'celesti' or 'celeste' (again with several variants), the genitive plural being 'coelestum' or 'celestum': in the mediaeval sense, the word meant 'heavenly'. One of the classical meanings of 'Caelestia', 'the heavenly bodies', does not appear to have carried into mediaeval use, which seems to have been restricted to a theological concept of heaven, as a place of state of divine entities.

NVMINE is a difficult word to translate in mediaeval Latin. 'Numen' is one of those terms the precise meaning of which depends very much on context. However, as NUMEN carries from classical Latin the idea of the spiritual working of the gods, then it is reasonable (given the context) to translate it freely as 'divine image'. We may therefore suppose that the CELESTUM NUMEN, the 'divine image of the heavens', refers to the zodiac which is set in the marble floor beyond the Latin verse. Having said that, we must also note that by the thirteenth century the word 'numen' had also been thoroughly grounded, to mean 'domain' or 'property', so that the phrase CELESTI NVMINE might be read as being the ablative absolute for 'heavenly domain' – again, however, such a reading may be taken as referring to the zodiac near the inscription.

We may take it that the phrase CELESTI NVMINE DANTE does not furnish the name of one of the planets: its real significance will be revealed in relation to the second level of meaning within the inscription, relating to the date when the zodiac was set down.

Let us therefore turn our attention to the second line. Here we shall find not so much the incorporation of planetary names, as reference to the person responsible for the setting down of the zodiac, as well as to the idea that the inscription (and basilican church) contain hidden mysteries. The secret-script names of planets are contained only on the outside lines of the three lines of Latin.

METRICUS ET IUDEX

In classical Latin the word 'metricus' refers to a prosodian or poet. By the twelfth century it also contained within it the idea of measurement relating to geometry, as well as versification. The words may be taken as meaning:

'One skilled in measure, and a judge'.

Almost certainly the phrase refers to the person named in the following half of the hexameter (Ioseph). This Joseph was clearly a poet, but it is not quite so certain as to whether he was a 'judge' or not: he may have been the sculptor or designer.[12] We may take it for granted that he was a monk, possibly a Benedictine. In fact, by the twelfth century there were several different ecclesiastical 'judicial' posts available to monks: without a verbal qualification, the word IUDEX did not then mean anything like the word 'judge' in any sense which might be used in a modern translation. Whilst there were a large number of different kinds of judges, both secular and ecclesiastical,[13] the word could even be applied to someone who was a judge of horoscopes. The related verb could refer to the act of making judgments about horoscopes – or as we might say nowadays, to 'one who casts and reads horoscopes'. The title of Alkindi's important book on astrology was the *Judicia*, for example, and the word is found in very many European titles, including the influential text and tabulations by Roger of Hereford, the *Iudicia Herefordensis*. Even well into the eighteenth century the word 'judgment' was often used of a horoscopic reading. As the modern mediaeval historian Eugenio Garin points out,[14] the term 'scientia iudiciorum stellarum' was used to distinguish astrology (as the science of judgments) from 'astrologia doctrinalis' or 'astrologia quadrivalis', as the science which we would now call 'astronomy'. However, it is not necessary to labour this point, for we do not know what kind of a 'judge' (if any) our Joseph was – my wish is merely to show that the word IUDEX has many possible meanings within its context of the thirteenth century, and that the word might well apply to an astrologer.

We may therefore assume that a reference to one skilled in measurement, and one who is a judge of such matters as horoscopes, is also an astrologer. There are several possible meanings in this interesting piece of Latin, but at least one of them seems to suggest that Ioseph was an astrologer. Curious as the phraseology is, we may be sure that it has been adopted because of its potentiality within the framework of the code.

One gets the impression that the sentence is constructed mainly to give the name of a planet:

MEtRiCUS et IUdex = MERCURIUS

To obtain this word in full it is necessary either to carry over a letter R from the following half-line (from CONDERE) or to repeat the letter R from the same half-line from which one derives the other letters (specifically from METRICUS). The former method of deriving the R is well in accordance with the activity of Mercury, which is that of moving between spheres. One inclined to read sigillic influences in mediaeval inscriptions may see the form of the first M of this line (figure 1) as a design to represent two letter Rs, back to back. It is interesting that none of the other M forms in the inscription are of the same design – however, I would not wish to make too much of this argument. In deriving the R from CONDERE there is an additional esoteric depth of meaning, for (as we shall see) it is possible to interpret the Latin infinitive as relating to the idea of 'secrets', and it is from the conveying of secret knowledge for which Mercury was so famous that we derived the word 'hermetic', as applied to secret or hidden lore, from the Greek name for the god, which was Hermes.

Now MERCURIUS, as messenger between gods and man, is concerned with poetry, as well as with judgment: he is indeed the god of speech, and in the horoscope it is Mercury which is considered in relation to how a person expresses himself or herself. The Mercury of the classical lore was partly derived from the Anubis of the Egyptian lore, one of the judges in Hades, and many early images survive which show Mercury as dog-headed, as a survival from this role of judge, with the caduceus wand as symbol of this rank. We see therefore the same relationship between the sentence meaning and the planetary term derived from it as in connexion with LUNA.

The Latin of the next half-line sentence

HOC FECIT CONDERE IOSEPH

would appear to be fairly straightforward. If we read the HOC as an accusative, then almost certainly it would be taken as reference to the work or 'opus', in the form which became standard among artistic signatures. The work is of course the zodiac, and perhaps also the inscription. IOSEPH is perhaps the one previously identified as the poet and judge:

'Joseph caused this to be built . . .'

or

'Joseph caused this to be founded . . .'

However, we must note the important double meaning in the verb CONDERE. Besides meaning 'to build' or 'to found', the verb CONDERE also means 'to hide'. The Latin noun 'conditus' means both 'a foundation' and 'a secret': it is therefore a most interesting word to use in this context. 'Condere' may be applied to the idea of 'hiding within', or 'putting away for protection'.[15] Here then we have a reference by means of wordplay to the idea of Joseph hiding something. A 'second-level' translation might run:

'Joseph caused (or made) this to hide . . .'

What was Joseph hiding? Was he secreting in this inscription a clue to the mysteries of the zodiac contained in esoteric form within the church? We shall discover later that he is hiding something even more remarkable within this inscription.

HOC FECIT CONDERE IOSEPH does not provide the Latin name for any planet in terms of the code rules we have so far observed. This may be seen at a glance, for it contains no U or V. We might therefore pass on at this stage to analysis of the hidden content of the third line. The last line of the inscription also presents linguistic problems:

ERGO ROGO CRISTUM . QUOD SEMPER UIVAT IN IPSUM

This might be translated as:

'Therefore I pray Christ, that he may always live in him.'

There is a curious change of person, and the phrase is rather unexpected in structure. Who is praying? And who is intended in the accusative-case 'him'?

The Latin is ambiguous in its use of person, and there is the same discontinuity in the two phrases that we observed in the other lines of Latin. Who is the third person, and who is speaking in the first person? Again, though QUOD is sometimes used as an alternative for UT, the Latin is weak, though, as we should expect by now, only in order to permit a mixed acrostical reading. Why does the word ERGO appear: why should I 'therefore' pray, as there is no linguistic connexion between this line and the preceding one? However, let us forget for the moment the sense, and look at the most obvious acrostic derivations.

ERGO ROGO CRISTUM
ERgo rogo CRIStUM = MERCURIUS

'Mercurius' appears a second time, and we must therefore decide which of the two was intended to represent the planet of the horoscope. This second Mercury is not derived in quite the same way as the previous one, for a reduplication of the letter U is necessary – yet we have noted that this U is one of the important leitmotifs of the coding. Again, within the fragmentary sense of the sentence, we find a connexion with the nature of the planet contained within the sentence. 'Rogo', besides meaning 'I pray', also means 'I speak': Mercury is the planet which rules over speech – yet another link with the important concept of the Logos. Mercury, as the 'messenger of the Gods' (esoterically, the messenger between the realm of man and the realm of the gods), is hidden within a sentence relating to prayer – which itself is petition made from the earth plane to the celestial plane of the gods. The esoteric connexion is apparent also in this notion of Mercurial speech, for it is the Word (the Logos, which is one of the names given to Christ in relation to the Trinity) which communicates between God and man, just as the Mercurial word communicates between man and man. From a point of view of pure sense (another key to the code), it might be argued that this second MERCURIUS holds the field against the one derived from the previous line of the inscription.

However, if we consider the last line, we see that it is possible, without any straining of the letters, to arrive at the names of all four of the planets so far un-named, including the two remaining names for the planets in the stellium, VENUS and SATURNUS.

quod SempeR UivAT iN ipSUm = SATURNUS
quod sEmper uiVat iN ipSUm = VENUS
quod SeMpeR vivAt in ipsum = MARS
quod semPER vivaT In IPsUm = IUPITER (or IUPPITER)

Now, while there may well be some profound significance in this fact, the originating of a planetary name from a given sentence is not itself the main standard by which the secret communication works. The planetary name so derived must be linked in its esoteric planetary nature with the notion expressed in the sentence from which the word is derived. There does not appear to be any linguistic or astrological sense within the sentence which could be applied to Venus, Mars or Jupiter, while there is a very good reason for interpreting it in relation to Saturn.

To derive the words SATURNUS and VENUS from this sentence would involve the repeat of the letter N of IN. However, we should note that there is an N expressed by the contraction mark of MONTEM, and it would be possible to regard this word as being part of the line.

We noted earlier how the natures of the Moon, of Venus and Mercury were reflected or 'hinted at' within the meanings of the relevant Latin sections – what is the relationship between Saturn and Venus in QUOD SEMPER VIVAT IN IPSUM?

There is actually a sort of mediaeval joke in connexion with this derivation of the word SATURNUS from this last part of the hexameter, for the next word in the colophon is 'temporem' (time). The joke is that in the mediaeval cosmology, Saturn itself marked the end of time – beyond the sphere of Saturn there was only 'eternity', time no longer existed. Was this one of the reasons why the colophon was split up in this curious way, to make a subtle joke? As we shall see eventually, it was not the only reason.

136

Fortunately, the relationship between the word SATURNUS and the meaning of the sentence from which it is derived does not depend merely upon a sort of esoteric joke. The inner meaning of the Latin phrase is connected with the idea of life, and the inner life: it is in this context that the word Saturn has a deep meaning. Anyone who is familiar with the modern occult tradition will know that the mystery tradition teaches that human life began in what is called the 'Saturn Period'.[16] However, as it would be very difficult to show from external literature that mediaeval thinkers were familiar with this esoteric notion, I will not labour the point, even though it is apparent that all the ancient mystery wisdom was available to initiates of the order that built San Miniato al Monte. Instead, I will examine this relationship between Saturn and life from a different standpoint.

In mediaeval astrological lore, Saturn rules the skeletal system. It is therefore the 'planetary virtue' which gives structure to the human body, and which, so to speak, lends form to the living being. However, the skeletal system is also (quite reasonably) a symbol of the death-force, for it is the skeletal system which continues in material existence long after the life-force has departed the body. It is to these ideas – well entrenched in mediaeval astrology – that Saturn applies in connexion with this snippet of the inscription. The prayer for life in a sentence which contains a coding for Saturn is of deep esoteric significance.

In contrast, it is Venus which has rule over the external body, over the physical flesh which clothes the skeletal system. We may see, therefore, that a sentence relating to life, in both its inner and outer senses, is an excellent framework in which to insert the two planetary names SATURNUS and VENUS.

The missing planet of the five is the Sun (we would reasonably expect SOL in Latin, or (less likely) the Greek HELIOS). We might expect to find some reference to the Sun somewhere in the inscription, but it is significant that neither of the words may be construed from this inner line: neither SOL nor HELIOS may be made from reassembling the letters in any of the sentences. However, the Sun as a symbol is not missing in the church symbolism: indeed, the Sun is the central symbol of the San Miniato imagery. The fact is that the Sun is the only planet to figure as a planetary symbol in the marble image of the zodiac (figure 13). It is placed in a twelve-rayed pictorial form (in what might appear to be a most surprising anachronistic heliocentrism) at the centre of the zodiac. The orientation of the axis of Saturn–Moon passes through the Sun, in its course along the centre of the nave.

The presence of the Sun in the centre of the zodiac reminds us of a passage in Alexander of Neckam which links Christ with the Sun: it is from this solar light that the faithful take their light, and are therefore equated with the reflective Moon itself. The whole congregation is seen as the Moon, taking sustenance from the solar Christ. It is this Sun which participates in both the annual and diurnal rhythms observable within the basilica, yet which itself is always hidden beyond the outer fabric of the church, manifesting only in the dim lighting of the church and once, miraculously in the annual shaft of sunlight which illumines the foot of Christ, as the cosmic Fish.

We may be certain that the last line is not constructed in such a complex form, bearing within it a prayer, merely to carry the idea of Venus and Saturn! A further analysis will show that the mediaeval inscription is of a far more complicated and magical nature than we have imagined so far. The inner, cryptographic content of the inscription has so far been revealed as relating to the unique planetary configurations – the conjunction of the four named planets with the Sun – which were in the constellation of Taurus when the zodiac and the inscription were laid down. We have not yet exhausted this cryptographic content, however, for the inscription bears a deeper content of hidden material, and indeed shows a numerological and magical content which, almost regardless of any secret content, makes it one of the most remarkable esoteric devices of the thirteenth century.

It would seem now that it remains only for us to make some sense of the three lines of the colophon or finial which begin with the Roman dating M.CCVII:

M.CCVII . RE
TINENTDE
TĒPOREM̄TĒ

The last line is the only one in the whole inscription to be marked with (quite standard) contraction signs. While it is possible to read the abbreviations in different ways,[17] the full Latin is probably intended to read:

M.CCVII. RETINENT DE TEMPORE MONTEM

This is far from simple Latin, and it gives rise to many difficulties. A translation might be:

'1207. They preserve the mountain from time'.

Actually, the verb 'Retinere' (to preserve) has many meanings, all linked with the idea of holding fast, or restraining. However, perhaps the most relevant to our present study is that meaning linked with the idea of 'keeping back for future use', which would give a translation something like:

'1207. They keep back the mountain (from the passage of time) for future use.'

Who are 'they', and what is the 'mountain' which is so preserved – and, indeed, is it from 'time' they are being saved? Is it the mountain (or the church on the 'mountain') which is being preserved, or something else? In fact, by the twelfth century the word TEMPOREM was already beginning to acquire its other meaning, approximately linked with our idea of 'those not directly concerned with ecclesiastical matters' – the lay congregation, the ordinary people, the profane – the 'temporal'. We might therefore be tempted to see yet another pun in this inscription: 'These things (whatever they are) preserve the mountain from the profane.' Which is, of course, the whole matter of esoteric art.

It would seem that once again we are being provided with a difficult Latin codification which makes some kind of sense, yet with obvious and important grammatical deviations designed to disguise a code. If we assume this to be the case, then we must expect the hidden word or words to relate to time – perhaps to the dating of the zodiac.

We must assume that MONTEM (Mountain) refers to the church of 'San Miniato al Monte'. Yet even with this assumption the Latin does not make sense. Does the Latin mean that the years preserve the basilica from time? Or does it rather mean that the hidden words (the planets, and hence the horoscope) preserve the mountain from time? Or is there something else which preserves the time of the basilica? In any case, what is this 'time of the basilica' (tempus montis) – perhaps it is the dating of the basilica's foundation? In fact this part of the inscription becomes more clear when we read it as a continuation of the first line of the hexameter. For the full force of this reading to reveal itself however, we must examine a further level of hidden meaning in the first line of the inscription as a whole.

We are led to ask ourselves if this short text does indeed point to a hidden date or 'time'? In other words, does the whole hexameter preserve within its structure the 'time of the church'?

In fact, we shall soon see that this is precisely the case – the short text is intimating quite correctly that hidden within the inscription is information relating to the time when the church and zodiac were founded. Since the three short rhymed lines of the colophon begin with the year, we might reasonably assume that they point acrostically to a system of dating by means of calendrical abbreviation. We may reasonably assume that such abbreviation will be presented in the form of mixed acrostic such as we have seen within the preceding analysis.

In the thirteenth century, and indeed for several following centuries, it was the normal procedure to date horoscopes according to the Roman method, even to the extent of using the bisextile year dating. We must therefore assume that if the Latin inscription does contain an acrostic for a date (to be read alongside the given year M.CCVII), then this will be in one of the forms frequently used contemporaneously with the founding of the basilica and/or zodiac. We may further assume that as the entire symbolism of the Taurean element of the San Miniato symbolism is concerned with sunrise, then there will be no attempt in the acrostic to denote the time (in hours and minutes, as is standard form with horoscope charts) of the Ascendant degree – the mediaeval 'horoscopos'. This is not necessary for a sunrise chart for which the latitude and longitude is known, the solar degree and horoscopos being identical.[18]

If these assumptions are taken as being reasonable, then we must expect the inscription to involve the key mediaeval Latin words (or abbreviations) for dating.

There are only three such terms – kalendae, idus and nonae – all derived ultimately from an early Roman system of lunar dating long-abandoned by the mediaeval period. By the thirteenth century there were several different ways of writing these words.

The Julian (Old Style) date on which the stellium of five planets took place is the 28 May 1207, which in the Latin system equivalent would be written 'Ante diem V kalendas Iunii' or 'Ante diem V kalendae Iunias', or, in accordance with several mediaeval variants, sometimes given in different cases and spellings.[19]

We must take it for granted that it is extremely unlikely that the short inscription would refer to something preserving from the passage of time the 'mountain' (which we hypothesize as being the founding date of the basilica or zodiac) without there being, somewhere in the Latin, an acrostic pointing to the date of foundation. In fact, this date may be read acrostically from the first line which precedes the year:

HIC UALUIS ANTE . CELESTI NVMINE DANTE .,. M.CCVII RE

The first clue is the word ANTE, which is always the first word in Roman dates, the 'Ante diem'. The word is emphasized by being the 'rhyme', and it appears twice in the same line. This word ANTE, is derived in this context from the Roman insistence on counting a period of time so as to include both the day on which it began and the day on which it ended. The word is therefore almost an open indication that a dating system is hinted at in the inscription – a notion which is supported by the fact that the last ANTE of DANTE is followed by a year in Roman numbers.

It is interesting to reflect on some of the hidden references or 'occult meanings' within this line, relating to both numerical value and to the gods. VALUIS may refer in mediaeval Latin to a numerical value related to payment.[20] CELESTI NVMINE DANTE is remarkably apposite as an 'occult blind' for a solar-lunar system of measurement. Could this be a reference to the goddess Juno, whose name is most apposite for a system of measurement in that the Kalendae were sacred to her? Whatever the underlying anagogic references within the Latin, the line may be interpreted approximately as follows:

HIC UALUIS ANTE . CELESTI NVMINE DANTE . M.CCVII RE
hIc uALuIS ANTE . CelESti nVMINE DANte . M.CCVII re

=

ANTE DIEM V CALENS IUNIAS MCCVII

A few standard variants for IUNIAS might also be drawn from the Latin, but it is more usual for the uninflected IUN to be used. In mediaeval dating, there were other forms, which might not be so derived: there are several ways of expressing dates, as for example 'kalendae sextae', which means 'the kalends of the sixth month' (that is, 'the first of June'), but the variant given appears to be the only one which may be derived from the inscription.

The word CALENS is found in many mediaeval scripts, and is derived from the earlier form 'calendae' or 'kalends' (and variants) relating to the first day of the month. It is specifically in relation to this dating that we may see how the V of NVMINE comes into its own, as the equivalent of the Roman V, or five. The 'V Junias' or 'V Junius' or 'V Jun' or even 'V Junii' (there are several ways of writing the same date) does not refer to the fifth of June, as one unversed in mediaeval dating might suppose, but to the 'fifth day prior to the Kalends of June'. The Roman method of counting involves including the two days at the beginning and end of the sequence. Following this method, we find that the Roman date is the equivalent of 28 May, the very day on which I had originally (as early as 1976) independently arrived at the most suitable date for founding the church in 1207.[21]

One might argue that the inscription could be read as referring to either the IV or the VI day prior to the Kalends, for these figures might be abstracted from the first half of the inscription thus:

hIc ualuis or hic ualuIs

However, I am convinced that the V of NVMINE is there precisely as a pointer to the isolated Roman numeral. Even so, as a reading of the conclusion will indicate, while these two alternative dates would still relate to a satellitium in Taurus, on the last day (the 'VI Kalendae') the Moon itself would have left Taurus, so that the latter of the two alternatives must be dispensed with on purely astrological grounds. Since the V Kalends does correspond to the day of the completed satellitium in Taurus, we should perhaps feel safe in taking this as a reading.

The date at which we arrive through this mixed acrostical reading is an example of the standard mediaeval method for providing a date of a horoscope, and for providing feast-days in religious calenders. The 'Kalends' (or 'Calendae', later the 'Calends' or 'Calens') marked the first day of the month, and were originally linked with the New Moon. It is of course a new moon which would have been seen in the skies on the night of 28 May 1207. Naturally in classical times, as in mediaeval times, the Kalends no longer referred to the condition of the Moon, but to an actual date – the first day of the month (the 'moon-ath', of course).

It is this date, 28 May 1207, which 'preserves from the passage of time the mountain for future use'.

In fact, since it is reasonable to assume that mediaeval astrologers relied more upon direct observation of the skies than upon tables of planetary movements set out in the Ptolemaic system, it is likely that the visible effect of the stellium would have been observed over a period of at least a couple of days prior to the final syzygy of Sun and Moon. In this survey of mediaeval astrology and its methods (and shortcomings) we see that while modern ephemerides are able to pinpoint fairly accurately the relationships of the planets, the mediaeval astrologer was less fortunate, and it is frequently the case that early horoscopes are inaccurate within one or two degrees. This makes the correlation between the acrostically derived date and the putative date for the stellium – itself derived some years ago, all the more remarkable.

However, let us return to our analysis of the hexameter. What happened on this date? Do we find a clue to what is intended in this hidden message relating to a specific day in 1207? In fact, the further information on an astrological kind which may be derived from the following lines of the inscription leads to many different readings. However, the following are probably the most accurate:

METRICUS ET IUDEX . HOC FECIT CONDERE IOSEPH . TINENTDE
metricUS et iudex . HOc fecit COideRe iOSePH . tinentde

= HOROSCOPUS
and:

ERGO ROGO CRISTUM
ergo rOgo cRiSTUm

= ORTUS
and:

QUOD SEMPER UIVAT IN IPSUM . TEPOREMTE – TE(M)PORE M(ON)TE(M)
quod sempeR UivAT IN ipSUm . teporeMTE – te(m)pore M(ON)TE(m)

= TAURUS IN MONTE
A variant for the latter reading could be TAURI IN MONTE.

If this series of readings is acceptable, then we are able to derive from all three lines of the verse, acceptable variants of the following Latin:

ANTE DIEM V CALENS IUNIAS HOROSCOPUS ORTUS TAURUS IN MONTE

along with a variety of different cases which might or might not have been used by a Latinist astrologer writing in the thirteenth century.

The word HOROSCOPUS is not quite what it would appear to the eyes of a modern reader. The HOROSCOPUS is the technical name for the Ascendant, or degree rising over the horizon at a given moment, in what is now the 'horoscope figure'. In mediaeval astrology the word did not relate to a 'horoscope figure', but to the ascendant degree. It was from the name used for this ascendant degree in early astrology that the modern word 'horoscope' for the entire figure was derived.[22] In the thirteenth century, it was used only to denote the sign, constellation or degree arising on the eastern horizon at a given moment. Thus HOROSCOPUS ORTUS TAURUS, or HOROSCOPUS ORTU TAURO, or HOROSCOPUS ORTUS TAURI, are mediaeval designations for a Taurean

Ascendant. By the thirteenth century there were many variants, as for example, 'ortus Tauri', 'Taurus in oriente', 'oriens Tauro', 'horoscopus Taurus', 'ascendens Taurus', 'Taurifer', and many variants in terms of cases. Technically, there is no need to repeat the concept of 'rising signs' by using the words HOROSCOPUS and ORTU together, and it is therefore quite possible to argue that the former relates to the ascendant sign or constellation (Taurus), while the latter (as either ORTUS or ORTU) relates to the sunrise: such short-forms are often used in astrological documents to relate to the sunrise. More formal methods of recording the event might also be used, as for example 'ortus solis in Tauro', and several linguistic and orthographic variants. However, most of the forms for 'Ortus Taurus' may be derived from the line of Latin, and it is reasonable for us to take this as the probable interpretation. One cannot help observing the sheer brilliance of the mediaeval construction which (in its role as a code-derivative) associates the word TAURUS with the notion of 'life', for, as we have seen from our examination of the symbolism of San Miniato, Taurus is symbolically regarded as the sign of incarnation.

The word ORTUS relates to the ascendant planets – to those planets rising over the horizon at a given time. Sometimes, in astrological documentation, the word is applied (without the qualifying SOLIS) to the Sun: thus in this case we could read the single word as meaning 'sunrise', even though this is not strictly necessary within the framework of the decoding.

The three technical words used in mediaeval astrology to denote a gathering of planets ('satellitium' and 'conjunctio' or 'conjugatio') do not appear in the coding. If we were to translate into modern English the Latin which we have just derived from the inscription, it would be something like:

> 'On the 28th May, Taurus was the ascendant constellation at sunrise at San Miniato al Monte.'

Within the acrostic reading of these lines we find the precise date (A.D.V.CAL.IUN.M.CCVII), the time (HOROSCOPUS or ORTUS) and the place (IN MONTE), relating to the foundation of the church, or of the setting down of the marble zodiac, and the time of that remarkable stellium in Taurus.

Without any dislocation of terminologies we arrive logically at a breakdown of the curious hexameters to a point where they: (i) reveal the names of four planets in the constellational horoscope; (ii) give the date and year in which they are said to rise over the horizon; (iii) name the sign or constellation in which they so rise, and; (iv) link these celestial events with San Miniato al Monte. This coded inscription may well be described as the most remarkable to have survived from the mediaeval period.

Remarkable as the encoding is, the analysis has not yet exhausted the content of this San Miniato inscription. There is another important factor in the inscription which is of great esoteric importance, relating to the numerology implicit within the form of the Latin. There are three lines in the inscription, which might or might not be linked with the notion of the Trinity, in conventional ecclesiastical symbolism. That there is an insistence of three lines is evident from the way the colophon has been split into three, and incorporated as finials. There are three lines, each made up of three sections. Is there anything relating to astrology or chronology which may be read into this division in three?

There may be little doubt that within the secret symbolism of the Latin we are considering, there is an attempt to confront the pessimism inherent in the Joachimism of the thirteenth century. This pessimism, which was profound in the first decades of that century, was connected with Joachim di Fiore's prophecy (widely believed) that the Antichrist would come during the early years of the century, and bring the world to an end by 1260. This prediction of the coming end of the world (which was widely believed in the first decades of the thirteenth century) had a devastating effect on the social life of those times, and was a cause of deep concern to the Church.

As we have already noted, Joachim had proposed Three Ages of the world – a concept derived from earlier theological writings.[23] What was special was that he gave a nominal term to these ages. Each age was said to last for 42 generations – in seven ages of six generations. That is to say, that the Joachimite world period consisted of $3 \times 42 = 126$ generations. Joachim was not specific about the length of time which he visualized a generation to represent, but later interpreters (following hints in his original texts) usually interpreted it as being 30 years. The first age was that of the Father, and had closed with Zacharias, the father of John the Baptist. The second age had begun with the birth of Christ, and was expected to last until 1260, when there would be the Last Judgment, followed by the third age, the 'Age of Spirit', to be lived in a non-ecclesiastical state of grace, as a sort of perfected monasticism. The numbers used in this structure of ages are all magical, and properly belong to the neoplatonic numerology, even if Joachim himself did not realize this.

The 3 and the 7 are the basic esoteric numbers, while the 6 derives its magical potency from being 2 times 3. This is no place to dilate on the magical properties of the 3 and 7, but we should note that Joachim himself had a specialist graphic method of drawing from 2 the magical trinitarian number 3.

At the turn of the twelfth century, when the Joachim prophecies were at their highest point of influence, it was believed that the two ages were coming to an end, and that the third lay before the world, after the coming of Antichrist. Joachim himself made much of the relationship between the number 2 and the number 3, even to the point of showing the magical sigillic nature of the 3 as a container of 2. We find this interesting relationship of '2 and 3' is reflected within the San Miniato inscription on several levels. For example, the interesting caesura symbol .,. is almost a sigillic statement of '2 from 3', while the secret code makes use of two lines from the three to give the names of the planets, and two lines from the three to give the horoscopic time. One wonders if this specifically mediaeval (and indeed Joachimite) numerology could be accidental?

This simplistic numerology is reflected in the San Miniato inscription. Altogether there are 3 lines of letters in the marble inscription (figure 1). This need to retain the trinitarian symbolism probably explains why the colophon itself is broken into three lines, and merged with the hexametric verse. The symbolism of deriving 2 from 3, which was important to Joachim, is also hinted at in the strange symbols which separate the verse from the severed fragments of the colophon, which have the forms .,. (figure 1). This strange graphic reminds us of the way Joachim derives the form of the number 3 from two crescents, joined at an invisible centre: ⌣.⌣ . In certain periods, some mediaeval scriptoria adopted a convention of using the three dots (∴) as marking a period, two dots and a comma (..,) as a semi-colon, and one dot at half the height of the letter as a comma. However, while this method is used at times in the eighth-century *Book of Kells*, it was by no means uniform as a convention, and it is likely that there is significance in the important deviation (.,.) in the San Miniato lapidary inscription. For some notice of the convention, see Edward Sullivan.[24]

Altogether there are 129 letters in the inscription. However, three of these letters bear abbreviation or contraction marks: one disguises the presence of 2 further letters, and 2 disguise the presence of single letters, according to the norm of such abbreviation lines. Three contraction marks indicate the invisible presence of four letters of the alphabet: what is important, however is for this contraction method to be operative, only three letters have contraction marks over them, even though four letters are contracted out:

TEMPOREMTE
TE(M)PORE M(ON)TE(M)

Let us assume that what is important is the fact that three letters have contraction marks over them. Let us assume further that these abbreviations are not there merely for reasons of lapidary economy: this assumption will lead us into a most interesting view of the whole inscription.

If we assume that the 3 letters have been abbreviated for a reason, then it could be that they are marked so as to be deleted from the total number of letters in the inscription. Such a deletion would give 126 letters in the inscription. This number may be divided by the total number of lines, namely 3 to give 42 letters:

$$(13) + (18) + (8) = 39$$
$$(15) + (21) + (8) = 44$$
$$(15) + (22) + (9) = 46 \text{ (less 3)} = 43$$

TOTAL   126 by 3 = 42

If this assumption is correct, then we find in this inscription the same number of

145

unabbreviated letters as are in the generations of the entire periodicity of the Joachim prophecies. Further, this total is symbolically divided into three, in much the same way as are the periodicities of the Joachim ages: the structure of the three lines presents two complete sentences, and one incomplete – perhaps a reference to the idea that two ages are past, and one is still in conception. Surely such a coincidence of numbers cannot be accidental? The prayer to Christ (whom Antichrist is to oppose) in the last line of the Latin takes on a deeper significance within the framework of this analysis, and its position within the inscription is justified. Additionally, we may see that the setting down of a zodiac at the beginning of an 'age' or 'periodicity' linked with a vast cycle of time beginning in Taurus, makes quite a different promise of coming security to that threatened by the supposed appearance of Antichrist. In the light of this anagogic and numerological symbolism, the zodiac and the inscription may be seen as a most profound esoteric response to the popular esotericism of Joachimism which was disturbing thirteenth-century society and religious life. The zodiac was a symbol that San Miniato would endure for all time, in the open reference to the promise made by Christ that he would remain with the earth itself until the end of time.

The numerological basis of the inscription is well in accord with the magical outlook of the mediaeval builders. If one of the purposes of the San Miniato symbolism was directed against the pessimism of the Joachimite prophecies, and against the notion of the imminent appearance of the Antichrist, there could be no more open form of symbolic warfare than this. The zodiac and the inscription make use of the same numerological structures as the heretic to present an entirely constructive and optimistic view of the durability and security of the present and coming age, under the stellar protection of the fixed sign Taurus, and under the aegis of Christ the Logos.

Conclusion

One could write the history of . . . a philosophy considered 'occult' because occulted by official scholarship.

(G. DURAND, *'On the Disfiguration of the Image of Man in the West'*, Ipswich 1977: a condensed version of the central portion of a lecture given at the Eranos Conference of August 1969.)

What conclusions may we derive from the preceding study of San Miniato? In a sense, no further conclusions are required. A work of art is rather like a flower, like the over-quoted rose of Gertrude Stein, for it exists in its own right, within a kingdom of its own, and needs neither explanation nor gloss to account for its being. However, the implications in our study of the symbols in San Miniato al Monte point to its being something more than a work of art: it is surely a philosophical machine, a cosmically ordered structure of arcane symbolism, which hints at some hidden meaning or function. Within this esoteric structure there are important theological and esoteric implications which demand some further treatment, even if this carries us beyond the more usual realm of architectural or astrological studies, into areas of speculation generally disregarded by ordinary scholarship.

Even as I write, I am all too well aware that the following sentences will be understood or appreciated only by those who are already to some extent familiar with the literature and style of esotericism. It is, however, sometimes necessary to write in this way, otherwise new ideas and speculations foreign to ordinary thought do not find their way into our cultural life.

There is a sense in which the argument contained within the previous text is its own conclusion. I argue that the zodiac of San Miniato is the hub of an arcane symbolism which unites heaven with earth, sunrise with sunset, the end of an age with the beginning of an age. I argue that the inscription in front of the zodiac is no ordinary mediaeval verse, but both a code and a numerological device which challenged a contemporaneous heresy. The secret of San Miniato al Monte appears to be essentially 'astrological', or 'zodiacal'. For this reason it is certainly possible to explore the significance of this remarkable church entirely within the framework of the anagogic astrological symbolism which the zodiac radiates within the church. However, it could be that the zodiac itself is a sort of occult 'blind'. It is quite possible for us to examine the zodiac, and its ramification of symbolism throughout the basilica, and still miss its underlying esoteric meaning.

It is my belief that the arcane symbolism of San Miniato, which is intimately woven into an early thirteenth-century theology quite acceptable to the church at that time, is a little more complex than would meet the eye of even a seasoned student of the esoteric. It is my belief that the symbolism of San Miniato is derived from the impulses arising from one or other of the esoteric movements which proliferated in the thirteenth century – sometimes in orthodox realms, at other times in the more shadowy realm of the heretical. Because of this, I think that in order to appreciate more deeply the symbolism of San Miniato we should look beyond the astrological stream of thinking which so obviously animates the basilica. This is another way of saying that we should glance at the symbolism hidden behind the arcane-seeming forms which appear in San Miniato as 'astrological' or 'zodiacal'.

On reflection, we may see that rather than being essentially a 'zodiacal' system of symbolism, San Miniato is really a 'solar' system of symbolism. This much is evident from the curious survival of solar imagery in the twelve-rayed sun at the centre of the zodiac itself: the symbolic centre of the basilica is certainly the zodiac, but the hub of the zodiac itself is the Sun (figure 11). A dispassionate appraisal of the design of the church leads us to admit that its arcane symbolism rests much more upon the use of sun symbols and sunlight, than upon the zodiac itself. If Pisces were not linked with the annual effect of sunlight, and if Taurus were not orientated towards the daily sunrise, then the zodiacal symbolism would be flat and unprofitable indeed. These considerations alone should lead us to identify the stream of esotericism with which San Miniato al Monte is connected.

After some years of pondering, it has become my conviction that the basilica of San Miniato is involved with what has been called by esotericists the 'Sun-Mystery', concerning which most occultists admit it is difficult to write even today. This Sun-Mystery was one of the ancient – perhaps indeed the most ancient – of all the esoteric streams within the mystery centres. There are traces of the Sun-Mystery in the Ancient Persian epoch, the indications being that the Persians, whose cultural flowering preceded that of the Egypto-Chaldean epoch, saw the Sun as a divine source of Light. Such mysteries were later woven into the external religion of Zoroastrianism, which laid emphasis on the warfare between the Light of Ahurah Mazdao and the Darkness of Angra Mainyu, the Ahriman of certain modern schools.

In the Egypto-Chaldean epoch, the Sun was seen as the divine source of Life. The symbolism for what is now called the 'Etheric', the invisible quintessential life-force which permeates all living creatures, was linked with what has become the modern sigil for the Sun in the system of Egyptian hieroglyphics,[1] reminding us of how the most potent ideas of ancient mystery schools often survive in misunderstood sigillic forms. More important, however, was the fact that the creative gods were all linked in one way or another with the solar forces. It is of course no accident that the sun-disk played so important a part in Egyptian symbolism: the appearance of the sun sigil between the horns of a hieroglyphic for a bull transforms it into the god-like Apis of the mystery lore.

In the Greek epoch, the Sun was seen as the divine source of Love. In the Hesiodic stream of symbolism, through which the ancient esotericism of the east was carried into Greece, the god Eros was born of Chaos. Chaos was ever seen as the 'naturally' formless and fissiparous four elements, separating from each other in a formless disintegration. It was the quintessence, the invisible fifth essence, later called the Etheric and linked with the Sun, which gave form to the four elements, made of chaos a cosmos. The mediaeval esotericists inherited this wisdom of the five elements, and turned it into the basis of their alchemical hermetic study: it is of great importance and significance that exoteric historians still write and speak of the four elements, as though there were and are only four, when all the esoteric lore has always insisted that there are five elements.

The Greek myth of Psyche and Eros encapsulates an esoteric truth, which is that in the time of ancient Greek civilization man was not yet spiritually prepared to look upon the fifth element, on the quintessential forces which gave form to matter. When Psyche looks upon this forbidden fifth element of solar Eros, then she loses her love, and has to relinquish her contact with a great god.

This truth, encapsulated in the beautiful Greek myth, is changing in modern times. It is one of the important teachings of modern esotericism that man now stands on the edge of the Etheric, as though on the edge of a new and undiscovered territory. Such a teaching points to a simple truth, which is that many people living in the present age can already see and experience the wonderful soft warmth of the vibrant quintessence which lies behind the forms of nature. When esotericism was to some extent banished at the end of the last century by the secret fraternities,[2] one of the most important ideas expressed in writing for the first time was that in the coming twentieth century people would be enabled to see into the Etheric realms, into that fifth level hitherto denied all humans save those who had been initiated.[3]

In the early days of Christianity, it was held that Christ was indeed linked with the solar forces. In esotericism He was linked with the now misunderstood solar beings, the Elohim of the Jewish tradition. It was recognized that as a spiritual being Christ had descended from even beyond the ranks of the Seraphim. More pertinent to our theme is the fact that within esotericism it is recognized that Christ lives within the Etheric. It is this spiritual truth which has led to many misunderstandings about the so-called 'second coming'. In terms of esotericism, the second coming occurred a very long time ago, in the then invisible realm of the Etheric. The modern esotericism insists that the new visibility of the Etheric forces is connected with the visible Christ.

The Christ of the New Mysteries did not come unannounced in the pre-Christian esoteric schools. Indeed, for many centuries prior to His coming, these schools prepared the way, in a cosmic, spiritual and social sense. After His descent into incarnate being, He was hailed in the ancient literature as Jupiter-Mithras, and was thus linked with the Persian mystery wisdom.[4] He was called 'the new Amun', and many of the sigils for his being were derived from the Egyptian mystery wisdom.[5] He was called Apollo, and in being so named he was hailed as the embodiment of the solar god whose name among all the gods remained unchanged in Greek and Roman times. The sun-disk, either in overt symbolism or in aureole form, was used in connection with each of these three solar beings. The wise-men, the Magi, who were later reduced to three, and given names in the mediaeval mythologies, have always been seen as initiates, gathering from different esoteric streams to bear witness to the new Initiation which was to flood over the earth. Herod is the type of non-initiate, who cleaves the earthly power at all costs, and confuses the spiritual power with the temporal. In this respect he is symbol of the darker forces in Rome, with which the esoteric stream of Christianity has ever been forced to fight since those early days.

The link between Christ and the Sun was most profound in pre-Constantine Christian times. Not only were the Elohim of the old dispensation solar gods, who became the Exsusiai of the later hierarchies of angels, but Christ was himself often symbolized in solar terms, the most obvious being the anthropomorphic sun-image of Apollo. We have already noted the willingness of the early writers to link Christ with solar imagery. By the fourth century of our era, however, there was a change, and the ancient stream of Sun-Mystery wisdom was first diluted, and then consciously sluiced away. Scholars are aware of this major change in the direction taken by the ancient mystery schools,[6] but it is Rudolf Steiner who has written with most insight of this critical period in the history of civilization. It is therefore worth quoting Steiner's view of the Sun-Mysteries at some length:

> Then, from about the fourth century A.D. onwards, came the time when, fundamentally speaking, the sun was no longer regarded as anything but a physical orb in space, when the sun was darkened for man. To the ancient Persians the sun was the actual reflector of the Light weaving through space. To the Egyptians and Chaldeans the sun was the Life surging and pulsating through the universe. The Greeks felt the Sun as that which infused Love into the living organism, guiding Eros through the waves of sentient existence.
>
> This experience of the sun sank more and more deeply into man's being and gradually vanished into the ocean-depths of the soul. And it is in the ocean-depths of the soul that man bears the sun-nature today. . . .
>
> In the fourth century A.D. there were schools which taught that the sun-mystery must remain untold, that a civilization knowing nothing of the sun-

mystery must now arise. Behind everything that takes place in the external world lie forces and powers which give guidance from the universe. One of the instruments of these guiding powers was the Roman Emperor Constantine. It was under him that Christianity assumed the form which denies the sun.

Living in the same century was one whose ardour for what he had learnt in the Mysteries as the last remnants of the ancient, instinctive wisdom, caused him to attach little importance to the development of contemporary civilisation. This was Julian the Apostate. He fell by the hand of a murderer because he was intent upon passing on this ancient tradition of the threefold Mystery of the Sun. And the world would have none of it.

Today, of course, it must be realised that the old instinctive wisdom must become conscious wisdom, that what has sunk into the subconsciousness, into purely organic activity and even into sub-organic activity (within the human being), must once again be lifted into the light of consciousness. We must re-discover the Sun-Mystery.[7]

I have already noted that the solar centre of the San Miniato zodiac points back to a manuscript tradition of late antiquity, which placed personifications of the sun at the centre of zodiacs or melothesic figures. In examining one such drawing, in its mediaeval copy (figure 13), we could not help but observe (along with the modern art-historian Saxl) that the figure was reminiscent of the Sun-Mysteries associated with the programme of revival initiated by Julian the Apostate. I chose to put a different slant of interpretation on the Latin inscription written at the top of this illustration, mainly because I feel that the monk who wrote it was aware of the heretical implications in the image – but such differences in opinion and interpretation are of no real significance. The fact is that in the mediaeval period such images of a solar-centred zodiac were known in the monastic scriptoria. Indeed, such images proliferated in the eleventh and twelfth centuries, and it is perhaps significant of the extent to which they reminded later scholars of heretical strains, that the tradition was cut short. The material in the melothesic image of figure 15 would shortly be transformed into the image of a human being, the familiar 'zodiacal man', surrounded by the signs of the zodiac, and the deific personification of Sol would be dropped entirely, in place of the now-familiar image of the planetary Sol.

The material in the zodiacs was shorn of its classical solar references. One has the impression that there was a concerted effort in the monastic scriptoria to delete this image of the solar-god, however faint a reference it might be to the Sun-Mysteries, and however far it was from the heresies described in the ancient literature with which such monks were all too familiar.

It must by now be evident that I am convinced that the solar symbolism of San Miniato is concerned with the ancient pre-Constantine Sun-Mysteries, which, by the thirteenth century, had sought a new symbolic form by way of zodiacal symbolism. In esoteric circles, these mysteries are sometimes called the 'three-fold mysteries', because it was taught that there were three spiritual bodies making up the physical sun, just as there were three spiritual qualities within the whole physical man. This three-foldness is evinced within the symbolism of San Miniato, by means of solar symbolism. The daily rhythm of the Taurean solar orientation, the annual rhythm of the Piscean symbolism and the epochal rhythm of the satellitium, are all reflections of the three-foldness of the experience within the basilica. The marble zodiac is linked with the lower will of man, the wall-fishes are linked with the emotional life of man, whilst the Piscean foot of Christ, transmuted by the sunlight itself, is linked with the spiritual or mental life of man. The threefold levels in man (which had different names in the mediaeval epoch) find a correspondence in the three levels of the church – the nave, the raised 'choir', and the higher apse mosaic. Below these three levels, in a region virtually untouched by the symbolism, is the crypt within which are the remains of San Miniato. One need hardly point out that within the symbolism which we examine here, the tomb is the physical body, the great mystery, recalling the etymology of the word 'sarcophagus' from the Greek word 'sarx' meaning 'flesh'.

There are elements in the Sun-Mysteries concerning which it is still not proper to speak or write openly. Even those who know of the esoteric truths connected with this ancient wisdom must remain silent about its deeper aspects. One factor which must be made available to modern consciousness, however, is that the Sun itself, in a spiritual sense, is a reflector of the planetary lights. This was one of the important traditions in each of the three epochs of Persian, Egyptian and Graeco-Roman. It was this wisdom which Julian the Apostate had wished to preserve in historical records, and it was precisely this wisdom which Constantine attempted to destroy, to make way for the new mystery wisdom of Christ. It is this mystery which is expressed in a most profound astrological symbolism dealt with by Trithemius, but derived from the Arabic astrological lore,[8] concerning the Secundadeian beings and their periodicities. The Secundadeian beings were the ancient 'movitori' or 'intelligencies' which governed the movements of the spheres. There is abundant evidence to show that the sigil is derived from the esoteric literature built around the seven Secundadeian beings, with the outer six representing the planetary beings of Saturn (Oriphiel), Jupiter (Zachariel), Mars (Samuel), Venus (Anael), Mercury (Raphael) and Moon (Gabriel), circling the central solar being of Michael. These six planets are reflecting their light to the Sun. Such a heliocentric arrangement was expressed in the sigil which research shows was used in several of the ancient mysteries, and the sigil has been linked with what in esotericism is called the 'Michaelic Mysteries'. The sigil is associated with the modern sigil for the Sun, which is really no older than the early Renaissance,[9] and with the ancient symbol called the 'Seal of Solomon'.

More important, however, is the fact that the sigil is used as a secret symbol in proto-Renaissance and Renaissance art as the outer sign of the solar esotericism of what has been called the Michaelic stream. A most lovely example is the picture of St Michael in the panel attributed to Piero della Francesca[10] in the National Gallery, in London. On the blade of Michael's sword is painted the secret sigil of the Trithemian beings. There is surely no accident that this sun-centred sigil was used as a decorative motif by Michelozzo when he designed the cappella in San Miniato al Monte in the mid-fifteenth century. All works of art which carry this symbol (save when it appears as an accidental decorative insert) appear to be linked in some way with the Sun-Mysteries, and we may take its presence in the cappella as a recognition on the part of Michelozzo that his cappella (which so disfigures the thirteenth-century basilica), recognizes the stream of Sun-Mysteries within the basilica, which the new mystery-wisdom of the Medici was to some extent to adjust in preparation for the coming age of materialism.[11]

The external symbolism of this almost-forgotten Christian Michaelic Sun-Mystery is expressed in the legends attached to the Palladium. In the exoteric tradition, the Palladium was the sacred image of 'Pallas Athena', the maiden goddess Athena. It was said to have been sent down from heaven by Zeus to the founder of Troy, Dardanus, the legendary son of Zeus and one of the Pleiades. In some stories his descent is traced to Ilus,[12] but in each case he becomes the ancestor of the royal house of Troy. It was maintained that the safety of the city, and hence of the civilization of the Trojans, depended upon the safety of this image, which would radiate its protective talismanic power through the city. Legends tell that Odysseus and Diomede carried off the Palladium and thus made possible the destruction of Troy, a cosmic necessity if the ancient wisdom was to be transmitted further west in a language born of the Greeks, first to Greece itself, then to Rome, then to Franco-Spanish Europe, then to the confines of Europe, which was Ireland, as far west as the islands of the Skelligs, and then across the western ocean to the Americas. There are several different accounts of the first part of this fascinating history, but the one made famous by Virgil[13] is perhaps the best known. It is certainly the one most directly linked with the esoteric truths contained in the history and mythology of the Palladium.

Tradition continues, insisting that the Palladium was rescued from Trojan soil by Aeneas, who eventually carried it with him to Rome. It was placed in the 'Penus Vestae', where it became the tutelary guardian of the new civilization of Rome.[14] When the temple of Vesta caught fire in 241 BC, it was rescued by the Pontifex Maximus, Lucius Caecilius Metellus. The legends attached to the Palladium became rather complex, and were often amended to allow for historical realities. The existence of the Palladium in Rome itself was a secret guarded by the initiates. These initiates and a few priests, even the first Emperors (Augustus, for example) participated in historical events in direct consciousness that the greatest of all spiritual treasures lay beneath the foundations of the most venerated Roman temple, radiating its power into the world through the ancient city. To this, Steiner adds,

. . . in a spiritual sense it had become known to those whose task it was to bring Christianity to the World. And out of the knowledge that the Palladium was guarded in Rome, the early Christians made their way thither. A spiritual reality lay behind these journeys.[15]

When Constantine began the secularization of the Christian mysteries, the Palladium was removed from Rome. It was taken to his new Constantinople. It is this act which accounts for the much-misunderstood movement east of the early Christians, with all the implications to which this decision led in later times. It is said that Constantine had the Palladium buried in the earth under a pillar erected there by his order. It was around this pillar that those Christians of the fifteenth century (following a widely known prophecy) gathered in the hope of being saved from slaughter by the Turks, in 1453, not realizing that by this time the Palladium had gone.[16] Esotericists know that it was necessary to remove the Palladium from Rome in order that the Christian religion might become the state religion, divorced from the ancient Sun-Mystery, of which the Palladium is the ancient symbol. With the Palladium went the last living powers of the ancient mystery wisdom.

It is after the Palladium had been carried to Constantinople that it was lost to external history. Many traditions have survived, but almost all of them are rooted in wishful thinking. It is interesting indeed that when Constantinople was lost to the Christians, there emerged in Christian literature the story of the Grail, that great symbol of Christian initiation wisdom. The Palladium legend travels east, so to speak, while the Grail legend travels west. It is as though the Grail symbol replaced the Palladium symbol, and there is probably no accident in the graphic and symbolic associations drawn in some astrological images between the Virgo of the skies and the Grail, as for example in the melothesic image which links Virgo with the sacred cup (figure 5). Pallas Athena had herself been the Virgin, and her later descendant was Diana of Ephesus – her symbolism adorned with the seven-ringed Secundadeian sigil, later taken over by Michael, who carried the sword and helmet of Athena.

It is of interest that some scholars have seen the zodiac of San Miniato as a survival from the destruction of Constantinople itself. The academics are certainly wrong in a direct sense: the zodiac was made in Florence, and was not carried from Constantinople, after 1204, as a few of them have suggested. And yet, we might ask if there is not a hidden wisdom running through such academicism – perhaps a trace of a subconscious memory of the esoteric reasons for the Fourth Crusade? This Crusade, organized like all others to bring back Jerusalem into the western map, was diverted to the Christian city of Constantinople. In the light of esotericism, it is possible to see this radical change of direction and plan as an attempt by those involved in the esoteric-heresies of that period to reclaim the Palladium, and with it the lost knowledge of the Sun-Mysteries. Perhaps there was more behind the diverting of a crusade than the cupidity of Venetians: perhaps it was an example of history being made by schools of initiates? There is much evidence that the legends of the Cross within the 'Golden Legends' of Voragine are derived from the Palladium legend – even to the details of the burial of the Cross in the earth, and the initiation sleep of the Jew. Certainly this solar context is emphasized in the cycle by Piero della Francesca in Arezzo.

Is San Miniato al Monte one of the surviving art-forms linked with this solar wisdom of the Palladium, and with esoteric lore of which the Palladium image is the external form? Even on the superficial levels beloved by modern historians, the Palladium must be seen as a symbol of the ancient wisdom. The esoteric tradition sees the Palladium as being bound up with the holiest traditions of western esoteric lore. As Steiner writes,

> The Palladium, the ancient heritage brought from Troy to Rome, from Rome to Constantinople, and which, as it is said, will be carried still farther into the darkness of the East – this Sun-treasure must wait until it is redeemed spiritually in the West, released from the dark shadows of a purely external knowledge of nature. Thus the task of the future is bound up with the holiest traditions of European development.[17]

As we have noted, in the zodiac Aries is protected by Pisces on one side, by Taurus on the other. It is as though Aries were poised between the spiritual excarnation of Piscean spirituality and the pull to earth which manifests in Taurus. What is the esoteric content in this symbolism? Aries was the Ram, linked with that other ancient esoteric symbol, the Golden Fleece. Surely it is no accident that the earliest images of Christ show him as a young man, carrying a ram or sheep upon his back? Aries is ruled by Mars, whose symbol is the warrior. Athena was the warrior-maiden, with her helmet and spear, reminding us to some extent of the later traditional image of the archangel of the Sun, Michael, who wears armour and carries a golden blade. The sunlight glinting on the spear of the statute of Athena high on the Athenian Acropolis, could be seen by ships approaching the Greek mainland off Sounion, thirty miles away: that sunlit spear was symbol of the ancient sun-wisdom. Aries rules the head in the human frame, and it also rules all cutting tools, as well as the cutting intellect of man, that place and process by which the human is most intimately woven into the spiritual world.

Is it not possible, in the light of this connection between Aries and the Sun, to see a beautiful esoteric symbolism in the story of St Miniato? The story tells how Miniatus was an Armenian prince, beheaded in the Roman arena in Florence for being a Christian. The historical account is dubious, for it mixes oriental traditions with western traditions, but this is of no great account, since what is important in the story is the esoteric elements relating to Florence. In the Arietan city of Florence, shortly before the Palladium is removed from Rome, Miniatus is beheaded. 'Aries commonly expects death from bloodshed or iron,' writes Michael

Scot.[18] The sword of Mars cuts off the head of Miniatus, and his vision is removed. Yet, in spite of this, he takes up his head and carries it across the Arno (crossing the waters of Pisces). He climbs the hill, that Taurean mount of earth and, on reaching the top, he places it on the ground. Later, is admitted to the rank of the saints, a church is built over his tomb, and still later, a basilica, replete with solar and zodiacal imagery, replaces this early church. Later still, Dante echoes the story of St Miniato's climb by way of mediaeval anagogic technics, and uses its symbolism in the greatest of all esoteric poems.[19]

Stories of such 'miracles' are commonplace in early Christian symbolism, of course, but no similar story contains the hidden wisdom which links decapitation with the ancient sun-wisdom, and with strains of symbolism connected with Aries, Taurus and Pisces. The extraordinary symbolism projects the planet Mars – still ruler of the head, still the ruler of Aries, still the ruler of Florence (though now Christianized under the tutelage of St John, who was also beheaded as a martyr) into the foundation of a building. Is this symbolism a type for the future? Is it possible that those men who used their esoteric knowledge to make Florence an instrument for their will, to make of it a centre to radiate a new wisdom and outlook through the world, knew of the coming needs of man? They adopted the name proper to healers, and called themselves the Medici, and gathered around them a core of great esotericists, many of them now among the most famous of their times. This group worked mainly through the instruments of banking and art. Were they aware that all men would gradually lose the ancient vision of the world spiritual, feel the taste of death, lament the loss of the Palladium? Could they sense that all men would soon have severed heads (severed not from the body, but from the spiritual cosmos) as a spiritual seed for a new church within, which must grow from a hill linked with their Taurean bodies? Was this the reason why the Medici were the ones to adjust overtly the thirteenth-century symbolism of San Miniato, by building within the nave a cappella? With such questions we touch upon the mysteries of the Palladium concerning which it is still impossible to speak openly, and not only for fear of ridicule.[20]

Like Miniatus, the Palladium had come from the east, and like Miniatus, its coming had been intimately involved in the solar mysteries which permeated early Christianity in Italy. The heretical strains of Christian thought were mingled in a rich classical loam of cyclical historicism. One age would follow another, whether the ages be in ternaries or septenaries, whether the present age be Golden or of Iron. Such cycles were almost always linked with planetary or zodiacal cycles, with the result that even today there are predictions derived from the supposed prophecies of the End of the World, and the end of zodiacal cycles, as Pisces merges into Aquarius. Such predictions are made by people who have little knowledge of the cycles they are supposed to have studied, and who usually have no sure understanding of what is meant by the theories of zodiacal cycles or World Ages.[21] The theories of world ages which Joachim di Fiore dreamed up in the twelfth century were just as chimerical, and the coming of the two Antichrists he foresaw were just as imaginative. Joachim, almost certainly because of his historical position, did not choose to clothe his predictions in astrological imagery (unlike almost all other predicators of woe in following times). Instead, he chose a personal view of cyclical history and merged this with a misunderstood theory of numerology in order to lend credence to his predictions. However chimerical his ideas, however terrible the effect of a prediction which put a term to life, they were of such an order as to catch at the heartstrings of those who lived in the thirteenth century. We have in the prophecies of Joachim di Fiore a taste of the ancient black magic working through fear. Joachim called the Antichrist who was supposed to come before the end of the world by the name of 'Gog', which came originally from the book of Ezekiel in the Old Testament. This Gog had almost certainly been a genuine personage, or a land, yet, under the impress of St John's apocalyptic vision, the reality of Ezekiel was transformed into a fearsome image which Joachim darkened even more.[22]

The Antichrist of the Christian lore is essentially a product of the literary imagination, the febrile result of biblical exegesis.[23] It is a spectre which has borne different names at different times: it is one which most esotericists see as the personal or group embodiment of an inner entity, which in modern occult circles is sometimes called the 'dweller'. Steiner is one of the few modern esotericists to have thrown a new and disturbing light on the nature of this being, in lectures which challenged the accepted teachings.[24] The white magicians, the genuine esotericists who are dedicated to working on behalf of the evolution of mankind, must counter this dark image which threatens to strangle and cripple the life-forces of our civilization. The esoteric story of the pagan Palladium, as of the later Christian Grail, may be seen as the embodiment of that esoteric impulse which will reject the dark lunar shadows of the many-named Antichrist. In place of fear, the Sun-Mysteries proclaim love: in place of an imminent end, the Sun-Mysteries proclaim the healing power of the solar god, who will stay with the earth until the end of time.

Perhaps I should make myself clear about the Palladium. Not for one moment do I suggest that the Palladium as a physical image is buried in San Miniato al Monte. The *soi-disant* geomancers, the ley-line hunters and the archaeologists alike may leave the zodiac marble undisturbed. The physical Palladium is in some senses as unnecessary as a concept as the 'treasure of the Templars' or the physical blood-line of Christ – both products of a materialistic mode of thinking. No doubt the Palladium, like the Grail, and like the blood of Christ, does have a material imprint on the physical plane, but what is most important in our present age is the symbolism of these things as spiritual ideals. We must not confuse legends with esoteric realities, for in that direction lies nothing but sensationalism. What I suggest, therefore, is that in San Miniato the ancient Sun-Mysteries, linked with the Palladium, have been given by unknown esotericists a formal symbolism in marble. This symbolism is so sophisticated and refined, so intimately woven into the ethos and cosmology of the thirteenth century, that it is almost beyond the grasp of modern man, who has become accustomed to a far more materialized art of symbolizing.

The solar symbolism of San Miniato al Monte, and the anti-heretical device of the lapidary inscription, unequivocally point to the basilica as the product of an esoteric school. In this sense, and perhaps in this sense alone, I may describe San Miniato al Monte as belonging to the esoteric stream which has its earliest tributaries in the Palladium wisdom, and finds its Christian significance in its capture of the Grail legends. The solar image of the San Miniato zodiac proclaims itself as symbol derived from an ancient wisdom of solar healing: it has an antiquity that reaches back beyond the first pages of history, and which carries an almost palpable feeling of this ancient healing power into our modern age.

Appendix 1 · Glossary

Ascendant The term is properly applied to the degree of the tropical zodiac arising on the eastern horizon of a horoscope chart, or indeed to the degree rising over the eastern horizon. The ascendant degree was the 'horoscopus' of the mediaeval astrologers. The word is also sometimes applied to the degree of a constellation arising on the eastern horizon of such a chart, though it is usual to distinguish the constellational ascendant from the tropical. The ascendant for the San Miniato horoscope (figure 36) is in constellational Taurus.

Asterism Literally a collection or group of stars (figure 32), but usually a configuration of such stars (a CONSTELLATION).

Ayanamsa A term used to denote the difference in degrees for any given point in time between the fiducial of the tropical zodiac and the sidereal zodiac.

Chorography A term used to denote the various attempts made to relate geographic areas to planetary or zodiacal influences. Italy is ruled by Leo, Florence by Aries, the latter of which is ruled by the planet Mars.

Constellation A distinctive pattern of star-groups (figure 33). The term is often confused with SIGN. The 'constellation zodiac' is the projection of a number of constellations associated by name (and in no other way) with the ZODIAC. The positions of these twelve zodiacal constellations correspond neither in location nor in extent with the signs of the ZODIAC.

Fiducial In astrology, the fiducial is a point (very often a fixed star) which is used as the basis for comparative measurement. The term is ultimately derived from the Latin 'fides' (faith), and refers to something in which one may place trust.

Horoscope In modern times the term is used to denote a chart which presents in symbolic form a relationship between the stars and the earth at a given moment of time and place – usually a birth-time and a birth-place – but sometimes, as for example in the San Miniato zodiac, for important or significant stellar events (figure 36). In mediaeval times the Latin term 'horoscopus' or 'horoscopos' was used to denote the ASCENDANT degree.

Image A technical term used in astrological literature to denote each of the twelve symbols for the twelve constellations and signs. The image for Aries is a ram, for example. The term must not be confused with SIGIL or with SIGN.

Lemniscate The lemniscate is a closed figure, having a resemblance to the figure 8, the word being derived from the Greek 'lemniscos' (ribbon). In astrology the word is used in modern esoteric circles to describe the movements of the planets and earth, but in mediaeval symbolism the lemniscate appears to denote the union of the sun and moon. The relevance of the lemniscate to San Miniato is discussed on page 000.

Melothesic man A technical term for the 'zodiacal man', an image of a human being (man or woman) demonstrating the relationship between the parts of the body and the zodiac or planets (figure 5). In such figures, the head is ruled by Aries, the feet by Pisces.

Precession In ordinary astrological use, the term is short for 'precession of the equinoxes', and is used to denote the retrograde movement of the vernal point through the constellations. The phenomenon is perhaps connected with the nutation of the earth upon its poles. In relation to the San Miniato zodiac and horoscope, it is necessary to visualize the CONSTELLATION zodiac and the ordinary (tropical) ZODIAC as overlapping, with one fixed and the other moving. Since the two zodiacs are of unequal segmentation (the tropical zodiac consisting of equal arcs, the constellational of unequal and variable arcs), there was never any point at which the two could correspond exactly in space. The movement due to precession is slight – just over 50.25 seconds of arc per year – therefore, since 1207 the fiducial point has moved approximately $(780 \times 50.25) = 10.89$ degrees.

Rulerships In astrology this term covers very many different relationships, but in connexion with the foregoing study it is restricted to describing the rule which planets are said to have over signs of the zodiac, or over certain things in the material world. In this sense, Mars rules Aries, and all cutting tools or weapons; Cancer has rule over birth, and so on. The word is also used in connection with CHOROGRAPHY, in which a sign of the zodiac or a constellation may be said to have rule over a particular country or city.

Satellitium see STELLIUM.

Secundadeians The name given to a group of spiritual beings or Archangels, the 'movers' or rulers of the ancient planetary spheres, who are assigned rule over a sequence of repeated historical periods of approximately 354 years duration. Oriphiel is linked with Saturn; Zarchariel with Jupiter; Samael with Mars; Michael (the group leader) with the Sun; Anael with Venus; Raphael with Mercury, and Gabriel with the Moon.

Sign	Sigil	Image
Aries	♈	Ram
Taurus	♉	Bull
Gemini	♊	Twins
Cancer	♋	Crab or Crayfish
Leo	♌	Lion
Virgo	♍	Virgin (with ear of corn)
Libra	♎	Scales (Woman carrying scales)
Scorpio	♏	Scorpion
Sagittarius	♐	Half-man, half-horse (with bow and arrow)
Capricorn	♑	Goat fish
Aquarius	♒	Water-pourer
Pisces	♓	Fishes, with mouths joined by silver cord

Sigil A term used to denote a graphic cypher or symbol, and in astrology used widely to denote the graphic forms used in horoscope figures and manuscripts to represent planets, zodiacal signs and other astrological elements. A sample of modern sigils for the zodiacal signs are given under ZODIAC – however, the sigils used in the thirteenth century were very different from these.

Stellatum A mediaeval term (from a now defunct cosmic picture) for the imagined sphere in which the stars and asterisms were supposedly fixed.

Stellium A term used in modern times to denote a group of three or more planets conjuncted in one zodiacal sign or constellation. The mediaeval term was Satellitium (sometimes conjunctio).

Tropical zodiac See ZODIAC.

Zodiac The zodiac is the belt centred on the ecliptic. This has been divided into twelve arcs of 30 degrees, called SIGNS, which run in a circular order, from Aries to Pisces. Properly speaking this is the 'tropic zodiac', and must be distinguished from the zodiac of the constellation. Each sign of the zodiac is accorded an IMAGE and a SIGIL. The zodiacal images on the San Miniato zodiac (figure 2) are standard mediaeval forms, with the exception of Pisces.

Appendix 2   Chronology of San Miniato

The following notes are culled from a variety of architectural and theological histories, supported by a few images. So far as I can gather, the early manuscripts relating to the fabric were destroyed at the expulsion of 1774, if not before: however, they may be preserved in some archives unknown to me. The most interesting surviving pictures of San Miniato are the fresco by Vasari in the Palazzo Vecchio, Florence, and a series of early-nineteenth-century engravings, one of which is reproduced in P. Bargellini, *San Miniato al Monte dans l'histoire et dans l'art*, Florence, 1967. Vasari's image is stylistic in the panoramic sense, with distances reduced, but it does give some idea of the layout prior to the nineteenth-century restorations. The building which appears to block the façade of San Miniato in the fresco is perhaps the Franciscan church lower down the hill, near the beginning of the modern via Giramonte. One observes that even such a stylistic representation succeeds in preserving the different orientations of these two churches. In Vasari's day, the most important thing about San Miniato was that it was an exterior fortification, a useful defensive for Florence. An interesting, if amateurish, drawing by Emilio Burci (1811–77) shows the church during its period of neglect, and indicates just how much in need of the restorations it would appear to have been.

1018–1062 San Miniato al Monte built on site of earlier basilican church: see, however, 1200–1207. The present crypt, though much restored, is of this period, though the crypt altar has been dated to 1013.

1073 Pope Gregory VII (Hildebrand, Pope 1073–85) gives the abbey and church of San Miniato to the Benedictine Monks of Oliveto, in place of the diminishing incumbents of the Cluniac order. This document of Hildebrand is the earliest known relating to the basilica.

1070–1270 Façade of basilica constructed – but see also 1401.

1198 Pope Innocent III elected.

1200–1207 Major restorations and rebuilding of San Miniato at the hands of the Olivetan monks.

1207 Zodiac, marble pavement, pulpit and the main decorative motifs and symbols of San Miniato constructed. Basilica built in present style.

1228 Calimala guild took on responsibility for administering the church fabric of San Miniato.

1295 Andrea dei Mozzi, Archbishop of Florence, built palace alongside basilica of San Miniato. This was to remain the summer residence of the bishops of Florence until 1553.

1297 Mosaic of Christ in Glory, between Maria and St Miniato, constructed in apse, perhaps over earlier fresco.

1320 Palace at San Miniato extended, to make Episcopal Palace.

1322 Timbered roof of San Miniato constructed and painted.

1387 Sacristy built in San Miniato, donated by Benedetto di Nerozzo Alberti. The fresco cycle depicting incidents from the life of St Benedict painted in the sacristy by Spinello Aretino.

1401 Gilded copper eagle placed on top of the façade of San Miniato as symbol of the Calimala guild – see 1228.

1448 Michelozzo finishes the cappella of the Crucifix in the apse of San Miniato, on the orders of Piero de' Medici.

1466 Antonio Rossellino finishes the tomb for the Cardinal of Portugal. This work necessitated the destruction of part of the ancient wall of the basilica of San Miniato: see ground-plan (figure 14). The entire design for the chapel and (perhaps) the tomb was that of Antonio Manetti, who died prior to completion of work.

1491 Apse mosaic (see 1297) depicting Christ in Glory restored by Alesso Baldovinetti.

1499 Ancient campanile of San Miniato pulled down.

1518 Documents and plans drawn up by Baccio d'Agnolo for new campanile, built between 1524 and 1527.

1529 Fortification walls built around the basilica and monastery of San Miniato (these walls are still intact, save at front).

1553 Benedictine monks expelled from San Miniato monastery, when Cosimo I decided to make it and the basilican surrounds into fortifications for defensive and military purposes.

1707 Abbey and church of San Miniato made over to the Jesuits.

1774 Jesuits expelled on orders of Grand Duke Leopold of Lorraine.

1784 Benedictine monks of Oliveto return to San Miniato monastery.

1808 Benedictine monks expelled from San Miniato by Napoleon. For some years the basilica and palace remain unoccupied.

1839 Cemetery laid out by Matas between ancient buildings and sixteenth-century fortification walls.

1849 Spinello Aretino frescoes (in sacristy) much restored.

1850 First complete art-historical guide to San Miniato al Monte published in Florence – see Berti, below, chapter 6, note 1.

1860 The basilica of San Miniato restored, though not on a grand scale. Certain of the 'inlays' on the clerestory are painted fictions. Marble-stucco encasings on some of the columns were probably added at this time, though others had probably been made in the Renaissance 'restorations'.

1868 Giuseppi Poggi constructs a grand stairway connecting the so-called West front of the basilica of San Miniato with the present Viale Michelangelo.

1924 The Benedictine monks of Oliveto return.

Appendix 3 · Data relating to the San Miniato horoscope

The original foundation horoscope, published in 1978 in *The Mercury Star Journal*, vol. IV, no. 2, gives the rounded-off placings for the seven traditional planets as Sun, Moon and Saturn 29 Taurus, Venus 24 Taurus, Mercury 7 Taurus, Jupiter 18 Gemini and Mars 24 Leo. A more detailed table of data might be considered useful, however. The geocentric tropical material tabulated below is derived from a computerized print-out ephemeris (in daily intervals for the inferiors, alternate days for Sun and superiors) for 2500 BC to AD 2000, prepared under the direction of Robert Powell, and in the possession of the author. The longitudinal positions are given Old Style. The material corresponds closely to that given in the five-day and ten-day intervals in Bryant Tuckerman's *Planetary, Lunar, and Solar Positions – AD 2 to AD 1649* (1964), also given Old Style. Precessional rates must be calculated in converting to constellational: the precessional rate adopted in calculations for the San Miniato constellational chart of figure 36 is a nominal 50.25 seconds per year, degree symbolism only being required. For ease of reference, the material is divided into two parts: the first contains material relating to the satellitium in constellational Taurus, the second contains material relating to the remaining traditional planets and the lunar node.

Date	Satellitium				
	Moon	Venus	Mercury	Sun	Saturn
26 May 27	49.6– 61.6	65.38–66.61	47.80–48.91	70.98	72.26
28 May 29	73.6– 85.5	67.84–69.06	50.07–51.30	72.89	72.52
30 May 31	97.6–109.8	70.29–71.52	52.58–53.91	74.80	72.78

Date	Remaining traditionals		
	Mars	Jupiter	Node
26 May	156.39	91.20	334.51
28 May	157.34	91.64	334.40
30 May	158.31	92.08	334.29

The following notes relate to the ground-plan in figure 14.

The dimensions of the San Miniato zodiac (Z) are as follows: the diameter averages 2.945 metres, ranging from 2.946 to 2.936. The heights of the images vary, in centimetres: AR 55, TA 53, GE 48, CN 40, LE 59, VG 53, LB 54, SC 55, SG 62, CP 61, AQ 54, PI 51. The central solar image is 27 cm in diameter. Although they are much worn by the passage of feet and time, only Aquarius is defaced. Cancer is partly restored.

The wall-fishes (F) are 12.7 cm high, the tip of their heads being 1.92 metres from the floor.

The distance from the corner of the tomb of the Cardinal of Portugal (T) to the centre of the zodiac (Z) is 19.52 metres. The inscription (INS), given in full on page 5, reproduced in figure 1, is 3.036 metres in length by 35.2 cm, with an average letter height of 8.6 cm (note, however, that the letter heights vary considerably – for example, the first vertical column gives H 8 cm, M 9.4 cm and E 8.6 cm).

Appendix 4 · Zodiacal material related to zodiacs mentioned in the text

1 The zodiacal sculpture at Sacra di San Michele, Val di Susa

This is early twelfth century, with zodiacal and constellation imagery derived from a manuscript tradition. The zodiacal motifs are now located vertically on the supports of the so-called 'zodiacal arch' at the top of the 'Scalone dei Morti', within the main building. This is really a constellational arch, for the sequence of images is derived from asterisms (figure 34). It is evident that this 'portal' is an (early) rebuilding from stones used at another site: very likely the entire portal, along with the carvings and the inscription, is originally from the old octagonal Baptistry (of which remains are still to be seen) before the main entrance to the monastery. The heights of the sets of images on each pillar is approximately 2.10 metres, the column width, including inscription, averaging 21.6 cm.

Along the right-hand column of the portal (set in foral-edged roundels, approximately 17.5 cm in diameter) is a vertical series of constellations, named alongside in the following sequence, from above down:

AQUARIUS, PISCES, ARIES, TAURUS, GEMINI, CANCER,
LEO, VIRGO, LIBRA, SCORPIUS, SAGITARIUS, CHAPRICORN(US).

There is no accident in the curious arrangement (even though the arch has been moved), for the division in the two pillars of the arch runs across the head of Cancer. From AQUARIUS to CANCER the images are read vertically, from LEO to CHAPRICORNUS they are read from the side. The Latin names all run to the top left of the pillars, and are read from the side. The images are clearly constellational, but it is evident that in this order they are being treated as zodiacal, as the sequence points to the formal order of the planetary rulerships set out by both Ptolemy and Firmicus (both texts available in the twelfth century through Arabian translations).

Of particular interest in the zodiacal images are GEMINI as two embracing men: CANCER is a 10-footed beetle-like crab: SCORPIUS, as a long-tailed creature grasping the scales of Libra in its claws, and CHAPRICORNUS, which is not fish-tailed, but a goat-headed long-tailed and winged dragon.

On the same column (though on the inner side within the entrance), reading vertically upwards, are the inscriptions:

VOS (LE)GITE VERSUS QUOS DESCRIPSIT NICHOLAUS

and:

166

VOS QUI TRANSITI(S) SURSUM VEL FORTE REDITIS

(This might be translated: 'Read (these) verses which Niccolo has inscribed, you who are passing, on the way up or perhaps on the way down'.) On the left-hand vertical column (in floral-edged squares) are depicted 18 of the constellations, named alongside the floral squares which separate them, in descending order:

(AQUILA), DELFINUS, PEGASUS, DELTOTON, ORION, LEPUS, CANIS, ANTICANIS, PISTRIX, ERIDANUS, CENTAURUS, CETUS, NOTHIUS, ARA, HYDRA.

Alongside HYDRA is the un-named Corvus and Amphora. The creature in the hand of CENTAURUS is a useful clue, for this is clearly a hare: the 'Bestia' of the constellational tradition. Aratus names this as 'Bestia', but in later times it was called the 'Fera' or 'Wolf'. In the British Museum mss. Harley 2506 it is depicted as a wolf, and even in modern times it is often confused with Lepus, which is actually located near to Orion in the skies, and not at all close to Centaurus. Manilius confuses this 'Beast' with CETUS. This might suggest that our sculptor is not working from texts derived directly from either Aratus or Manilius, though it is also possible that a mistake has been made, in some confusion with an earlier source. Note that the obscure term NOTHIUS is the equivalent of the 'Southern Fish', our Piscis Australis, who in legend was parent of the zodiacal pair, and was (rarely) in early texts called simply 'Notius', which is the Greek for 'southern'. Aratus calls the constellation 'Ichthyes Notios'. The PISTRIX is the short-form for the Roman equivalent of our 'Cetus', usually qualified with an adjective such as 'aequorea' or 'squammifera'. This in itself is of course something of a puzzle because CETUS is given in the series already, as a mediaeval image of a kind of whale, or rather threatening fish-monster. It is possible that the mediaeval carver was unaware that his image, which is that of a sailing ship, referred to the constellation Argo Navis, and knowing that 'pistris' (sometimes 'pristis' – which was one of the alternative names for PISTRIX) was a sailing ship, he confused the alternative name for Cetus with the image of Argo Navis. I can think of no other way of explaining this image and name, for 'pistrix' is not used in connection with a boat-image in any astrological source I know. The word DELTOTON is interesting, for it points to a Hyginus manuscript as a source for the words, if not for the pictures: the image is that of a standard Christian 'trinity' device. This Christian symbol reminds us that the images have been Christianized wherever possible. It is no accident that this NOTHIUS, in the image of a large fish, is placed in the same floral surround as ARA the 'Altar', which is not a pagan temple image with the sacrificial flame (as it is pictured in classical pagan images), but a Christianized altar, covered by an altar-cloth. The fish of NOTHIUS, hovering above the altar, is not only a thoroughly Christianized symbol – it is a direct reference to the body of Christ, and hence to the Eucharist.

Along the inner side of this same vertical column, to the left of the images, and reading vertically upwards, the top partly hidden by a later cornice, is the inscription:

HOC OPUS ORTATUR SEPIUS UT AUSPICIA(T)UR

(which translates approximately: 'This work exhorts the viewer to study it more often'). On the inside (within the entrance) of the same column, to the right:

HOC OPUS INTENDAT QUISQUIS BONUS EX(PENDAT)

(which translates approximately: 'Let every virtuous person pay attention to this work of art . . .'). On the inside (within the entrance) of the same column, to the left:

FLORES CUM BELUIS . COMIXTOS C(ERNITIS)

(which translates approximately: 'You see flowers mingled with beasts').

Of particular interest to those attracted to esoteric astrology is the series of seven roundels on the inside of the right front of the zodiacal arch: these are probably derived from early sigillic forms for the seven planets, and remind us of some of the 'characters' and 'images' of the later mediaeval sigillic tradition. The standard symbolic forms for the Sun, for the Moon and Venus are easily distinguished. The remaining forms are from a manuscript tradition which appears to have been lost, but there is an interesting echo, if not a graphic relationship (though technically anachronistic), between the sigils given by Agrippa and Steiner for the planetary forms. I know of no significant study of the astrological material of San Michele, but a general guide, by G. Gaddo, in which the zodiacal arch is described, is still in print: *La Sacra di San Michele in Val di Susa*, 1977, ed. For an examination of the sigils relating to the planets, see Gettings, *Dictionary of Occult, Hermetic and Alchemical Sigils*, 1979, and F. Kempter, *Rudolf Steiners Sieben Zeichen der Planetarischen Entwicklung*, 1967.

2   The floor zodiac in the Baptistry of San Giovanni in Florence

The diameter of the zodiac to periphery of concentrics averages 2.82 metres. The zodiacal roundel (figure 10) containing the images averages 33 cm. Some of the images carry names. The Libra roundel has been defaced. The workmanship and design of the zodiacal images are distinctly inferior to that of San Miniato, though it is probably approximately contemporaneous with this. It is possible that the zodiac was moved in the fifteenth century: see Leonardo Ximenes, *Del Vecchio et Nuovo Gnomone Fiorentino*, p. 17. At one time it is likely that the zodiac was orientated in meaningful relationship to the planetary associations of the spiritual hierarchies in the octagonal ceiling mosaics. These run clockwise, from the image of Christ, named: Dominions, Potestates, Archangeli, Angeli, Principatus, Virtues, Troni. The mediaeval planetary equivalents for these were JU, MA, ME, MO, VE, SU, SA respectively, though traditions vary even in mediaeval sources: see F. Gettings, *Dictionary of Astrology*, 1985, under Celestial Hierarchies. At present the zodiac is orientated on an Aries–Libra axis on the nominal east–west line of the Baptistry and Duomo.

The inscription in the centre (figure 12) has not been adequately translated: it almost certainly is linked with an alchemical concept, and is designed to be read in repetitive circles, ROTOR TE SOL CICLOS ET ROTOR IGNE ENCI. The curious ENCI is perhaps a play on the Latinized Greek ENCICLIOS (actually 'belonging to a circle', but linked with the idea of belonging to a hermetic circle, or to an academic discipline). However, the inscription can be viewed in several ways: for example, if the ENCI is read as an ENGI, then the sentence ENGI ROTOR TE SOL CICLOS ET ROTOR IGNE is a palindrome. There are several ways of interpreting this short inscription, but the general idea is that it invites one to stand upon the solar centre and revolve or whirl in the hermetic fire. In so revolving, one is directed to the much longer (and partly defaced) Latin inscription on the periphery of the zodiac. The 36 letters may possibly be arranged into a magic square of 6 × 6 letters, according to occult practise. However, this is not the place to deal with this coded system, which appears to belong more to the alchemical tradition than to the astrological.

Notes

Preface

1 A. K. Coomaraswamy, *The Transformation of Nature in Art*, Harvard, 1934.
2 E. Begg, *The Cult of the Black Virgin*, London and New York, 1985.
3 I mention such star wisdom in the chapter on mediaeval astrology – see, however, Esoteric Astrology in F. Gettings, *Dictionary of Astrology*, London and New York, 1985, and bibliographic notes therein.
4 H. Stierlin, *L'Astrologie et le pouvoir*, Paris, 1985.
5 The view that the French Revolution was supported by esoteric and masonic groups is widely held in occult lore: see for example R. Steiner, *The Temple Legend. Freemasonry and Related Occult Movements* – English translation (1985) of a series of twenty lectures given in Berlin between May 1904 and January 1906.

Introduction

1 The Serapeion orientation, which I shall touch upon later, is mentioned in a contemporary text by P. Schmitt, in *The Mysteries. Papers from the Eranos Yearbooks*, Princeton, 1971.
2 F. Gettings, 'The Nave Zodiac of San Miniato', in *The Mercury Star Journal*, vol. IV, no. 2, 1978: and *The Hidden Art*, London, 1978 (published in the USA as *The Occult in Art*, New York, 1978).
3 F. Gettings, *The Secrets of San Miniato al Monte*, Florence, 1982 – translated as: *Les Secrets de San Miniato al Monte* (trans. Nicole Marque); *I Misteri di San Miniato al Monte* (trans. Cristina M. de Mariassevich); *Das Geheimnis von San Miniato al Monte* (trans. Helga Kahnert).
4 A useful bibliography of relevant esoterica in relation to the history of art is included in Gettings, *The Hidden Art*. Surprisingly little satisfactory work has been done on the occult background to mediaeval art – see however R. Klibansky et al., *Saturn and Melancholy*, London, 1964; M. Schneider, *Pietro che cantano – Studi sul ritmo di tre chiostri catalani di stile romantico*, Milan, 1976; and G. Richter, *Ideen zur Kunstgeschichte*, Stuttgart, 1982. There is still no satisfactory history of esoteric influence on art, however. In connexion with the symbolism of mediaeval esotericism, see also Fulcanelli, *Master Alchemist. Le Mystère des Cathédrales*, translated from the French by Mary Sworder, with prefaces by E. Canseliet, London, 1971, and to a lesser extent, M.-M. Davy, *Initiation à la symbolique romane*, Paris, 1977. Further relevant material will emerge in the notes below. R. Steiner's *Das Kunstlerische in seiner Weltmission*, Dornach,

1961, based on eight lectures given in 1923, and *Art in the Light of Mystery Wisdom*, based on eight lectures given at various times prior to 1923, throw much light on the history of esoteric thought in relation to art. For a study of esoteric lore in general, see also H. P. Blavatsky, *The Secret Doctrine*, Pasadena, 1888. To a lesser extent, see also P. D. Ouspensky, *Tertium Organum*, London, 1922, and *A New Model of the Universe*, London, 1931.

5 F. Gettings, *Dictionary of Astrology*, London and New York, 1985.

Chapter 1 San Miniato al Monte, Florence

1 C. S. Lewis, *The Discarded Image: An Introduction to Mediaeval and Renaissance Literature*, Cambridge, 1964.
2 For example, R. Wittkower, *Allegory and the Migration of Symbols*, London, 1977, 'II – Eagle and Serpent', pp. 35ff.
3 For a popular book dealing with the esoteric background to the building of Chartres, especially in relation to the Templars, see L. Charpentier, *The Mysteries of Chartres Cathedral*, trans. R. Fraser, London, 1972. For a study of the masonic techniques, see J. James, *Chartres. The Masons who built a Legend*, London, 1982. For something of the masonic background, see Steiner, *The Temple Legend* (preface, note 5 above).
4 H. Waddell, *The Wandering Scholars*, London, 1927.
5 The 'colophon' of this inscription, which is involved with the code, may be translated in several ways, as we see in Chapter 5, but it is quite possible to read within it the promise that the zodiac or the church will outlast time. The Latin is M.CCVII . RETINENT DE TEMPORE MONTEM, which may be translated as 'The years 1207 preserve from time San Miniato al Monte'.
6 J. Chydenius, 'The Theory of Mediaeval Symbolism', *Societas Scientiarum Fennica Commentationes Humanarum Litterarum*, vol. 27, no. 2, 1, Helsingfors, 1966.
7 The specific reference to 'objective art' is derived from Ouspensky's account of Gurdjieff's view of art: see P. D. Ouspensky, *In Search of the Miraculous*, London, 1949. However, it is clear from his previous publications (especially *Tertium Organum*, London, 1922) that Ouspensky had a sense of this idea before his meeting with Gurdjieff. For 'objective art', which links with the notion of 'philosophical machines', see ch. 4, n. 9.
8 R. Wittkower, *Allegory and the Migration of Symbols*, p. 36.
9 Ibid., pp. 16ff. One of the mediaeval symbols for Christ was, of course, the Eagle, the bird of the sun.
10 P. D. Ouspensky, *A New Model of the Universe*, London, 1931.
11 Naturally, when I insist that this symbolism is elusive for the mind, I do not think for one moment that it does not carry deep significance for the subconscious. Art is much more the food of the human subconscious than of the conscious mind. It is, however, very easy to trip up over the imprecise words used in most modern psychological models of man, as may be seen from several examples in G. Devereux (ed.), *Psychoanalysis and the Occult*, London, 1974 ed.
12 See Appendix 4.
13 Such multi-layer, non-focussed, thinking appears to have been typical of the

astrological symbolism of mediaeval thought. For a view of how the Christian religion related to the ancient mystery wisdom, see, for example, Hugo Rahner, *The Christian Mystery and the Pagan Mysteries* from the same source as given in note 1.

14 See, for example, O. Neugebauer and H. B. van Hosen, *Greek Horoscopes*, Philadelphia, 1959. Few modern astrologers would be able to read Greek and Roman, or even pre-fourteenth-century charts in a contemporaneous sense, not only because the graphic symbolism is different, but also because the methods of interpretation are different.

15 An interesting account, and a provocative tabular synopsis, is contained in R. Collin, *The Theory of Celestial Influences*, London, 1954, ch. 16, served by Appendix 8, pp. 361ff.

16 R. Steiner, 'The Search for the New Isis – Divine Sophia' (trans. of four lectures given in Dec. 1920) typescript, n.d.

17 See, for example, G. Schiller, *Ikonographie der christlichen Kunst*, 1969 – at the time of writing only the first two vols of the English translation (by J. Seligman) are available, as *Iconography of Christian Art*, London, 1971.

18 R. H. Allen, *Star-Names and Their Meanings*, 1899, pp. 460ff. The quotation from Shakespeare's *Titus Andronicus* is not accurate, however, and Allen's conclusions in this matter are incorrect.

19 F. Gettings, *Dictionary of Occult, Hermetic and Alchemical Sigils*, London, 1979.

20 For the Spica symbol, and the related solar and Piscean symbols, see O. Neugebauer and H. B. van Hosen, *Greek Horoscopes*, pp. 460ff, and Collin, *The Theory of Celestial Influences*. Also, F. Gettings, 'The Sigils for Pisces and Spica', *The Mercury Star Journal*, vol. IV, no. 1, 1978.

21 For Notre Dame, Paris, see Fulcanelli, *Master Alchemist*. For Chartres, see Gettings, *The Hidden Art*, and Charpentier, *The Mysteries of Chartres Cathedral*; for the zodiacal schema of Vezelay, see F. Vogade, *The Basilica of Vezelay* (trans. E. Sinz), Bellegarde, 1972. I know of no esoteric treatment of this sculptural programme. An example of the academic approach to arcane astrological symbols at Chartres may be gleaned from A. Katzenellenbogen, *The Sculptural Programs of Chartres Cathedral*, Baltimore, 1959, notes 67 and 88 especially.

22 See the interesting version *The Art of Spiritual Harmony by Wassily Kandinsky*, trans. with intro. by M. T. H. Sadler, London, 1914. Kandinsky's relationship to Theosophy and the later Anthroposophy, so played down and misunderstood by contemporary art-historians, is dealt with admirably by S. Ringbom, *The Sounding Cosmos. A Study in the Spiritualism of Kandinsky and the Genesis of Abstract Painting*, Abo, 1970.

23 E. M. Smith, *The Zodia*, London, 1906, pp. 81ff.

24 Alexander of Neckam, *De Naturis Rerum* – see T. Wright, 'Alexandri Neckam de Naturis Rerum' in *Rerrum Britannicarum Medii Aevi Scriptores*, London, 1863. Neckam was probably paraphrasing the *Introductorium in Astronomiam* of Albumasar when touching upon astrological points.

Chapter 2   The secret symbolism of the zodiac

1 The relevant pages dealing with sigils used by Arnaldus de Villanova are given in

Appendix XIV, 'Die Sigille der zwölf Zeichen', of K. A. Nowotny, *Henricus Cornelius Agrippa ab Nettesheym. De Occulta Philosophia*, Graz, 1967.

2 See Gettings, *The Hidden Art*, pp. 17ff. For the significance of the Ru symbol and Ankh in relation to Christian symbolism, see for example Blavatsky, note 9 above, Part II, xxii 'The Symbolism of the Mystery-Names Iao and Jehovah, with their Relation to the Cross and Circle'.

3 For the well-known acrostic treatment of the Fish usually attributed to St Augustine, see Appendix 5. The symbolism of the man-fish has been dealt with by G. Massey, *A Book of the Beginnings. Containing an attempt to recover and reconstruct the lost origins of the myths and mysteries, types and symbols, religion and language . . . Part 2, The Natural Genesis*, London, 1881–83.

4 See Allen, *Star-Names and Their Meanings*, pp. 342ff. The tradition of the two fishes is found in several ancient alchemical texts, but see the excellent engraving in Lambsprinck, 'De Lapide Philosophico' of 1678 in the *Musaeum Hermeticum* reprint, Graz, 1970.

5 Lewis, *The Discarded Image*.

6 The eleventh-century figure is from mss. Lat 7028, fol. 154r. See F. Saxl, 'Macrocosm and Microcosm in Mediaeval Pictures', in *Saxl Lectures*. Unfortunately, this essay-lecture, and the following one in the collection, 'The Revival of Late Antique Astrology', contain considerable numbers of inaccuracies, and demonstrate a lack of familiarity with mediaeval astrological terminologies and imagery.

7 The mediaeval Latin might be translated as relating to the 'absurdities of the alchemists'.

8 Neckam, *De Naturis Rerum*.

9 Clemens, 'Recognitions', II viii. See also J. Danielou, *Primitive Christian Symbols*, London, 1964. In view of what I claim about the solar mysteries in the Conclusion, it is perhaps worth noting here that according to F. C. Bauer, *Das Manichaeisches Religionsystem*, 1831, the Manicheans believed that Christ dwelt on the sun. For interesting note of the solar-centred zodiac in the baptistry, see L. Ximenes, *Del Vecchio e Nuovo Gnomone Fiorentino e delle osservazioni astronomiche . . . etc.* Florence, 1757.

10 Steiner, *The Search for the New Isis*. Steiner's highly relevant view of the Sun-Mysteries is touched upon later – see Conclusion, note 7.

11 Because of the relationship which the sun holds with the earth, there is a period of days in which the phenomenon of the lighted foot is visible, though the most powerful effects are towards the end of August. The 'surviving' sunlight effect on the wall-fish is at its best when the Sun is in 17 degrees of tropical Pisces and 14 degrees of tropical Libra, which means that the effect will be centred on the 7/8 March and the 6/7 October over the next few decades. Those who wish to study this mystery of lighting are advised to be in the church some time before the 4.50pm optimum effect (last noted in 1987), if only to watch the gradual movement of sunlight up the wall towards the fish. The actual effect, of the sunlight moving across vertical fish itself, lasts only for a minute or so, however.

12 For the light effects, see O. Demus, *Byzantine Mosaic Decoration*, London, 1976 ed., pp. 35ff., and Schmitt, *The Mysteries. Papers from the Eranos Yearbooks*, Princeton, 1971. There are of course several well-known buildings which involve special light effects, as

for example the funerary temple of Rameses II in Egypt, the Greek temple of Apollo at Bassae, the Buddhist temples in Pagan (see H. Yule, *Narrative of the Mission to the Court of Ava*, London, 1855), and the castle of the Albigensians at Montsegur (see R. Nelli et al., *Les Cathares*, Paris, 1960). Of the several I have seen, however, that at San Miniato is by far the most remarkable. For a notice of esoteric symbolism which makes of the temple or church nave a symbol of the body of a god, see T. Burckhardt, *Sacred Art in East and West*, London, 1967; R. A. Schwaller de Lubicz, *Le Temple dans l'homme*, Paris, 1949; M. M. Davy, *Initiation à la symbolisme romane*, Paris, 1977; and (though in a different sense), M. Schneider, *Pietro che cantano*, Milan, 1976.

13 I do not wish to place too much reliance on this ossary symbolism, as it is possible that it has not been in the present position since the thirteenth century. The altar itself is usually dated AD 1013, and the reliquary containing the bones of the martyr is said to be pre-Roman (some claim it to be Etruscan). The sigil for Pisces is definitely thirteenth-century in form, but may of course be a late forgery.

14 See, for example, G. R. S. Mead, *The Doctrine of the Subtle Body in Western Tradition*, London 1967 ed.

15 B. L. van der Waerden, *Science Awakening II – The Birth of Astronomy*, London 1974.

16 For what I have called the 'missing bull' literature, see Gettings, *The Hidden Art*, p. 17ff. The nearest related pulpit symbolism to San Miniato is that in S. Leonardo in Arcetri, which is usually closed to the public.

17 In the talons of the eagle there is a small figure, which I have not been able to identify, though it is clearly a quadruped. It may be linked with that held in the talons of the eagle in the Pisan baptistry pulpit by Pisano, which I have to some extent dealt with in reference to this symbolism in *The Hidden Art*.

18 G. Durandus, *Rationale Divionorum Officiorum*, ed. V. d'Aquino, Naples, 1859. For a partial translation, see J. M. Neale et al., *The Symbolism of Churches and Church Ornaments*, Leeds, 1843.

19 Prior to the sixth century, there was greater flexibility in orientation. For a recent study of what has been called 'astro-archaeology', see J. Michell, *A Little History of Astro-archaeology. Stages in the Transformation of a Heresy*, London, 1977. It is interesting to note that Michell appears to support Penrose's notion that the Parthenon was orientated to the Pleiades in 1150 BC. One presumes that this orientation was for the earlier pre-Athenian temples. The Arabian astrologer Albiruni, in his study of the lunar stations, notes a tradition that the vernal equinox once coincided with the rising of the Pleiades: see Chapter 5, note 3 below, page 341. The zodiac in San Miniato might be said to lie on exactly the same orientation line. For all that many of Penrose's views have been superseded, or ignored, the fact is that his great teacher, Nissen is still one of the great authorities on problems of orientation: see, for example, H. Nissen, *Die Orientation Aegyptische und Griechische Bauwerke*, 1885. The work most consulted in this field is F. C. Penrose, 'A Preliminary Statement on an Investigation of the Dates of some of the Greek Temples as derived from their Orientation', in *Proceedings of the Society of Antiquaries*, Feb. 1892. If only there were a Nissen or a Penrose for mediaeval orientation problems. The problem of the arc of sunrise, as presented in relation to temple-orientations and ancient circles indicates something of the symbolic problem arising from the attempt to adjust a 30 degree zodiacal arc (that of Taurus) to what is

175

probably an arc of about 40 degrees on the mountainous horizon line to the east of San Miniato. The line of solar orientation appears to be centred on the 30 degree arc towards the end of May (Julian calendar), however. I have assumed that the central line of this arc was that adopted to the sighting of the sunrise on 28 May 1207, but I have done this in terms of visual sightings, rather than by means of sophisticated calculations, as it is in terms of the former that the thirteenth-century builders would have worked.

20 The horoscope for the foundation chart of San Miniato was first published in an article 'The Nave Zodiac of San Miniato', *The Mercury Star Journal*, vol. IV, no. 2, 1978. For details of ephemeris data, see Appendix 3.

21 See Appendix 3.

22 M. Scot, *Liber Introductorius*, quoted by L. Thorndike, *Michael Scot*, London, 1965 ed., p. 95. Unless otherwise stated, the quoted translations from Scot's influential and highly relevant *Liber Introductorius* are from Thorndike.

23 For Penrose, see note 19 above.

24 There are several mediaeval horologia in Italy. Perhaps the most impressive inside a church is that constructed under the direction of Gassendi in San Petronius in Bologna (see A. Chiarini, *La Meridiana della Basilica di S. Petronio in Bologna*, Bologna, 1975). The most lovely external horologia is in Bergamo, under the protective arches adjacent to the Duomo: this has been restored several times, but it still has the solar gnomen to channel the light of the sun into its lemniscatory pattern. Perhaps more apposite to our theme, however, is the ornate and gilded solar light-mask in the wall of the upper room of the Palazzo della Ragione in Padua. Here the gilded sun placed over the hole is linked both with astrological considerations and with the Eucharistic symbolism of the fresco around it. So far as I am aware, the esoteric importance of this horologium has been missed by art historians. However, for treatment of the zodiacal imagery in this Salone, see N. Ivanoff, 'Il problema iconologico degli affreschi', in *Il Palazzo della Ragione di Padova*, Padua, 1963. The calendrical marble and metalwork on the Salone floor is now almost entirely removed, so that the significance of the solar beam is lost.

25 M. Scot, *Liber Introductorius*, p. 57.

26 The standard works on Mithraism are F. Cumont, *Textes et monuments figures relatifs aux mystères de Mithra*, Brussels, 1899, and M. J. Vermaseren, *Corpus Inscriptionum et Monumentorum Religionis Mithraicae*, The Hague, 1956–60. See, however, *Journal of Mithraic Studies*, vol. I, no. 1, 1976. It is likely that Scot would have been familiar with the Roman images of the bull being conducted for sacrifice, but it is the link he makes with Taurus which is important within the present context.

27 Thorndike, note 22 above.

28 Some of the imagery for 'planetary conjunctions', to which are ascribed dire calamities are treated in F. Boll et al., *Sternglaube und Sterndeutung*, Stuttgart, 1966; the planetary conjunctions for 1521 and 1524 are reproduced in popular prints in Table XXIII. See also L. Thorndike, *A History of Magic and Experimental Science*, vol. 5, pp. 178ff. which deals at some length with the 1524 conjunction prophecies. In connexion with specific mediaeval prophecies, see L. Thorndike, vol. V and VI, chap. xi. One of these relates to 1377, made by Conradus Stollus, another to 1430 made in Milan by Vernadigius, while another, linked with the supposed coming of the Antichrist, was composed by

John of Lübeck in Padua, 1474. It is interesting to note that in the second of these (BM Mss. Harley 3731 f.176r) which is almost certainly contemporaneous with the prediction, mention is made of the Secundadeian periodicities which are generally supposed to have been introduced to the west by Trithemius almost a century later. See note 30 below.

29 For an early-thirteenth-century view of the effects of the Great Year (which is often confused with the precessional cycles), see Alexander of Neckam (ch. 1, note 24 above). Albumasar suggested a trepidation, involving an oscillation around an arc of 7 degrees, in periodicities of 900 years. Albategni gives a precessional rate of 1 degree every 60 years and 4 months. Alfraganus assumes an even rate of 1 degree per century. Each of these different views was known to the mediaeval astrologers: the rate of 25,920 years was known only in comparatively recent times. For a survey, see Gettings, *Dictionary of Astrology*, under Precession.

30 J. Trithemius, *De Septem Secundadeis, id est intelligentiss, sive spiritibus moventibus orbes* . . ., Nuremberg, 1522. The periodicities of 354 years and 4 months appear to be derived from the length of the lunar year (twelve synodic months), extrapolated according to the ancient astrological system from days into years. See J. Meeks, 'Cosmic Rhythms and the Course of History', in *The Golden Blade*, London, 1979, p. 19.

31 Trithemius (above) mentions Abano under his mediaeval literary-honorific in the first paragraph of the book. This is often overlooked by modern scholars. In any case, the periodicities of these movitori were mentioned in earlier astrological texts, though under different names – see for example note 28 above: Vernadigius gives the periodicities correctly.

32 For a study of the esoteric Piscean symbolism in connexion with Chartres, see Gettings, *The Hidden Art*.

33 Blavatsky, *The Secret Doctrine*, Pasadena, 1888, was probably the first text to point openly to the connexion between the etheric and the pentagram. For a Christian view of the symbolism, see A. Heidenreich, *The Catacombs*, London, 1962 ed., p. 25. The connexion between Venus and the (heliocentric) pentagrammic cycle is dealt with by J. Schultz, *Rhythmen der Sterne*, Dornach, 1863 – see in particular pp. 141ff.

34 In mediaeval geomancy the Moon is linked with crowds and the laity by virtue of its rule over the geomantic symbol called 'Populus'. For a thirteenth-century view of geomancy, see for example Scot, *Liber Introductorius*.

35 G. Adam, in a letter to Vreede published as 'The lemniscatory related surface in space and time'.

36 G. Davison, *Astronomy and the Imagination*, London and Boston, 1985, p. 137. E. Vreede, *Anthroposophie und Astronomie*, Stuttgart, 1954. See also Schultz, note 33 above, pp. 55ff.

37 Joachim di Fiore, *Liber Concordie*. The relevant passage relating to the numerology is given in Latin by M. Reeve, *The Influences of Prophecy in the Later Middle Ages*, Oxford, 1969, pp. 19ff. For a good survey on Joachim, see E. Jordan, 'Joachim di Fiore', *Dictionnaire de théologie catholique*, vol. VIII. The moral and theological roots of this heresy are studied by G. Leff, *Heresy in the Later Middle Ages*, Manchester, 1967. The figures I give for the second age of 42 generations are set out on page 144. Few

interpreters or popular followers of Joachim bothered to record Joachim's ambiguity concerning the length of a generation, however. I am aware that there are other interpretations for Joachim's view of history, as, for example, set out in the 'etatulae' recorded by Robert of Auxerre – see Reeve above, pp. 40ff. The outcome – the End for 1260 – is, however, much the same, and it was this which took hold of the fancy and fantasy of the time.

38 The apse mosaic is said to have been finished by 1297. As is evident from such sources as James, *Chartres*, London, 1982, it was normal for a church or cathedral to be built over a very long period of time, and for the original ideas of the architects to be expressed to perfection, even so. It is possible that the apse mosaic would have been preceded by a fresco, but there does not appear to be accessible documentation. The mosaic is said to have been restored by Alesso Baldovinetti in 1591, and again in 1860. The alpha and omega are interesting, as are those in the Baptistry of Florence (where the omega is purposely placed upside down). It was more usual for the Byzantines to use the abbreviated IC XC, but the general symbolism of the mosaic is western rather than eastern. A full survey of this mosaic would be extremely useful from an esoteric point of view, but is well beyond the limits of the present inquiry.

39 Quoted by Thorndike, note 22 above.

40 In spite of all the romantic claims made by popular occultists in modern times, this is not a labyrinth. The mediaeval literature refers to it as though it were a Cretan labyrinth symbol, but views it from a mythological point of view, it being taken for granted that the labyrinth itself was a symbol for something else. See for example James, *Chartres*, London, 1982. I refer the labyrinth to the idea of a dance, and this immediately calls to mind the remarkable paper by M. Pulver, 'Jesus' Round Dance and Crucifixion According to the Acts of St. John', 1942, in *The Mysteries. Papers from the Eranos Yearbooks*, Princeton, 1971.

41 Bodleian Ms 266 f.178v. This is quoted by Thorndike (note 22 above), as though astronomy were the subject of Scot's praise. The context clearly refers to astrology, however.

Chapter 3 Astrological considerations

1 L. Thorndike, *A History of Magic and Experimental Science During the First Thirteen Centuries of our Era*, New York, 1923, Ch. 30.

2 The Diocletian ban, continued by Theodosius is mentioned in Bouche-Leclercq, *L'Astrologie Grecque*, Paris, 1899, pp. 566ff. The quotation relating to thirteenth-century astrology is from Thorndike, note 22 above. For further notes on the relationship between theology and astrology in this formative period, see Thorndike, *A History of Magic and Experimental Science*, vols I and II; E. Reiss under 'Astrologie' in *Realencyclopaedie der Classischen Alterthumswissenschaft* (Pauly-Wissowa), Stuttgart, 1896, and T. O. Wedel, *The Mediaeval Attitude Towards Astrology*, Folcroft, 1920, which provides a useful bibliography for general astrological lore and history, even though it is concerned specifically with the English school. The two basic texts with which the mediaeval non-Arabic astrology was involved were Firmicus Maternus, *Julii Firmici Materni Matheseos Libri VIII*, now the W. Kroll and F. Skutsch edition, Leipzig,

1897–1913, and Ptolemy's *Quadripartium* (in modern editions), Claudius Ptolemaeus, *Claudii Ptolemaei Omnia quae extant Opera*, the E. O. Schrekenfuss edition, Basel, 1551. Many of the modern arguments used or quoted in academic literature are derived from, or parallel in thought to, those formulated by Ficino in his attack on astrology, which was to a large extent based on the writings of Carneades, known only through such references as appear in Augustine and Cicero.

3 See for example C. G. Harrison, *The Transcendental Universe*, London, 1893, and R. Steiner, *The Occult Movement in the Nineteenth Century and its Relation to Modern Culture*, London, 1973, translations of ten lectures given in Dornach in 1915. Some familiarity with the literature of theosophy is required for an appreciation of these books.

4 F. A. Yates, *The Rosicrucian Enlightenment*, London, 1972.

5 There are several seminal works by Steiner in this field, all of them derived from his lectures: see, for example, *Rosicrucian Esotericism*, London, 1978, translated from ten lectures given in Budapest in 1909, and *Rosicrucianism and Modern Initiation. Mystery Centres of the Middle Ages*, translated from six lectures given in Dornach in 1924: see also note 3 above, and *The Temple Legend*, London, 1985. For an excellent compilation within the Steinerian spirit, see Allen, *A Christian Rosenkreutz Anthology*, New York, 1968. The oft-quoted source by M. Heindel, *The Rosicrucian Cosmo-Conception, or Mystic Christianity*, London, 1937 ed., is largely derived from Steiner lectures and books. The most influential of the Rosicrucian texts is the *Fama*, which is essentially incomprehensible save when read as an esoteric document: see *The Fame and Confession of the Fraternity of R:C Commonly of the Rosie Cross*, by E. Philalethes (actually Thomas Vaughan), London, 1652. There is a useful reprint issued for the Societas Rosicruciana in Anglia, Margate, 1923.

6 Something of the importance of Roman astrology may be gleaned from F. H. Cramer, *Astrology in Roman Law and Politics*, Philadelphia, 1954. For the Hellenistic and later forms, see also O. Neugebauer and H. B. van Hosen, *Greek Horoscopes*, Philadelphia, 1959.

7 Augustine is among the first to put on paper his ignorance of the old mystery wisdom concerning the names given to the constellations: his *Civitate Dei*, intended as a guide for the new Christianity, therefore marks the final break with the ancient initiation tradition. See *De Doct. Christ.* 2. 21. His comments show that he did not know much about astrology, but this did not prevent him from making his influential stand against it – see for example *Civitate Dei*, 5. 4–5. His arguments may be traced back to Cicero and Carneades.

8 Macrobius, in *Somnium Scipionis* (see the Leipzig edition of 1840). His approach, while predominantly philosophical, is rooted in the ancient mystery lore, and evinces no knowledge of exoteric astrology.

9 For a useful summary of Thomian views of astrology (as is so often the case, more liberal than his later interpreters assume), see Wedel, note 2 above, pp. 67ff.

10 G. Sarton, *Introduction to the History of Science. Vol. II – from Rabbin ben Ezra to Roger Bacon*, Washington, 1950.

11 See Bib. de l'Arsenal Mss. 1036. See also H. F. C. Schjellerup, *Description des étoiles fixes au milieu du dixième siècle de notre ère, par l'astronome persan Abd-al Rahman Al-Sufi*, St Petersburg, 1874. See also E. Wellesz, 'An Islamic Book of Constellations', Oxford,

1967. Although only a booklet, the text contains several errors: for example, Centaurus does not grip Lepus in his hand. Lepus is a different constellation, and the figure in the Centaurus asterism is the Beast or Wolf of classical astronomy. In some mediaeval Arabic-derived images the Beast certainly looks like a hare, but this does not mean that it is the constellation Lepus. Centaurus is 2LB–28SC, 28S–68S, Lepus is 5GE–3CN, 14S–25S, according to the 1923 figures of V. Robson, *The Fixed Stars and Constellations in Astrology*, London, 1923.

12 For note of Marbodus and Firmicus, see Wedel, note 2 above, p. 32.

13 For the esoteric view of the background to this period, see R. Steiner's *Rosicrucianism and Modern Initiation*, translated by M. Adams from shorthand reports of lectures now bearing the title *Die Weltgeschichte in anthroposophischer Beleuchtung und als Grundlage der Erkenntnis des Menschengeistes* (No. 233 in the Bibliographic Survey). In particular, Chapter 2.

14 See Wedel, note 2 above, p. 39.

15 See Gettings, *Dictionary of Astrology*, under relevant headings.

16 See F. Saxl, 'Macrocosm and Microcosm in Mediaeval Pictures', in *Saxl Lectures* pp. 177ff.

17 See Chapter 2, note 41 above, I, pp. 385ff.

18 Hildegarde of Bingen, *Causa et Curae* – it is often argued that this text combines many late interpolations (though I would assess most of the astrological material to be contemporaneous): see for example Sarton, note 10 above, p. 387. One must be careful of the Hildegarde texts since the Benedictine nun, 'The Sibyl of the Rhine', as she was sometimes called, appears to have been a bad Latinist, and it is likely that the text was partly worked by her secretary. For a survey of Hildegarde's cosmic view, see M. Davy, *Initiation à la symbolique romane*, Paris, 1977. I have no idea why F. Saxl (note 16 above), should write of Hildegarde as one 'who held astrology in abhorrence . . .'.

19 See Neckam, *De Naturis Rerum*.

20 R. Scot, *Liber Introductorius*, p. 102. The Latin is 'Ymagines huius seculi subiciuntur ymaginibus supercelestibus' – 'The images of this life are subject to the higher celestial images.'.

21 Alexander Halensis, *Summa Theologica*. Much of the astrological lore is based on the Latin translations from the Arabs, which is perhaps why Roger Bacon claims that Alexander did not write the *Summa*.

22 Gerardus of Cremona, *Elementa Astronomica*, printed probably for the first time in Ferrara in 1493, but available in several manuscripts from after 1187.

23 For a useful modern notice of the influence of Alfraganus on Dante, see E. Moore, *Studies in Dante – Third Series, Miscellaneous Essays*, Oxford, 1908 ed.

24 See, for example, the collection of figures (which are not genitures) in the British Museum, Mss. Royal App. 85 f.1–2. Either the dates suggested in the catalogue for these horoscopes (converted from the Arabic) are not accurate, or they are very inaccurate figures. For example, the figure marked b. in the catalogue cannot be cast for 10 May 1162, for the figure clearly gives the Sun in 13 degrees of Leo, Moon in 17 degrees Scorpio, Jupiter in 20 Gemini, Saturn in 12 Leo. The day is wrong (Moon position), the month is wrong (Sun position) and the year is wrong (Saturn position). It would appear that the figure is cast for 23 July 1123 – though this is not the equivalent

date given according to the Arabian calendrical system.

25 See *Liber Introductorius*.

26 For a popular treatment of Sacra di San Michele, with special (non-esoteric) mention of the 'zodiacal arch', see G. Gaddo, *La Sacra di San Michele in Val di Susa*, Susa, 1977.

27 For a brief notice of these mediaeval sigils, see Gettings, *Dictionary of Occult, Hermetic and Alchemical Sigils*, London, 1979. The twelfth- and thirteenth-century sigils for Taurus, used in some horoscopes, in place of the standard abbreviations, were variants on the forms.

28 For a survey of the pre-mediaeval chorographies, see Bouche-Leclercq, *L'Astrologia Grecque*, Paris, 1899. For a brief note of the various chorographies adopted into western astrology and merged into one, see Gettings, *Dictionary of Astrology*, under Chorography.

29 So far as I am aware, the esoteric element in the melothesic images have never received an adequate treatment. For an academic survey of the earliest forms, see Saxl, note 16 above.

30 Alexander of Neckam, *De Naturis Rerum* – see Th. Wright, 'Alexandri Neckam de Naturis Rerum' in *Rerrum Britannicarum Medii Aevi Scriptores*, London, 1863.

31 M. Capella, *Opus Martiani Capelle de Nuptijs Philologie et Mercuris . . .*, Vicenza, 1499.

Chapter 4   Sunlight, Bull and Fish as secret symbols

1 See G. R. S. Mead, *Thrice-Greatest Hermes. Studies in Hellenistic Theosophy and Gnosis*, 1964 ed. The commentary is on Plutarch's *Mysteries of Isis and Osiris*, IX, i, p. 190 of vol. 1.

2 St Ambrose of Milan, in the translation of Heidenreich, *The Catacombs*, London, 1962 ed.

3 One calls to mind the so-called 'Strict Observance' of Freemasonry mentioned by R. F. Gould in his *History of Freemasonry*, London, 1886. The Mithraic mysteries were solemnized in a consecrated cavern on the 25 December, beginning at the moment when the priests observed the constellation of Virgo appear. On setting, it issued forth the sun 'which appeared as a son supporting itself on its mother's lap.' See I. Cooper-Oakley, *Masonry and Medieval Mysticism. Traces of a Hidden Tradition*, London, 1900.

4 See M. Davy, *Initiation à la symbolique romane*, Paris, 1977, p. 157.

5 See O. Demus, *Byzantine Mosaic Decoration*, London, 1976 ed. The use of light in such symbolic directions, and formal patterns, cannot be separated from orientation-theory – see therefore above, ch. 2, note 19.

6 For some note of the Albigensian use of light, see Nelli et al., *Les Cathares*, Paris, 1960.

7 The hymn is one quoted by Davy, note 4 above, p. 230, and quite rightly linked with the 'Sol Invictus' of Mithraic literature. See also Demus, note 5 above.

8 Hugo de St Victoire, *Mystical Mirror of the Church*. There is a useful English translation in J. Neale et al., *The Symbolism of Churches and Church Ornaments*, Leeds, 1843.

9 As a matter of interest, I happen to believe that this should be the *sine qua non* of every aesthetic judgment, but realize that in saying that I am flying in the face of contemporary historiography, which is rooted in archaeological methods. Even so, the idea seems to be the cornerstone of Goethe's methodology, which is sure to find

popularity in some future time.

10 I have treated the Piscean symbolism of Chartres in *The Hidden Art*, London, 1978. The curious (and entirely esoteric) use of Virgoan–Piscean symbolism at Chartres is directed on a north–south axis, but it is difficult to determine whether this has any specific significance in relation to the rest of the zodiacal symbolism in this cathedral. Naturally, the zodiacal window in the southern wall is designed to take advantage of the best sunlight.

11 Thorndike, *Michael Scot*, London, 1965 ed., p. 57.

12 See H. P. Blavatsky, *The Theosophical Glossary*, London, 1892, p. 323. However, the posthumous nature of this text makes it sometimes unreliable, in spite of the care taken by G. R. S. Mead. The scholar is advised to consult her two major works *Isis Unveiled*, 1878, and *The Secret Doctrine*, 1888.

13 H. G. Gundel, 'Zodiakos', *Realencyclopaedie der classischen Altertumwissenschaft*, Pauly-Wissowa, 1972, pp. 611ff.

14 R. Beck, 'Interpreting the Ponza Zodiac', in *Journal of Mithraic Studies*, vol. I,. no. 1, 1976. The Ponza zodiac is actually a constellation chart of unequal arcs, the images of which concentrate on zodiacal asterisms.

Chapter 5   Astrological considerations in relation to San Miniato

1 He would speak like this because the space into which he looked, whether it be the sun-strewn light of day, or deep into the shadow of the earth at night, was filled with spiritual beings. The zodiacus was a living entity, its very name charged with life, while the stellatum was studded with the stars which some thought were higher animals, others spiritual quintessences, and the Cherubin (so named because of a misunderstanding about the Hebraic plural) were of the highest spiritual beings near the throne of god. It is quite impossible for us to look into the skies above us with the same awe as someone of the mediaeval period would have done. Our mechanical model has done far more than displace the earth from the centre of the cosmos: it has influenced our way of seeing.

2 The nomenclature of the spiritual hierarchies accorded rule over the planetary spheres of the Ptolemaic model of the cosmos is, ranging from the lowest (the ninth hierarchy): Moon – Angels, Mercury – Archangels, Venus – Archai, Sun – Exsusiai, Mars – Dynamis, Jupiter – Kyriotetes, Saturn – Thrones. In Florence, these ranks are pictured and named in the mosaic dome of the Baptistry, above the circular thirteenth-century zodiac. However, this sequence, adapted from Dionysius the Areopagite, was not universally accepted in Christian art: for a useful note of variations, see F. Zauner, *Das Hierarchienbild der Gotik. Thomas von Villachs Fresko in Thorl*, Stuttgart, 1980.

3 For a definition of the IAU zodiac, see E. Delporte, *Atlas Céleste*, Cambridge, 1930, and *Délimitation scientifique des Constellations*, Cambridge, 1930. For a well-argued criticism of this zodiac, see R. Powell and P. Treadgold, *The Sidereal Zodiac*, London, 1979.

4 For mediaeval manuscript examples of lunar mansions, and useful explanatory diagrams and text, see Nowotny, *Henricus Cornelius Agrippa ab Nettesheym*, Graz, 1967.

5 The late-mediaeval astrologers depended upon the so-called 'Alfonsine Tables' of

Arabian origin, but these were not compiled until 1252, long after the laying down of the San Miniato zodiac: the San Miniato horoscopist may have used the Toledo tables. Arabic texts aside, the *Phainomena* of Aratos (circa 270 BC), the Hyginus *Poeticon Astronomicon*, and the stellar lists preserved by Ptolemy were used as a basis for earlier calculations and image-making. For texts which link with the modern versions of the mediaeval tradition, see (for example), V. Robson, *The Fixed Stars and Constellations in Astrology*, London 1969 (ed.), R. H. Allen, *Star Names. Their Lore and Meaning*, 1963 ed., from the 1899 edition of *Star-Names and Their Meanings*, and Powell and Treadgold, note 3 above.

6 See ch. 3, note 18 above, Bk. I, pp. 12, 10–22.

7 C. Fagan, *Astrological Origins*, Minnesota, 1971, p. 2.

8 See, for example, BM Mss. Sloane 3883, the so-called *Liber Toc* – 'Dixit Toc Graecus observa Venerem cum perveniret ad pliades et coniuncta fuerint.'

9 Robson, note 5 above, pp. 49, 62.

10 Aratos, note 5 above.

11 There have been many attempts to reallocate and redefine the asterisms, to redraw the skies in the image of contemporaneous man. The attempt to revamp the asterisms in terms of materialistic Christian images was made by Julius Schiller in 1627. A reliable bibliography, and a brief history, is provided by Allen, *Star-Names and Their Meanings*, 1899, but see also Davison, *Astronomy and the Imagination*, London, 1985.

12 Steiner, *The Search for the New Isis* (trans. of four lectures given in Dec. 1920).

13 See Appendix 4.

14 See Moore, *Studies in Dante*, Oxford, 1908 ed.

15 F. J. Carmody, *Theoretica Planetarum Gerardi*, Berkeley, 1942. Gerardus says, '. . . et totidem versus occidentem in aliis 900 annis'.

16 For a further discussion, see Gettings, *Dictionary of Astrology*, under Precession.

17 For systems of dating according to the Roman method, see 'Hadriani Junii Fastorum Liber', in J. G. Graevius, *Thesaurus Antiquitatum Romanum*. Trajecti ad Rhenum, 1698. The standard procedure of translating dates into the modern equivalents, allowing for calendrical adjustments, does not always result in satisfactory correspondences in relation to horoscopic data. For a study of the ecclesiastical system, see J. G. and S. H. Butcher, *The Ecclesiastical Calendar, its theory and construction*, Dublin, 1877. The mingling of the Roman system with the ecclesiastical system is often found in horoscopes and documentation: see for example a document of the eleventh century (quoted p. 182 by G. F. Berti, *Cenni Storico-Artistici per servire de Guida ed Illustrazione alla Insigne Basilica di S. Miniato al Monte . . .*, Florence, 1850), which notes the 'Saint's Day of San Miniato' as 'Passio Sancti Miniatis VIII KL Nov. Festivitas S. Miniatis Martyris'. The festival is celebrated now on the 28 October.

18 An example of a twelfth-century solar list using such a system is in the British Museum Mss. 25031, which gives solar positions for the year at sunset (actually, even this designation is dubious, as the term used is 'vesperis', a monastic term, not related to what we now conceive as 'clock-time'). It is in the hand of an English scribe, and may have derived from Worcester. The solar position for 28 May, for example, is 12.27 tropical Gemini. The implication is that the figures have been copied from an Arabic source from tables relevant to late ninth-century tables. Some of the short-forms are

Byzantine Greek, whilst the numeration is in mediaeval-Arabic. See also above, ch. 3, note 24.

19 For example, a compotus in 5 books, dated 1176, and attributed to Roger of Hereford, is in the British Museum (Royal 12 F 17), and entitled *Herefordensis Iudicia*. A treatise on astrology, which sets out the signs, planets houses, elections, and so on, along with a useful list of astrological terms and tables in the thirteenth century, is British Museum manuscript Digby 149, 'Liber de quatuor partibus astronomie iudicorum'. See also Garin, below, ch. 6, note 14.

20 For some note of different rising times in various climata, see O. Neugebauer and H. B. von Hosen, *Greek Horoscopes*, Philadelphia, 1959.

21 For the story of Walcher, prior of Malvern, who could not observe the 1091 eclipse because he had no clock (horologium) see L. Thorndike, *A History of Magic*, vol. 2, p. 68, where the story is credited to C. H. Haskins. The account is an amusing one, but a familiarity with the documentation is sufficient to show that the tables themselves are not conducive to accurate readings (at least by modern standards). For example, the thirteenth-century tables in British Museum Mss. Arundel 377 give tables for lunar positions of the moon 'de apparitione Lune xxix die ad vesperum cum tabula'. The term vesperum is exceedingly imprecise, and we must assume that such tables were designed as guide for the practising astrologer, in a position to check the readings personally by observation. Conversion from Arabic to Latin was often careless – the Arabic astrological day began at sunrise, while the Julian day began at midnight, but this is often overlooked in the tables. Again, in the same manuscript (f.86ff), the tables attributed to Roger of Hereford, (f.86ff) at Hereford for 1178, and supposed valid to 1200 are also just as questionable. There are relatively accurate mediaeval methods, of course, but none of them have the simplicities obtained by modern methods, which astrologers take for granted nowadays.

22 In the twelfth and thirteenth century the word 'horoscopos' is used to denote the 'rising point' ('ortus' or 'Ascendens'). Thus, the word 'horoscope' originally applied to the Ascendant degree, and only in post-sixteenth century astrology was it used to denote the chart as a whole. This has led to much confusion among those non-specialists who have dabbled in the history of mediaeval astrology. For relevant bibliography, see F. Gettings, 'An Ancient Sigil Revived', in *Astrology*, vol. 51, no. 1, 1977.

23 The ayanamsa of the Babylonian (Kidinnu) system was believed to be fixed in 8 degrees of Aries: this system was used well into the Middle Ages. Ptolemy fixed his vernal point in the first degree of Aries, though the epoch for Ptolemy's catalogue should be for AD 48 and not AD 138, as is often stated. For a brief analysis of the ayanamsa, see G. Dean et al., *Recent Advances in Natal Astrology*, London, 1977, pp. 50ff, and Gettings, *Dictionary of Astrology*, under Ayanamsa.

24 Thorndike, *Michael Scot*, p. 93.

25 Allen (*Star-Names and Their Meanings*, 1899) suggests that Spencer called them the 'Moist Daughters' because of this connexion with rainy weather. However, Aratus (see E. Maass, *Arati Phaenomena*, Berlin, 1955) records that the Heliades are supposed to have wept because their brother Phaethon fell into the river Po (the 'Eridanus' of constellation lore). They were 'moist' because of their tears, not because of diosemeic considerations.

26 R. Ebertin, *Die Bedeutung der Fixsterne*, trans. I. Banks, *Fixed Stars and Their Interpretation*, Aalen, 1971, p. 28.

27 Powell (note 3 above) gives Aldebaran for the epoch 1950.0 as: Longitude TA 15.00.00: Latitude S, 05.28.14. In the map given by G. R. Mair, *Aratus*, London, 1921 (a text which incorporates material from Eratosthenes), Taurus starts at 20 Aries, and its horn tip touches 20 Taurus. However, Gemini does not begin until the end of 30 degrees of Taurus.

28 B. Tuckerman, *Planetary, Lunar, and Solar Positions. A.D. 2 to A.D. 1649 at Five-Day and Ten-Day Intervals*, Philadelphia, 1964.

29 See Allen, note 25 above.

30 It is worth observing that Aratus (note 25 above) puts the Hyades on the forehead of the Bull, but they were not so located in the majority of mediaeval images of the constellation.

31 For a modern treatment of Morin de Villefranche, *Astrologia Gallica*, see J. Hieroz, *L'Astrologie selon Morin de Villefranche . . .*, Paris, 1962. P. 99ff relates to heliacal visibility, but there appears to be an error in the figure given for Saturn.

32 William of Conches, *Philosophicarum et Astronomicaram*, Basel, 1531, calls the 49,000 year cycle the 'great year' (magnus annus). Neckam, *De Naturis Rerum*, gives a period of 36,000 years. The more accurate historian D. Petarius, *Uranologion, sive systema Variorum Authorum qui de sphaera . . . etc.*, 1630, gives the more reasonable periodicity of 350,635 years. The question of the great years, and the Sothic relationships, are dealt with from an esoteric point of view by Massey, *A Book of Beginnings*, London, 1881–3, pp. 339ff.

33 For Michael Scot's mention of foundation charts, see Thorndike (*Michael Scot*, London, 1965 ed.), p. 95. Thorndike quotes from a manuscript in Munich (Staatsbibliothek, cod. lat. 10268). An interesting academic note of the foundation chart for later structures is in R. Taylor, 'Architecture and Magic: Consideration on the Idea of the Escorial', in *Essays in the History of Architecture presented to Rudolf Wittkower*, London, 1967.

34 The cabbalistic view is different, for it is only at the Crown of Kether that the human soul peers into the 'quintessential nothingness', in Eckhart's apt phrase.

35 For the descent and ascent of the soul in the two major traditions which were later inherited by the West, see G. R. S. Mead, *Thrice-Greatest Hermes. Studies in Hellenistic Theosophy and Gnosis*, London, 1964 ed., vol. I, pp. 288ff.

36 Aristotle, *De Generatione et Corruptione*, II.x. It was in his *Meteoreologica* (I.ii) that he issued his oft-quoted lever for the new astrology – 'The earth is bound up by necessity with the proper motions of the heavens, so that all powers that reside in this world are governed by those above'.

37 Al Biruni, is properly Muhammad ibn Ahmal – see R. R. Wright, *The Book of Instructions in the Elements of the Art of Astrology . . . written in Ghazah, 1029 AD. Reproduced from the British Museum mss. Or. 8349*, London, 1934.

38 All the above data is provided in one form or another by Allen, *Star-Names and Their Meanings*, 1899, pp. 391ff.

39 See Wittkower, *Allegory and the Migration of Symbols*, London, 1977, p. 36. The tree, called the 'Peridoxion' is in the Physiologus literature. The same tree, called the

'Dragon Tree' figures in esoteric lore, as the name of Nagarjuna, the founder of the Madhyamika School of Buddhism. In this case, as always with the oriental occultism, the dragon is symbol of wisdom and knowledge. The tree element in this case is related to the Bodhi tree of buddhism, which is both a symbol of wisdom and of the human spine.

40 A Volguine, *Astrology of the Mayas and Aztecs*, Sidcup, 1969.

Chapter 6   The secrets of the Latin inscription

1 G. F. Berti, *Cenni Storico-Artistici per servire di Guida ed Illustrazione alla Insigne Basilica di S. Miniato al Monte . . .*, Florence, 1850. See especially p. 62. Berti's recording of the peculiar punctuation of the inscription is quite wrong. Additionally, in place of CRISTUS he gives CHRISTUS, and for the short-form MNT he hazards MENTEM, which is certainly imaginative but meaningless within the context. Berti also gives no indication of knowing what the inscription means. His only explanatory note to this section of his 'guide' (note 26), p. 62, gives the title of Ximenes' book on Florentine gnomens wrongly (see above, ch. 2, note 9).

2 W. and E. Paatz, *Die Kirchen von Florenz. Ein Kunstgeschichtliches Handbuch*, Frankfurt am Main, 1940.

3 Augustine, *City of God*, Bk. XVIII, 23. See also Gettings, *Dictionary of Occult, Hermetic and Alchemical Sigils*, London, 1979, under Secret Alphabets, and K. A. Nowotny, *Henricus Cornelius Agrippa ab Nettesheym. De Occulta Philosophia*, Graz, 1967. Acrostic verses were not uncommon in mediaeval scriptoria: an example is reproduced in a poem in the eighth-century Echternach Gospel Book, in J. J. G. Alexander, *A Survey of Manuscripts Illuminated in the British Isles*, vol. 1 – *Insular Manuscripts – 6th to the 9th Century*, London, 1978, repro. 116, text 51ff.

4 A number of mediaeval secret scripts are reproduced in Gettings, note 3 above – see series indicated under Secret Scripts.

5 J. Trithemius, *Steganographia*, ed. M. Becker, Frankfurt, 1606, and *Veterum Sophorum sigilla et imagines magicae*, Herrenstadt, 1932. For a modern analysis of the simple code, see P. Chacornac, *Grandeur et adversité de Jean Trithème . . .*, Paris, 1963.

6 See ch. 1, note 24 above.

7 Roger of Hereford, above, ch. 5, note 19. For J. J. G. Alexander, see *Insular Manuscripts – 6th to the 9th Century*, London, 1978.

8 See Gettings, note 3 above, under Leo. I have pointed to the anagogic use of precisely the same sigil in St Pierre, Geneva, in *The Hidden Art*, London, 1978.

9 R. E. Latham, *Revised Mediaeval Latin Word-List from British and Irish Sources*, London, 1965, p. ix.

10 William of Conches, *P. Honorii Augustudunensis Presbyteri . . .*, Basel, 1644, bk. 1, ch. 63 – 'De Caelis et Stellis et duodecim signis'. For example: 'Duae sunt ianuae coeli . . .'.

11 See T. Burckhardt, *Sacred Art in East and West*, London, 1969. See also note 10 above.

12 In the late twelfth century it was becoming usual to name the poet or sculptor of a fine work. Once again the Sacra di San Michele inscriptions (Appendix 4) come to mind, for these name the sculptor (or at least a poet) Nicholas. There is another Nicolaus

mentioned as sculptor ('Nicolaus Sacerdos et Magister') on the pulpit of the cathedral in Bitonto: see G. Mongiello, *Bitonto nella Storia e Nell'Arte*, Bari, 1970, pp. 81ff.

13 See for example G. F. Berti (note 1 above), who records in the *Decreto del Vescovo di Firenze*, the following subscription 'Hanc vero Cartulam ego Adalbertus Notarius et Iudex scribendo atque laudando confirmavi' (p. 182). This Adalbertus was of the early eleventh century. See also D. du Cange, *Glossarium Mediae et Infimae Latinitatis*, vol. 4, pp. 437–40. An interesting twelfth-century use of the word 'Judex' in an astrological context is in the Mss with the incipit 'Ista tabula Alfragani et Iosaphi sic operanda est circa iudices lunarum . . .' British Museum, Add. 34,018, 93v. This 'Iosaphus' is an Arabian astrologer, and not our San Miniato Ioseph. For a more general use of the verb 'iudicare' in connexion with astrology, see for example Roger of Hereford, Bodleian Mss. Digby 149 (thirteenth century). 'Liber de quatuor partibus astronomie iudicorum editus a magistro Rogero de Herefordia . . .' This is often called the 'Iudicia Herefordensis' – see Thorndike, *A History of Magic and Experimental Science*, vol. II, p. 186. This text is contained in the British Museum Royal Mss 12 F 17, which contains also a translation of *Haly de iudiciis*.

14 E. Garin, *Lo Zodiaco della Vita. La polemica sull'astrologia dal trecento al cinquecento*, Bari, 1976, p. 3: translated into English with the misleading title *Astrology in the Renaissance. The Zodiac of Life*, London, 1983. Much of the material deals with the proto-Renaissance, however. The importance of the meeting of east and west in the Council of Florence/Ferrara in 1439 is rightly emphasized, though the approach (as the Italian title suggests) is really from the point of view of the history of ideas, rather than from the point of view of the history of astrology.

15 See the *Oxford Latin Dictionary*, OUP, 1968, under 'Condo' – especially 5, 6 and 7.

16 For a description of this Saturn period which throws much light on many of the ancient symbols, see R. Steiner, *Die Geheimwissenschaft im Umriss*, available in English translation as *Occult Science – an Outline*, the reprint of 1979 being the best.

17 For a different reading of this abbreviation, see Berti, note 1 above. However, MCCVII . RE/TINENTDE/TEPOREMTE, with the standard abbreviation signs can only read MCCVII . RETINENT DE TEMPORE MONTEM.

18 For a brief survey of the word and its sigil, see F. Gettings, 'An Ancient Sigil Revived', in *Astrology*, vol. 51, no. 1, Spring 1977.

19 For a text on the Old Style computation, see above, ch. 5, note 17. Berti (note 1 above) gives a useful line relating to the Feast Day of San Miniato – VIII KL Nov.

20 For 'Valua', as used in the sense of 'emolumentum' or 'reditus', see D. P. Carpentier, *Glossarium Novum ad Scriptores Medii Aevi* . . . (du Cange), Paris, 1766, under VALUA. This new sense is not fully documented until 1235, and so it is not a point I will labour here, nor is it essential to my argument.

21 Gettings, *The Secrets of San Miniato al Monte*, Florence, 1982.

22 See note 18 above.

23 For references to the numerology involved in the Joachim prophecies, see M. Reeve, *The Influences of Prophecy in the Later Middle Ages*, Manchester, 1967.

24 See *The Book of Kells*, Sir Edward Sullivan, London, Paris and New York, 1914.

Conclusion

1 For something of the history of the Sun sigil, see Gettings, *Dictionary of Occult, Hermetic and Alchemical Sigils*, London, 1979. For the Egyptian symbolism, see note 5 below.

2 See for example C. G. Harrison, *The Transcendental Universe. Six lectures in science, theosophy and the Catholic Faith*, London, 1894. Steiner's ten lectures *Die okkulte Bewegung im neunzehnten Jahrhundert* . . . (No. 254 in the Bibliographical Survey, 1961), translated into English as *The Occult Movement in the Nineteenth Century*, London, 1973, is influenced by the Harrison lectures, but gives the source wrongly as C. J. Harrison.

3 The future ability to see into the etheric is expressed with uncharacteristic clarity by H. P. Blavatsky (*The Secret Doctrine*, Pasadena, 1888, vol. 1, p. 12): '. . . it must be stated that Occult Science recognises Seven Cosmical Elements – four entirely physical, and the fifth (Ether) semi-material, as it will become visible in the air towards the end of our Fourth Round, to reign supreme over the others during the whole of the Fifth. The remaining two are as yet absolutely beyond the range of human perception.'

4 See for example, Julius Africanus in *Patrologia Cursus Completus – Series Graeca 10* (Migne), 1857 – 'Africani Narratio de iis quae Christo nato in Persia Acciderunt'.

5 The Egyptian sigil ⊙ , which was resurrected in the fifteenth century, and later adopted by astrologers as a sigil for the sun, has a fascinating history in connexion with the early mysteries. The Apis Bull hieroglyph is nothing other than a standard bull with the sigil between its horns. See E. A. Wallis Budge, *An Egyptian Hieroglyphic Dictionary*, London, 1920, p. cix. for the hieroglyphic as representative of Sun, Day, Time, etc., and in connexion with the Sun-god Ra, see ibid., p. cxxiv. It is interesting to observe that this sun sigil was adopted in Early Christian times as symbol for Christ. A sixth-century example (on a tomb-slab, at the centre of a primitive cross) is still preserved in the crypt of the pieva in Gropina, Loro Ciuffenna. A tenth- or eleventh-century pulpit with a missing bull symbolism is located in the nave.

6 For some of the academic literature, see, for example, *The Mysteries. Papers from the Eranos Yearbooks*, Bollingen Series XXX.2, Princeton, 1971 ed. See in particular H. Rahner, *The Christian Mystery and the Pagan Mysteries*, of 1944. C. G. Jung's *Transformation Symbolism in the Mass*, in this collection, is one of the clearest examples of how much of Jung's philosophy appears to be derived from insights rather than from profound scholarship. In comparison, the esoteric literature may be approached through Blavatsky (note 3 above) or through (for example) R. Steiner, 'Contrasting Principles of Ancient and Modern Initiation' I–III, *Anthroposophical Quarterly*, vol. 18, nos 2–4, 1973, and *Alte und Neue Einweihungsmethode*, the text of fourteen lectures given in 1922. For an excellent survey of the influential Gnostic mysteries and initiation methods of other mysteries, see Mead, *Thrice-Greatest Hermes*, London, 1964 ed.

7 R. Steiner, *The Sun-Mystery in the Course of Human History* (English translation by D. S. Osmond, of a lecture given at Dornach on the 6 November 1921), London, 1955. So far as I know, there is no exoteric record of Julian the Apostate having being murdered. Eye-witnesses, such as Ammianus (XXV 3) record that he was killed in June 363 by a Persian cavalry javelin, thrown during a skirmish with the army commanded by Meranes. However, Steiner's account of history is often at variance with the traditional accounts – and certainly not through any lack of scholarship on his side. For further

information on the Sun-Mysteries of Julian, see W. C. Wright, *The Works of the Emperor Julian*, London, 1913, especially 'Orations IV: Hymn to King Helios', p. 404.

8 Trithemius, *De Septem Secundadeis*, Nuremberg, 1522, indicates that the reign of Michael will begin in 1881 (there are slight errors in his calculations), and this corresponds approximately with the dates set out in the theosophical tradition initiated by Blavatsky. For a treatment of the Michaelic urge, see in particular R. Steiner, *The Michael Mystery*, London, 1956 ed., with foreword by George Adams.

9 For a note on the development of this sigil during the Renaissance, see Gettings, note 1 above. See also note 5 above.

10 The St Michael in the National Gallery is from a polyptych, probably from one commissioned for the high altarpiece of S. Agostino at Sansepolcro, finished circa 1469. The sigil is on the blade of the sword, over the severed head of the serpent, as though imprinted there in triumph. The inscription around the low waist-band of the cuirass is ANGELUS POTENTIA DEI. . .HA. Although incomplete, it is possible that the inscription links with the classification of angelical beings given by Pope Gregory I, as one of the Potestates, the equivalent of the Exsusiai, who were the beings of the sun – see Zauner, ch. 5, note 2 above. In the occult tradition Michael is the solar leader of the Secundadeians, who are of course the 'intelligencies', or the spherical movers. In the fifteenth century, it seems to have been commonplace for the sigil to be inserted into the armoury-decoration of Michael's image.

11 The esotericism of the Medici has never adequately been dealt with in the academic literature, though it is hinted at in such general texts as Collin, *The Theory of Celestial Influences*, London, 1954. Modern occultist literature usually recognizes that the great artists, writers and musicians around the Medici were themselves initiates, and concerned with creating the secure foundations for the coming western culture, of which we are currently witnessing the death throes. The famous letter of Marsilio Ficino of 1492, proclaiming the 'seculum aureum' (Age of Gold) was written to an astrologer, Paul of Middleburg (see Reeves, *The Influences of Prophecy*, Oxford, 1969, p. 429), and the excitement within the letter seems to have carried the Florentine Platonists for a long time: they were truely 'the instrument of a total renewal of theological thought and customs, which opened a magnificent new view of human history'. Reeves is quoting Chastel, and finds later in her own study that the optimism concerning the optimism of history, like prophecy itself, was one of the unexpected links between the mediaeval and the Renaissance periods. The view of mediaeval history was inextricably interwoven with the deep-rooted belief in the veracity of prophecy, of which astrology was the most intellectualized department.

12 See N. G. L. Hammond and H. H. Scullard, *The Oxford Classical Dictionary*, Oxford, 1979. The descent from Dardanus is Arctinus ap. Dion. Hal. 1.69. The descent from Ilus is Ovid 'Fasti' 6 419ff.

13 Ibid. The legend is from Virgil's 'Aeniad' 2 116.

14 Ibid. The legend is from Dion. Hal. 1. 69.

15 Steiner, note 7 above.

16 See E. Gibbon, *The History of the Decline and Fall of the Roman Empire* (D. Milan et al., ed., London, 1903), book VIII, p. 172. It is interesting that the date of the fall of Constantinople was successfully determined by the Islamic astrologers for 29 May 1453

(Book VIII, p. 168). On that morning, the crescent Moon beloved by Islam would have hung over the horizon prior to the dawn light, but the actual astrological calculations would have been related to the chart of Meranes himself. Some modern historians emphasize the effect of the eclipse which occurred on the previous day.

17 Steiner, note 7 above.

18 M. Scot, *Liber Introductorius*, p. 97.

19 The esotericism of Dante often passes unnoticed. In 'Purgatorio', Canto XII, 100ff, the reference to San Miniato follows on what is perhaps the earliest literary reference to the Akashic Chronicles. It is usual for commentators to interpret the last line of this verse 'The city that so discreetly orders things' as an irony. However, in view of the mystery-wisdom hidden in San Miniato, it is possible to read the line in a very different way. In any case, in climbing the hill on the oltr'Arno, Dante has his back to Florence – he has turned his back on Aries, which reflects precisely on the preceding verse, in which the angel brushes from his forehead the P of pride. Pride is the sin usually associated with Aries.

20 Before the cappella was constructed, in anachronistic disfigurement of the thirteenth-century design, it was possible for one to stand on the central sun of the zodiac and see all the symbols to which I have alluded in my examination of the symbolism of San Miniato. The cappella now occludes the two wall-fishes, and thus breaks the sequence. I cannot imagine that this insertion of the Medici mystery-symbolism into the ancient sequence was unintentional. In fact, the clever use of orientation lines and symbolic forms by Michelozzo points to an astounding level of symbolism linked with the theme of redemption, and points to a profound level of symbolism within San Miniato which has so far gone unnoticed, making use of the tassellated symbols in the pavement of the nave (see Wittkower, *Allegory and the Migration of Symbols*, London, 1977). However, a full survey of this symbolism (which in any case belongs to a fifteenth-century symbolic symbology) is not possible within this present treatment. Within the present context, it is perhaps sufficient to point out the secundadeian symbols on either side of the cappella (note 9 above).

21 The most widely known ancient cycles were associated with the three ages of metal, and the seven planets, or their corresponding beings. Derived from this latter cycle, by way of Gnostic speculation, were the periodicities of the Secundadeian beings (see note 8 above), mentioned in mediaeval esoteric literature. Joachim's cycles of history were really a throwback to the 'metal ages', perhaps determined by the magical connotation of three so beloved by the Christian exegecists. His dire predictions were a demonizing of the ancient triune periodicities, but his numerology appears to be entirely personal. The 'Gog' who was the final Antichrist was derived from biblical speculation, which had turned a seemingly harmless leader or tribe into an adversary of humanity – see notes 23 and 24 below. This is perhaps no place to mention the modern interpretations of the Nostradamus prophecies. It is a commonplace for soi-disant commentators to claim that Nostradamus has predicted the coming of the Antichrist in 1999. In fact, Nostradamus refers to 'le grand roi de terreur'. Since Nostradamus employs codes and puns in all his other predictive verses, there is no reason why the interesting word 'terreur' should not be read as 'du terre' and 'erreur'. A terrible king who is of the earth and filled with error is not the mythical Antichrist. The point I wish to make is that the

prediction appears to be as baseless as the thousand or so others to which any historian might point in the past. There is simply no basis for interpreting the 'Centuries' literature of Nostradamus as pointing to the end of the world, in the final years of the present century. I find it interesting that the builders of San Miniato should oppose the lunar demonology of 'Gog' with the solar imagery of Christ. For a study of the 'Great Conjunctions' literature, see Garin, *Lo Zodiaco della Vita*, Bari, 1976.

22 So far as I am aware, Joachim is the first to name his second Antichrist 'Gog'. The name is derived from Ezekiel (xxxviii and xxxix), and is originally linked with a quite historical personage, tribe or place. The Apocalypse of John takes the name as referring to the leader of a great assault on mankind, uniting thereby with the distinctive yet literary figure of the Antichrist: see note 24 below.

23 The notion of the Antichrist is derived from biblical exegesis of such texts as Ezekiel, Thessalonians (II. ii) and 'Revelation'. However, none of these texts mentions Antichrist by name, and this fearsome being, who may be said to have 'possessed' the minds of men more completely than any other demon, is almost entirely a literary production, rising like an unlovely Venus from a foam of ink. The notion of the Antichrist is merged with the Beast of Revelation, a creature with many heads, who makes war with the saints. In Verse viii it is made clear that only those not true to Christ will be subjected to this beast. . . . The one biblical authority for the name Antichrist is the apostle John, who mentions him five times, once in the plural (I. ii). This last fact indicates that originally at least the idea of the Antichrist was not charged with the same sense of exclusivity as the name Christ. It appears to be used by the author of John's Gospel to denote either a heretic, or someone opposed to Christ's message. This view was supported by Tertullian (*De Praes. Haer.* c.4), and a few other early writers, yet this has not prevented a vast library of books being written about the Antichrist as though he were a mighty demonic being.

24 R. Steiner, *Das Johannes-Evangelium*, a cycle of twelve lectures given in Hamburg in May 1908, translated into English in a revised edition, *The Gospel of St John*, London, 1973. One question which we should be asking is of what inner urge or entity within man is the Antichrist the literary embodiment? In the opinion of some esotericists, the Antichrist is really a personal demon, the ancient equivalent of what some modern occultists call the 'Guardian of the Threshold' (another literary figure, though a personification of a quite real demonic entity – see E. G. E. Bulwer-Lytton, *Zanoni*, London, 1882). The notion, and its terminology, were adopted initially by the Theosophists, by which stream it passed into modern general occult use. It is a good name for a demon which each person must face at the 'end of the world', which is of course the end of the present incarnation.

Index